The End of Money and the Future of Civilization

The End of Money and the Future of Civilization

THOMAS H. GRECO, JR.

Floris Books

First published in 2009 by Chelsea Green Publishing,
White River Junction, Vermont
First published in the UK by Floris Books 2010

British Library CIP Data available

ISBN 978-086315-733-2

Printed in Great Britain by Bell & Bain, Glasgow

*Dedicated to the memory of my father, who made sure
I had a good education and, though he didn't always
understand, provided unfailing support
throughout his life.*

CONTENTS

1   My Purpose and My Journey   1
2   Mega-Crisis and Metamorphosis — Can Civilization Be Saved?   12
3   The Contest for Rulership — Two Opposing Philosophies   23
4   Central Banking and the Rise of the Money Power   33
5   The New World Order   47
6   Usury and the Engine of Destruction   56
7   The Nature and Cause of Inflation   70
8   The Separation of Money and State   87
9   The Evolution of Money — From Commodity Money to Credit Money   99
10 The Third Evolutionary Stage — The Emergence of Credit Clearing   115
11 Solving the Money Problem   124
12 Credit Clearing, the "UnMoney"   141
13 The State of the Alternative Exchange Movement   156
14 How Complementary Currencies Succeed or Fail   164
15 Commercial Trade Exchanges — Their Present Limitations and Potential
    Future   181
16 A Regional Economic Development Plan Based on Credit Clearing   193
17 The Next Big Thing in Business: A Complete Web-based Trading Platform   202
18 Organizational Forms and Structures for Local Self-Determination and
    Complementary Exchange   215
19 The Role of Governments in Establishing Economic and Financial Stability   232
20 Exchange, Finance, and the Store of Value   243

    Epilogue   259
    Acknowledgments   263
    Appendix A: A Model Membership Agreement for a Credit Clearing Service   264
    Appendix B: An Objective Composite Standard Measure of Value   275
    References   278
    Notes   281
    Index   289

1. My Purpose and My Journey

It may seem a bold assertion to suggest that the end of money might occur any time soon. Money is such a basic feature of our everyday lives that a world without it is almost inconceivable. It is a thing as necessary as air, water, and food — because, in a developed economy, it is by the process of exchange that we acquire virtually everything we need to live, and money is the instrument that enables that exchange. Exchange will certainly continue, but in quite a different way, and money as we know it will become obsolete. How this is occurring, and what will take its place, are the subjects of this book.

Very few people realize that the nature of money has changed profoundly over the past three centuries, or that it has become a political instrument used to centralize power, concentrate wealth, and subvert popular government. While there has been some talk about the "cashless society," what is being talked about does not constitute an end to money, but rather the enhancement of "political money" by the application of ever more effective instruments of social, economic, and political control. *When I speak about the end of money, I am referring to the growing recognition that money has become nothing more than an information system, and to the emergent mechanisms for managing exchange information outside of the conventional banking system and without the use of political monies.*

The implications of this are multidimensional and far-reaching. Dee Hock, CEO emeritus of VISA International, has said,

> we are at that very point in time when a four hundred year old age is rattling in its deathbed and another is struggling to be born. A shifting of culture, science, society, and institutions enormously greater and swifter than the world has ever experienced. Ahead, lies the *possibility* of regeneration of indi-

viduality, liberty, community, and ethics such as the world has never known, and a harmony with nature, with one another and with the divine intelligence such as the world has never seen. It is the path to a livable future in the centuries ahead, as society evolves into ever-increasing diversity and complexity.[1] [emphasis in the original]

In my view, that must be a shift from élite rule based on "command and control" hierarchies and military force to a more inclusive, participatory, just, harmonious, and sustainable order. I maintain, in all humility, that this book goes a long way in providing what is needed for that shift to come about. It describes the single most important thing that needs to happen, which is a fundamental change in the way we mediate the exchange of goods and services, and it provides specific advice that will enable a process I refer to as "reclaiming the credit commons" that can be achieved by the widespread implementation of direct credit clearing unions and private production-based voucher systems that I describe in later chapters.

My Personal Journey

I grew up in the 1940s and 1950s. That was a time of great confidence and optimism in America. Fascism had been obliterated, or so we thought. Through American generosity, Europe was being rebuilt — a magnanimous gesture toward our former enemies in the form of "the Marshall Plan." And despite the "cold war" and the "communist menace," it seemed as if progress was inevitable, that life could only get better for everyone. The United States was the greatest, richest, most productive, and most benevolent country in the world. Like the movies we saw, the world was mostly black and white, there were "good guys" and "bad guys," and on the world stage we Americans were (of course) the good guys.

As a young professor, I was dismayed by the student unrest on college campuses in the late 1960s and early 1970s and their seeming disrespect for established institutions. Even at conservative Rochester

Institute of Technology (RIT)[2] where I was teaching, there were frequent false alarms and bomb threats that disrupted the normal class routine as buildings had to be evacuated and searched for nonexistent bombs. I thought it was all part of a communist-inspired plot to destroy our educational system and our American way of life.

Seeds of Disillusionment

Some seeds of disillusionment had already been planted in my mind a few years earlier while I was working on my MBA at the University of Rochester. I happened to find a book in the Rush-Rhees library that piqued my curiosity. It must have been its provocative title that caught my interest. The book was *The Power Élite* by C. Wright Mills, published in 1956. At that time, the very idea of an élite class in our supposed "classless" American society was considered by most to be an absurdity. The predominant view was that America was a pluralistic society in which competing interests kept each other in check. That notion was supported by works like John Kenneth Galbraith's *American Capitalism: The Concept of Countervailing Power.* Mills challenged that myth, sketching a different picture and presenting evidence that there was a "power élite...composed of men whose positions enable them to transcend the ordinary environments of ordinary men and women; they are in positions to make decisions having major consequences."[3] He spoke of a "higher immorality" that was "a systemic feature of the American élite." Mills argued that "Of course there may be corrupt men in sound institutions, but when institutions are corrupting many of the men who live and work in them are necessarily corrupted... Within the corporate worlds of business, war-making and politics, the private conscience is attenuated — and the higher immorality is institutional-ized."[4] This was an insightful observation of what Philip Zimbardo's work would later prove, that perfectly normal and otherwise good people often do evil things as a result of the situations and systems in which they happen to be embedded.[5]

Awakening

I did not pursue the matter further at the time but went on with my life, married, started a family, began my academic career, and proceeded to live the "American dream." But life has a way of surprising us and upsetting our plans. Upon receiving tenure at RIT in 1972, I requested a sabbatical leave to work full-time on my Ph.D. at Syracuse University. It was during the 1973–74 academic year at Syracuse that I had what might be called an epiphany. I was awakened from my middle-class stupor and was able to see more clearly the way things actually are. From that point onward, I embarked upon a self-directed programme of personal reeducation. Despite having already acquired two university degrees and being well on my way toward my doctorate, I came to realize that I was ignorant of the most fundamental requirements for living a fulfilled life, including the basic motivations that determined my own behavior. Along with my new insights and a desire to broaden the scope of my knowledge, I developed a newfound concern for social justice, economic equity, personal freedom, self-expression, ecology, and peace. I found kindred spirits in various groups and organizations, including the Rochester Peace and Justice Education Center (PJEC).

In the Wake of Inflation

One day, as I sat at a desk in the PJEC office where I was a some-time volunteer, a colleague handed me a book that had just arrived in the mail, *In the Wake of Inflation Can the Church Remain Silent?* Skimming through it, I saw that the book was neither well-written nor adequately referenced, but despite the amateurish style of the work, it still managed to pique my interest. There were some shocking assertions about our money and banking system of which I was dubious but not sufficiently knowledgeable to dismiss out of hand. I decided to take a closer look. There were a few cited quotes that seemed as if they might be from credible sources, one of which was a pamphlet called *Money Facts − 169 Questions and Answers on Money* that had been commissioned by the US House of Representatives Subcommittee on

Domestic Finance, Committee on Banking and Currency, and produced by the Government Printing Office.[6] That was enough to convince me that the matter deserved further investigation.

I got in touch with the author, Edward Veith, who lived in one of the Rochester suburbs, and we eventually became good friends. Ed was quite elderly by that time and not well educated. He had been long retired, having worked many years as an elevator installer and repairman. Ed was a very religious Christian who paid perhaps a bit too much attention to television evangelists, but he had a good heart and the "money problem" had long troubled him. He could not reconcile the practice of usury that is inherent in our system of money and banking, nor the persistent official debasement of our national currency, with Bible scriptures and his religious beliefs. And while I didn't share in all the particulars of his religious convictions, it was through my conversations with Ed that I, too, became concerned about the same issues and about the credit monopoly in private hands that is our system of money and banking. As a result, I embarked upon this work that has been my main focus for almost thirty years. It has become my personal mission to unravel the mysteries of money, to share as widely as possible what I have learned, and to collabourate with others in creating new structures that can enable us to transcend what has become today a "mega-crisis."

Starting with *Money Facts*, I discovered that it was a supplement to a larger report of the same congressional committee called *A Primer on Money*,[7] which I duly acquired, read, and digested. Those sources provided quite a different picture from what is commonly believed about money and banking, but that was only the beginning. As in any investigation, one source leads to another, and a great body of evidence is gradually built up. I discovered that, in this field (as in any other) an orthodox view had emerged that pushed aside dissenting views and limited the academic debate. Fortunately, there is a great wealth of pertinent material that remains to be discovered if one is willing to dig deeply enough. It is the results of that searching and sifting that I present in this volume. Like Edward Veith, I hope that the insights and ideas presented in my book will stimulate others to action and guide them in the right direction.

E. C. Riegel

In the course of my research, I have benefited from the work of a great many monetary scholars from various countries of the world, many of whom are quoted in this work. But one source deserves special mention for the acuteness of his insight. I have often acknowledged that my quest to understand money has been aided more by the work of E.C. Riegel[8] than by any other source. Riegel left a great legacy of writings and correspondence,[9] a legacy that would have been lost to us except for the fact that Spencer MacCallum, during his student days at Princeton, happened to meet Riegel a year before his death and recognized the greatness of his work. Years after Riegel's death, MacCallum acquired Riegel's literary estate. He went meticulously through all of it – cataloguing and transcribing, publishing and republishing – and made it available to others who might appreciate Riegel's special insights and be able to build upon the conceptual foundation that he had so elegantly laid. MacCallum was acutely aware of the importance of Riegel's work to civilization's future, peace, personal freedom, and general prosperity. Riegel wrote about all of those things because, as he showed so clearly, they are dependent upon the liberation of the exchange process from the dominance of political and banking interests, and he showed how private initiative and voluntary action could achieve it.

Much of what Riegel envisioned, and tried to implement in the 1930s and 1940s, has been reinvented in more recent times in the form of the mutual credit clearing circles, like local exchange trading systems (LETS), that have sprung up from the grassroots and been proliferating around the world – along with extra-bank credit clearing services offered to businesses by commercial "barter" exchanges. These pioneering efforts have provided the foundation for the more perfected and complete systems that are now on the horizon. We now have not only the understanding but also the information and telecommunications technologies needed for the creation of the kinds of decentralized credit and finance networks that Riegel suggested many decades ago.

Why Yet Another Book?

This is my fourth book, each of which has had the word "money" in its title. It is not money as *wealth* that has been my subject. Rather it is the structures of money and the role of money as a *medium of exchange* that have been my concern and preoccupation for a period going on thirty years. This is not a mere academic interest but a means to an end. My work has been driven by a passion for social justice, economic equity, personal liberty, world peace, and ecological restoration.

My intention in writing this book is to provide the historical background and conceptual foundation necessary for understanding our current predicament, and to suggest (in some detail) courses of action that can lead us out of it. Gandhi is quoted as having said, "there is enough for everyone's need but not for everyone's greed." I sincerely believe that it is entirely possible to achieve a dignified quality of life for each and every person now on the planet or likely to be born in the coming two or three decades, if only we humans will organize our relationships and resources toward that end. As enhanced communications bridge the distance between peoples and cultures and enable us to apply our collective intelligence across traditional boundaries, the "global village" becomes a reality. The next step is to cooperate in removing the structural impediments to realization of a higher ideal and to build new structures that better serve our purpose. The structures being considered here are those that relate to power and wealth – in particular, the mechanisms for exchanging goods and services in the market. The means that I propose do not rely upon coercion or the forced redistribution of wealth, but upon voluntary, entrepreneurial, and cooperative initiatives organized at the local level but networked globally to achieve the liberation of money and the exchange process and the democratization of finance and economics.

What I have to say in this volume repeats little of what I have said before, and that which is repeated is merely for the convenience of the reader who may not have accessed my prior works. In 1989–90, I wrote and published my first book, *Money and Debt: A Solution to the Global Crisis*, which described in concise terms the basic dysfunctions and problems inherent in our present political money and banking regime, and presented a framework of principles and ideas upon which solutions to the money problem might be built.

In 1994, I wrote and published my second book to build upon that framework, to flesh out the ideas, and to suggest some new possibilities. *New Money for Healthy Communities* provided an overview of both historical and contemporary exchange alternatives, including the "scrip" and other monetary substitutes that proliferated during the Great Depression of the 1930s, and the local currencies and credit clearing systems that have emerged in more recent times. It also presented several original exchange designs that could be implemented at the local grassroots level to improve the health of local economies in the face of economic globalization and the damaging policies of the central banking system. My third book, *Money: Understanding and Creating Alternatives to Legal Tender*, published in 2001, was an expanded, updated, and much improved version of that previous book.

This present volume, based upon much additional research and experience, goes broader and deeper. From the start, I had intended to write a complementary currency handbook to provide more and better guidance to those who are undertaking to organize exchange alternatives. I had also planned that this volume would deal with the "money problem" in a broader context so that the reader who is new to the subject might grasp both the urgency and proper approach to its solution. I quickly realized that in order to adequately achieve my purpose, it would be necessary to expand the historical and conceptual aspects of my topic. That material is contained largely in the first half of the book. I believe that this volume achieves its intended goals, but in a way that might seem less direct than one would expect.

During my academic career I learned a very important lesson about teaching and learning. As a new faculty member in the College of Business at RIT, I was asked to teach a required course in statistics, a course that was to become my specialty. It was, in the beginning, a frustrating experience because my students did not seem to be learning what I expected them to learn. It took me a few years to realize that my students lacked the conceptual foundation they needed to understand the methods and meaning of statistical inference. This was not their fault, it was merely a gap in their experience. It was also my use of the "wrong" methods of instruction. I had assumed that the lecture method would be adequate and that I could begin at the higher level of abstraction common to college-level courses. But I came to realize that my students needed to have direct experience with the physical processes involved in taking samples and summarizing their data, and that they needed to see how their results compared with other samples from the same population that were taken by other students. I abandoned the lecture method and shifted my approach to using simulations, case studies, and group projects — all of which produced far better results. I actually had to invent and manufacture my own "population simulator," which consisted of a bucket filled with five hundred plastic chips of various colours, each imprinted with two numbers. I then asked each student to draw a sample at random, record the data and compare their results with those of other students in the class. Some of my colleagues asked how I would know if a student got the right answer. I replied that I was not interested in checking their arithmetic, the object of the exercise was to demonstrate the predictability of incomplete sample data. That lesson was conceptual, not methodological.

It is with that in mind that I have approached the writing of this book. I have tried to provide the necessary conceptual foundation for understanding money and the exchange process, at least in so far as that can be expected using print media. I have also tried to further demystify the subjects of money, banking, and finance by tracing historical landmarks and important evolutionary shifts that have changed the essential nature of money and have politicized money, making it an instrument for concentrating power and wealth. This book casts the inquiry within the broader context of civilizational evolution, showing both the forces that have shaped the present global regime of money and power and the urgency of transcending it. It seeks first to elucidate how the centralized control of money, credit, and banking has been *the key mechanism* for achieving ever greater concentrations of power and wealth, and to explain how the present global monetary system has inherent in it an economic growth imperative that has been destructive to the environment and also to democratic institutions and the fabric of society. Secondly, it provides specific design proposals, exchange system architectures, and prescriptions that are applicable to various sectors and levels ranging from the local to regional, national, and global, proposing actions to be taken by grassroots organizations, businesses, and governments. *The prescriptive elements address not only the details of exchange system design, but also strategies for their implementation.*

To borrow a phrase from Dee Hock, there is a need, "to reconceive, in the most fundamental sense, the very ideas of bank, money, and credit card."[10] I hope this book will help to stimulate that process among a wide audience, and that it will provide the necessary understanding for entrepreneurs, activists, and civic leaders to implement approaches toward monetary liberation that can empower communities, promote democratic institutions, and begin to build economies that are both sustainable and democratic. I agree with economist Irving Fisher, who said "it is no exaggeration to say that stable money will, directly and indirectly, accomplish much social justice and go far toward the solution of our industrial, commercial and financial problems ... among strictly economic reforms, it stands, in my opinion, supreme."[11] But I would go even further, adding that the solution of the money problem is essential to solving our environmental and political problems as well.

This book is written for a general audience, but it is concerned especially with informing four particular groups:

1. those who are already sensitive to the money problem and are curious to know more about how money and economies work;
2. social entrepreneurs who are motivated to organize alternative exchange and financing arrangements;
3. businesspeople, who are looking for ways to survive and thrive in an increasingly hostile economic climate and to protect themselves from the machinations of the monetary and financial establishment;
4. government officials at all levels who are searching for answers to the vexing problems of fiscal management and seeking to improve the health and sustainability of their local, regional, and national economies.

This book will meet their needs by providing information and insights that are not readily available from academic or journalistic sources, and offers specific advice to all groups.

I recommend that the general reader peruse the chapters in the order presented, as they build upon one another in telling the story. Those who already have some knowledge of the history of money and the basic concepts of reciprocal exchange might want to skip ahead to the second half of the book to read first about the proposed solutions and details of exchange system design and implementation. But a complete understanding requires a solid conceptual foundation, which the first part of the book is intended to provide. Those early chapters describe money – not as a historical artifact, but as an evolving process. Just as modern aircraft bear no resemblance to earlier modes of transportation, so does modern money bear no resemblance to the precious metal coins that preceded it as exchange media. More importantly, it is essential to understand the emergent systems of credit clearing that are making money as we know it obsolete.

Nietzsche described money as "the crowbar of power"; Henry George, more than one hundred years ago, observed that, "What has destroyed every previous civilization has been the tendency to the unequal distribution of wealth and power." The challenges before us today demand that we acquire a deep understanding of the relationships between money, power, and wealth. It is my belief that this book, in providing essential information, ideas, and specific advice, will help the reader to achieve that understanding, and motivate action that is in the right direction. It is my hope that Congressman Dennis Kucinich is correct in saying that, "We are at a teachable moment on matters of money and finance,"[12] and that people the world over will then be motivated to cooperate and organize themselves to help themselves.

2. Mega-Crisis and Metamorphosis — Can Civilization Be Saved?

What the caterpillar calls the end of the world,
the master calls a butterfly.
RICHARD BACH

Prospects and Prognostication

Prognostication is a hazardous business — something that is best avoided. Events have a way of confounding the expectations of even the wisest among us. There is a story that a young man once inquired of the powerful banker and financier J.P. Morgan what he thought would happen to the stock market. Morgan is said to have replied, "Young man, the market will continue to fluctuate."

And so it is, not just for the stock market but also in the markets for bonds, commodities, and currencies (foreign exchange). Like the weather, it is hard to predict the day-to-day ups and downs, particularly in light of the fact of market manipulations by the biggest players and interventions by governments and central banks. Those who play the markets and are not privy to those insider moves will have a hard time coming out ahead of the game. To give an analogy, an occasional hot spell in November (in the northern hemisphere) should not dissuade us from recognizing that colder temperatures are probable as winter sets in.

So in any particular system, despite the inevitability of short-term fluctuations, it may still be possible to discern a general tendency or long-term tend. But even trends sometimes reverse themselves. As spring approaches, temperatures stop falling and begin to rise. We can have confidence in such expectations because we have a solid theory to explain them and considerable experience that affirms it. The point is that, even though the timing may be impossible to pinpoint, we can often see where we're headed and where we will eventually arrive *if something does not change.* If a heavy smoker has been diagnosed as having lung cancer yet continues to smoke, there is little doubt as to her prospects. So where is civilization headed? Is it a happy prospect? If not, what can be done to change direction and the likely outcome?

In this chapter I will begin to explain why I believe that the transition to a steady state economy,* and, indeed, the very survival of civilization hinge upon the fundamental restructuring of money, banking, and finance. If the money problem is not solved, we can expect that the future will bring ever greater misery — continued wars for dominance over resources, accelerating despoliation of the natural environment, continued erosion of democratic institutions, the imposition of a global neofeudal society, and the beginning of a new dark age.

Exponential Growth

Growth, in many realms, has gone too far and too fast. There is a pattern of growth called *exponential* or *geometric* that describes growth that does not proceed at a constant rate (called *linear* or *arithmetic*), but at a rate that continually accelerates. There is a fable often used to drive home the concept. In one version, an Oriental king is presented by a courtier with a gift of a chessboard. The king, wishing to reciprocate, asks what the courtier would like in return. The king is surprised when he is asked to provide an amount of rice on each of the following sixty-four days according to the number of squares on the chessboard — on the first day a single grain of rice on the first square, on the second day two grains of rice on the second square, on the third day four grains of rice on the third square, on the fourth day eight grains on the fourth square, and so on, each day doubling the amount of the

---

* A steady state economy is one that does not require the consumption of increasing quantities of physical resources over time, while still producing enough of the right kinds of products and services to sustain human societies over the long term. Implicit in this definition is adequate distribution that matches supplies with basic needs, a focus on increasing quality of life instead of increasing quantity of material consumption, and improved resource productivity, i.e., increased efficiency in the use of physical resources whereby greater value is derived from smaller amounts of material used.

day before. The king readily agrees and orders that the rice be provided as requested. At first, the amounts are trivial, but the impossibility of the bargain soon becomes apparent. By the thirty-second day, the cumulative amount required would be 4,294,967,295 grains, or about 100,000 kilograms (220,000 pounds) of rice. By the sixty-fourth day, it would amount to a billion times as much as that — many times the amount of rice that exists in the whole world.[13]

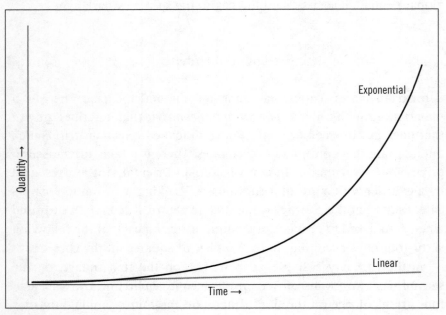

Figure 2.1 Exponential and Linear Growth over Time

Limits to Growth

How this applies to humans and our present global circumstances has been explored by a number of investigators over the years. Perhaps the most famous is Thomas Malthus for his *Essay on the Principle of Population*, published in 1826. Malthus postulated that human population grows exponentially and that it would eventually outrun food supplies, which he saw as having potential for only arithmetic growth. While humans have, up to now, managed to forestall a general global famine, localized famines have been numerous — though often the result of political and economic factors rather than resource limitation. Other factors and other resource limitations are now coming into play. These have been explored and reported more recently — for example, in the controversial 1972 book *The Limits to Growth*[14] and its recent update,[15] which focused specifically on five variables: world population, industrialization, pollution, food production, and resource depletion. Now, as we approach the second decade of the twenty-first century, it appears that the critical shortages will be in energy, fresh water, and food.

It is quite evident that explosive, exponential growth of anything cannot continue for very long. Nature amply demonstrates, in insect populations for instance, that such growth must eventually level off or the thing that has been growing exponentially will decline precipitously.[16] My concerns around these matters were first aroused in 1982 when I read a book by John Hamaker called *The Survival of Civilization*.[17] In it, the author described three things that were (and still are) growing exponentially — the level of carbon dioxide in the atmosphere, human population, and debt. While the first two of these have gained fairly widespread recognition, the "debt bomb" and its likely consequences remain obscure. About this, we will have much more to say in Chapter 6 and later chapters.

The intensifying mega-crisis that confronts the world today is multidimensional. It is not only environmental, but also simultaneously economic, financial, cultural, religious, and political. It seems that all of our institutions, and the structures upon which we depend, are breaking down. The news these days is filled with dire warnings and predictions about global warming, climate change, peak oil, and resource depletion. It is good that these reports have raised the general level of awareness, at least in the developed countries, that life on earth is facing challenges that may be unprecedented in recorded human history. On the economic front, there is news of recession, inflation, bank failures, business failures, and job losses. On the political front, we hear of insurgencies, terrorist bombings, civil unrest, the breakdown of order, and the loss of freedom. In the name of "homeland security," Americans, and to some extent Europeans, have surrendered cherished freedoms and checks on governmental abuse of power. Our education system fails to educate, our health care system fails to deliver health, and our criminal justice system fails to deliver justice. Are these things coincidental, or is there some underlying systemic cause that connects them?

Paradigm Shift

The present time seems to be particularly fluid, as we hear from various quarters talk about *the end of the era*, *spiritual awakening*, *the emergence of new paradigms*, and *societal transformation*. Such talk suggests far-reaching changes both in human consciousness and in the nature of civilization. The late Willis Harman repeatedly asked the questions "What in the world is it that is trying to happen?" and "What can, or should, we do to assist it?" and devoted the last part of his life to trying to answer them. During the late 1990s, I was privileged to be included in a series of colloquia during which a couple dozen fortunate individuals joined with Willis to inquire, probe, discuss, and strategize about those questions.[18]

We can hardly imagine the eventual outcomes of such monumental developments as genetic engineering, cloning, nanotechnology, computers, satellite communications, the Internet, a globalized economy, electronic money, global warming, and any number of predicted geophysical changes. These stresses signal an intensifying global crisis of unprecedented proportions. This is a time when far-reaching vision is urgently needed. What is the best word to describe the process we are experiencing — reform, revolution, transformation, metamorphosis, or emergence? There are a number of trends that common reason argues cannot continue, yet they seem to have a momentum that appears unstoppable: human population growth, increasing economic inequity among peoples and countries, erosion of democratic principles of governance, social alienation, climate change, despoliation of the environment, and the increasing inability of institutions to achieve their intended purposes.

Some current political figures in America and elsewhere have outlined planned economic policies and political programmes that sound appealing because they promise some needed "fixes." Many of these are aimed at propping up the "system" or reversing the looting and lopsided favouritism for wealthy and powerful élites that have characterized government policies of the past several decades. But even if politicians are sincere, they seem always to promise more than they can deliver — and what they promise is not a sufficient response to our present multidimensional crisis. The problem is more fundamental than that, and processes are required that can accomplish at least these goals.

- Put an end to unnecessary growth and wasteful production of weapons and junk.
- Enable a transition to a sustainable, steady state economy.
- Restore a large measure of local control over local affairs, and nurture the emergence of human-scale institutions.
- Enable the nonviolent resolution of inevitable conflicts and harmonize the interests of all.

It is my contention that the reinvention of money is a necessary prerequisite, and that the prescriptions outlined in later chapters are the right kind of medicine for achieving those goals.

Metamorphosis

That our global civilization cannot continue on its current path seems evident. What comes next is, of course, much harder to predict. However, I am at heart an optimist, and as such believe that the caterpillar's metamorphosis into the butterfly might offer us an apt analogy for our changing civilization. I believe that the "caterpillar" stage of human evolution is now coming to an end. The disintegrating caterpillar body cannot be sustained or reconstructed, it can only proceed with the metamorphic process, which means a complete disintegration as it becomes a resource "soup" that feeds the emergent butterfly. We are on the verge of a complete redesign and rebuilding of all our political, economic, social, and cultural structures − the things that are hard-wired through our laws, institutions, and social norms. The structures we need to create must be consistent with the values we espouse and the outcomes we wish to produce. These both determine and are determined by who we are, how we behave, and how we interact. If we are fortunate, we will succeed in emerging as the new creature that I think humanity was always destined to become.

The Egg, the Caterpillar, and the Butterfly

The physiological processes that we observe in nature may have sociopolitical counterparts. Metamorphosis of the caterpillar into the butterfly may be more than a metaphor; it might actually describe what is happening in the world.[19] It starts with the egg. A mature butterfly will lay a tiny egg on a leaf. Then, when the conditions are right, that egg will hatch. A tiny caterpillar will eat the eggshell and then it will start to feed on the leaf. It might actually eat *all* of the leaves of the plant, and then move on to another plant. Now in the *larva stage*, the caterpillar has one need − to eat and grow. That's what caterpillars do. This does not go on indefinitely − but while it is eating, the caterpillar can devastate the host plants. As a gardener, I've had ample opportunity to observe this firsthand. In our Tucson garden we had some hot chili pepper plants. One morning my friend Donna came and said, "Look at that plant. All the leaves are gone!" With the plant defoliated, it was easy to spot the culprits − two tomato horn worms. They're the big green ones, about as big as my thumb, that are commonly found on tomato plants − as we discovered, they like pepper plants too. It took only two of them and only one night to eat almost every leaf from that plant. Surprisingly, they ate not only the leaves but also the hot peppers. How this compares to the way in which human civilizations consume resources seems pretty evident.

As the caterpillar grows it goes through a process called moulting. When the caterpillar grows too large for its skin, the skin breaks open, and the caterpillar crawls out with a new skin. The social and political revolutions of the past few hundred years might be analogous to the molting process. They represented abrupt changes for societies but not the all-encompassing transformative change that the present circumstances seem to require. This molting process will happen four or five times, but at some point the caterpillar stops eating and stops growing, because nothing can grow forever. Somebody ought to tell our economists and politicians that.

So what does the caterpillar do then? It attaches itself to a twig, and its skin then hardens into a chrysalis. And what happens in the next phase, called the *pupa stage*, seems almost miraculous. From the outside, it appears that nothing is happening, but in fact a lot is going on inside the shell. The caterpillar body disintegrates, turning into a nutrient soup. But in the caterpillar body there are, and there were from the very beginning, what are called "imaginal buds" or "imaginal disks." These are clusters of cells that contain the programme of the emergent butterfly. These imaginal buds were in the caterpillar body all along, but they were dormant through the larva stage. Now they become active and start to grow and to play out the butterfly programme. This may take a period of days or even weeks. When conditions are right, the chrysalis breaks open and the butterfly crawls out, spreads its wings, and flies away. This is the *imago* stage, the mature adult butterfly. The adult butterfly behavior is quite different from that of the caterpillar. While the caterpillar devours plants and appears to be terribly destructive, the butterfly flies around, sipping nectar from blossoms and polinating plants in the process; it engages in sex and the females lay eggs to begin the cycle anew.

Now it is tempting to be judgmental about the caterpillar for its destructiveness because it often can devastate crops that we depend upon for food. But as destructive as the caterpillar may seem, it performs a necessary function. It accumulates the nutrients and prepares the space necessary for the butterfly to develop and emerge. And remember that chili plant? It sprouted new leaves; it recovered. We lost the peppers, but only on that one plant, and we had a couple others that were not damaged at all. So in the case of human and civilizational emergence, maybe this is a stage that we have had to go through.

Does the butterfly compete with the caterpillar? Does metamorphosis involve a battle for dominance? Is it a revolution? The picture is not entirely clear, but evolution biologist and futurist, Elisabet Sahtouris cites recent discoveries that suggest that the process may not be quite so peaceful as had been supposed. Of the imaginal disks, she says,

> Apparently the caterpillar's immune system battles the imaginal cells while it can, perhaps strengthening them in the process. But as the disks link together, the caterpillar's immune system fails and the butterfly in formation is nourished on the soupy meltdown of the self-digested caterpillar. It took a long time for biologists to understand that the butterfly has its own unique genome, carried by the caterpillar, inherited from ancient butterflies who acquired them long ago in evolution ([as described in] Margulis & Sagan, Acquiring Genomes, 2002). If we see ourselves as imaginal discs or cells working to build the butterfly of a better world, we will understand that we are launching a new 'genome' of beiefs, values and practices to replace that of the current unsustainable system. We will also see how important it is to link with each other in the effort, to recognize how many different kinds of imaginal cells it will take to build a butterfly with all its capabilities and colours.[20]

True, we are voraciously consuming resources – it looks like we are destroying the planet, and if we continue we undoubtedly will. But I think our collective consciousness is beginning to change. We are becoming aware of limits and are reaching that part of our evolutionary programme that says, "Stop!"

Get With the Programme

As we reach the end of our caterpillar stage of civilizational evolution, many are waking up to the butterfly programme and are diligently working to bring about the necessary changes to transform this world from one of strife, violence, injustice, inequity, and despotism to one of peace, harmony, justice, equity, and freedom. It appears that the imaginal buds are now beginning to stimulate one another into more intense activity that will result in what Dr Laurence Victor calls a "synergistic emergent eruption which will be as powerfully positive as its nuclear winter antipode is negative." There is no exclusive "butterfly" club, but an open process in which everyone can find their own role in their own time. We're being nourished by the accumulated resources of a dying civilization while we find ways to build the new. It is a process in which we rethink, reorganize, and restructure – first reducing our dependence upon the dominant structures, next reorganizing ourselves into mutually supportive clusters or affinity groups, then creating structures appropriate to serving the needs of both our affiliate groups and the common good.

There are already many notable examples of this process moving forward in local communities. One such example that I've had some contact with is the Conscious Community Network[21] that has been developing over the past six years in northern Nevada. Starting with a focus on improving the local economy, under the leadership of Richard Flyer this effort has evolved into a broad-based community-building phenomenon. As Flyer observes, people have a

> drive, for authentic connection, as basic as needing food and water [which] has become harder to realize in a globalized "top down" society and economy – so people have been forming new associations where they can get this felt need met... In every sector of society (business; political; religious; and social service) and all over the planet, people are forming small groups to get back to the basics of our common humanity and connect with one another. The future lies with groups like this, networked in a myriad of ways, and within all parts of society.

We are now seeing (especially with our energy crisis) the decline of "bigger is better" and the emergence of "small is beautiful" in local communities – like millions of blooming flowers all over the planet within the broken-hearted world that we live... The change that is happening goes way beyond economic and social – it is actually a spiritual rebirth showing signs of becoming visible – the emergence of a new society from within the old – and each of us, whether we know it consciously or not, have a vital role in being midwives to its birth.[22]

Coming from this perspective, I have focused my attention primarily on developing solutions that are entrepreneurial and innovative, based on bottom-up organization and voluntary association. As one sage once put it, "If the people lead, the leaders will follow."

3. The Contest for Rulership — Two Opposing Philosophies

There appears to be a general tendency for those who get a little power to try to acquire more of it — and like an addictive drug, power's ability to satisfy seems to depend upon its use in ever-larger doses. Lest the following be misunderstood, let me say at the start that I believe the same tendencies exist in every one of us, and that our efforts to improve our collective lot should not be cast as an "us versus them" contest. When I speak of ruling "élites" it is not to cast them as "evil" in opposition to the "virtuous masses," but to explain the distortions in human affairs that have developed over time and to suggest what may be needed to give civilization a chance of evolving toward higher levels of achievement and a more harmonious condition.

Élitist or Egalitarian?

In 1944, F. A. Hayek warned that the western democracies were on the same "road to serfdom" that had been followed by fascist Germany and Italy (and communist Russia) during the early twentieth century.[23] He characterized the political contest as being between socialism on the one hand, and capitalism on the other — equating the former with "collectivism" and the latter with "individualism."[24] Hayek's dichotomy is, I think, an overly simplistic characterization, and the fundamental struggle goes beyond particular political ideologies or economic systems however one might wish to define them. In my view there is a contest raging in the world that is more fundamental and less apparent than Hayek's. It is one that impinges directly upon our freedom, our dignity, and our morality. It is a struggle between what might be called *elitism* on the one hand, and *egalitarianism* on the other. By elitism I mean the centralized rulership exercised by a small privileged class, while egalitarianism implies the dispersal of power and popular self-government. As Lord Acton keenly observed, "Power corrupts, and absolute power corrupts absolutely." Whether that power be wielded through political office or economic dominance makes little difference; the outcome is the same. It is easy for those who live far above the masses to delude themselves into thinking that power and privilege are their "right," and that whatever serves the narrow self-interest of their class, or race, or religious group also serves the general interest.

Hayek was sensitive to the defects of communism, but he seems to have been blind to the defects inherent in capitalism that make it equally susceptible to becoming totalitarian and tyrannical. The defining feature of totalitarian systems is the centralization of power and control, whether it be economic, political, or social, for these three are but facets of one whole. Considering the millennia of institutionalized hierarchy in our societies, Laurence Victor goes so far as to say,

> I believe that [bureaucracies] are strong attractors for human psychopaths. In fighting their way to the top, individuals are selected who have the greatest tolerance for collateral damage of their actions. Today, the top [levels] of most power echelon hierarchies are populated by psychopaths... The greater the power, the greater the collateral damage required and the greater the deception — both to others done damage [to] and those who are indoctrinated to damage others.
>
> [There are] two alternative modes for coordinating activity so as to accomplish what only many hands in coordinated activity could accomplish. The egalitarian mode involves voluntary cooperation to achieve requisite coordination. An exemplar might be a tribe's collective effort in gathering materials and constructing a long house. The egalitarian mode can have leaders or managers, as roles to assist in coordination. Ideally, each person contributes as to their existing competencies and interests — and all essential roles are covered. The élitist mode involves forced labour in a top down command structure to achieve coordination (and even to

get persons to act as demanded). The force could be facilitated by slavery or wages, both essential for survival in the prevailing situation. Once a people settle into an élitist mode, it must be defended by force and the indoctrination of labour to accept their status.[25]

For that reason, *any* excuse for concentrating power and curtailing the personal rights and freedoms to which all are entitled, even national defense or a "war on terror," must be viewed with suspicion – for as H.L. Mencken observed more than seventy years ago, "The whole aim of practical politics is to keep the populace alarmed (and hence clamorous to be led to safety) by menacing it with an endless series of hobgoblins, all of them imaginary."[26] The real hobgoblins, often created by government itself, can be effectively addressed only by a responsible citizenry acting together from its community base.

Law, by itself, is incapable of restraining the behavior of the addict, for addiction creates imperatives that are stronger than the inhibitions induced by law. But, beyond that, power addicts' need for ever more power leads them to seek ways to control the very process by which laws are made, changed, and adjudicated. While the separation of governmental powers into executive, legislative, and judiciary functions was intended to offer some assurance of pluralism and impartiality, the ever-widening socioeconomic differences have the effect of drawing these functions together into the hands of power élites whose members possess shared interests that are typically antagonistic to those of the masses who comprise the rest of society. As legal constraints upon concentrated power are gradually nullified, government becomes a weapon against freedom, and the ruling class tightens its grip. The people must be ever watchful for the telltale signs of creeping totalitarianism – government secrecy, stonewalling, obfuscation, classified information, abuse of prisoners, surveillance of citizens, harassment of dissenters, appeals to national security and executive privilege, and covert interventions in the affairs of other countries. These signs have been plainly evident in America for some time, and the trend toward totalitarian government has been ramped up since the events of September 11. This is clearly shown in Naomi Wolf's book

The End of America, which outlines ten steps common to all transitions from democratic to totalitarian rule, and shows how they are already manifest today in the United States.[27] Chalmers Johnson, in his *Blowback* trilogy,[28] has clearly described how America's imperial overreach has all but destroyed our republican form of government.

It is said that "the price of freedom is eternal vigilance," but it cannot end there – vigilance is but the beginning of freedom. The acquisition and preservation of freedom require, in addition, responsible civic action. An informed, organized, and *politically active* citizenry is the only kind that has any chance of remaining free.

The Contest in American History: Monarchy or Republic?

A close examination of the early days of the American republic is worthwhile for gaining insights into the ideological struggle that continues to this day. In early American history, the contest between the forces that favoured élite rule and those that favoured pluralistic "government by the people" is epitomized in the persons of Alexander Hamilton, George Washington's Treeasury Secretary, and Thomas Jefferson. Jefferson, and Andrew Jackson after him, envisioned an American government that opposed aristocracy and enabled power and property to be widely shared. It is not commonly recognized that the forces in favour of élite rule were prominent in the formation of the government of the United States, or that their intentions, though seemingly stymied on the political front, have been subsequently and superbly carried out by surreptitious means on the monetary and financial front.

This ideological polarity is nowhere better described than in Arthur Schlesinger's brilliant historical treatise *The Age of Jackson*. Hamilton was of the opinion that "No society ...could succeed 'which did not unite the interest and credit of rich individuals with those of the state.'"[29] He was distrustful of ordinary people to rightly judge matters – indeed, "The rock on which Alexander Hamilton built his church was the deep-seated conviction that society would be governed best by an aristocracy, and that an aristocracy was based most properly and enduringly on property."[30] As Jefferson himself proclaims in his memoir, "a short review of facts will show, that the contests of that day were contests of principle, between the advocates of republican, and those of kingly government, and that had not the former made the efforts they did, our government would have been, even at this early day, a very different thing from what the successful issue of those efforts have made it."[31]

While Jefferson favoured a stronger union than that which emerged under the Articles of Confederation, he was vehemently opposed to the reconstruction of monarchist government on the American continent. He describes in detail how some high army officers suggested to Washington that, prior to disbanding the revolutionary army, Washington should use it to secure to himself the crown. "The indignation with which he is said to have scouted this parricide proposition was equally worthy of his virtue and wisdom." Failing in that attempt, these same individuals proposed "the establishment of an hereditary order ... to be ingrafted into the future frame of government, and placing General Washington still at their head." This, too, Washington resisted.

But the acquisitive forces are nothing if not persistent. Upon the convening of the states at Annapolis in September 1786, Jefferson described this situation:

> [So] general through the States was the sentiment in favour of the former [republican government], that the friends of the latter [monarchy] confined themselves to a course of obstruction only, and delay, to everything proposed; they hoped, that nothing being done, and all things going from bad to worse, a kingly government might be usurped, and submitted to by the people, as better than anarchy and wars internal and external, the certain consequences of the present want of a general government. The effect of their manoeuvres, with the defective attendance of Deputies from the States, resulted in the measure of calling a more general convention, to be held at Philadelphia. At this, the same party exhibited the same practices, and with the same views of preventing a government of concord, which they foresaw would be republican, and of forc-

ing through anarchy their way to monarchy. But the mass of
that convention was too honest, too wise, and too steady, to be
baffled and misled by their manoeuvres.[32]

Power by Other Means

Failing on the political front, the élitists, under the leadership of
Alexander Hamilton, moved forward their monetary and financial
schemes. Jefferson had been away on his mission to France during the
Constitutional Convention, but upon his return in December of 1789,
he was appalled to observe the extent of monarchist sentiment within
the executive branch of the government.

> Hamilton's financial system had then passed. It had two objects;
> first, as a puzzle, to exclude popular understanding and inquiry;
> second, as a machine for the corruption of the legislature; for
> *he avowed the opinion, that man could be governed by one of*
> *two motives only, force or interest; force, he observed, in this*
> *country was out of the question, and the interests, therefore,*
> *of the members must be laid hold of, to keep the legislative in*
> *unison with the executive.* And with grief and shame it must
> be acknowledged that his machine was not without effect; that
> even in this, the birth of our government, some members were
> found sordid enough to bend their duty to their interests, and to
> look after personal rather than public good.[33] [emphasis added]

Jefferson goes on to say,

> *But Hamilton was not only a monarchist, but for a monarchy*
> *bottomed on corruption!* In proof of this, I will relate an anec-
> dote, for the truth of which I attest the God who made me.
> Before the President [Washington] set out on his southern tour
> in April, 1791, he addressed a letter of the fourth of that month,
> from Mount Vernon, to the Secretaries of State, Treasury and
> War, desiring that if any serious and important cases should arise

during his absence, they would consult and act on them. And he requested that the Vice President should also be consulted. This was the only occasion on which that officer was ever requested to take part in a cabinet question. Some occasion for consultation arising, I invited those gentlemen (and the Attorney General, as well as I remember,) to dine with me, in order to confer on the subject. After the cloth was removed, and our question agreed and dismissed, conversation began on other matters, and by some circumstance, was led to the British constitution, on which Mr Adams observed, "purge that constitution of its corruption, and give to its popular branch equality of representation, and it would be the most perfect constitution ever devised by the wit of man." *Hamilton paused and said, "purge it of its corruption, and give to its popular branch equality of representation, and it would become an impracticable government: as it stands at present, with all its supposed defects, it is the most perfect government which ever existed."* And this was assuredly the exact line which separated the political creeds of these two gentlemen. The one was for two hereditary branches and an honest elective one: the other, for an hereditary King, with a House of Lords and Commons corrupted to his will, and standing between him and the people. [emphasis added]

Hamilton was, indeed, a singular character. Of acute understanding, disinterested, honest, and honourable in all private transactions, amiable in society, and duly valuing virtue in private life — yet so bewitched and perverted by the British example as to be under thorough conviction that corruption was essential to the government of a nation.[34]

The core element in Hamilton's financial schemes was to establish in America a central bank modeled after the Bank of England. He was able to achieve his purpose in large part because, as Jefferson observes, "[Washington] was not aware of the drift, or of the effect of Hamilton's schemes. Unversed in financial projects and calculations and budgets, his approbation of them was bottomed on his confidence in the man."[35]

It is easy for us in our time to see Hamilton as a villain and Jefferson as a saintly champion of the people, but nothing is ever as clear cut as that — a thorough reading of history enables a better understanding of the players' motives. Hamilton's overarching objective was to create a strong central government that might enable a weak and fledgling American union to withstand the pressures brought upon it by the imperial powers of Europe, most notably Britain and France. While one might grant the necessity of that time for concentrating more power at the federal level to protect its interests and its people from the then world powers, one must be extremely dubious about the necessity or wisdom of the United States becoming, as it has, a twenty-first century global hegemonic empire.

Hamilton's most often quoted assertion is this one: "A national debt, if it is not excessive, will be to us a national blessing."[36] One of Hamilton's first proposals upon taking office as Washington's secretary of the treasury was that the federal government assume the Revolutionary War debts incurred by the various states. Though it required the federal government to go deeply into debt, that debt had the desired effect of cementing the union of the states. An essential part of Hamilton's plan called for creating revenues sufficient to service the debt and to establish the credit of the federal government, which enabled it to attract much needed capital for development from abroad. Federal government revenues in those days, and even up until the twentieth century, were derived mainly from duties on imported goods and excise taxes on some domestically produced commodities. Hamilton's plan gave the federal government a monopoly on customs duties. With persistence and some dealing with Jefferson and Madison over the location of the new nation's capital, Hamilton succeeded in getting these proposals through Congress and signed by President Washington.[37]

Further along the lines of strengthening the union, Hamilton reasoned that it was essential to draw the loyalty of the moneyed class toward the union and away from their respective states. This was one reason for the assumption of the states' debts. As John Steele Gordon explains it, "The debts [of the states], of course, were largely held by the prosperous men of business, commerce, and agriculture — the oligarchs, in other words. These men's loyalties lay mainly with their respective states and the cosy local societies in which they had grown up. Although they had largely supported the creation of the new Union, Hamilton had every reason to suppose that their support would quickly fade if their self-interest dictated it. Hamilton, therefore, was anxious to make it in the self-interest of these men to continue their support of the Union."[38]

For us today, the most significant aspect of Hamilton's programme was his effort to establish an American central bank along the lines of the Bank of England. "Hamilton saw it as an instrument of fiscal efficiency, economic regulation, and money creation. Jefferson saw it as another giveaway to the rich and as a potential instrument of tyranny. Furthermore, Jefferson and Madison saw it as patently unconstitutional for the federal government to establish a bank, for the Constitution nowhere gives the federal government the explicit power to charter a bank or, for that matter, any other corporation."[39]

But Hamilton got his bank, and over the subsequent years the forces for élite rule have gotten a whole lot more. The courts subsequently ruled that the chartering of the central bank was constitutional, and by selling the idea of the "implied powers" of the Constitution, the élitists have managed to enlarge the power of the federal government vis-à-vis the states, far beyond anything that the framers of that document had intended or might have envisioned.

The battle for rulership has continued to rage throughout the history of the United States, even up to the present day. Except for occasional victories – most notably under the leadership of Jefferson, Jackson, and perhaps Franklin Roosevelt – the élitist forces have step-by-step tightened their grip on power, in the name of national security arrogating ever more power to the executive branch, until the Congress has become a mere rubber stamp. While the United States maintains the trappings of a democratic republic, it is in truth an imperial power under the control of a global oligarchy. As the only remaining superpower, it has been used to achieve "full spectrum dominance" that can assure control of the world's major resources, and usher in a "new world order" in which the mass of the population in *all* countries is increasingly dominated and exploited by a very small ruling class using whatever means it may deem necessary.

As Jeffrey Sachs observes, "When a society is economically dominant, it is easy for its members to assume that such dominance reflects a deeper superiority — whether religious, racial, genetic, cultural, or institutional — rather than an accident of timing or geography." He notes the historical emergence of all kinds of theories that justified "brutal forms of exploitation of the poor through colonial rule, dispossession of the properties and lands of the poor by the rich and even slavery."[40]

President Bill Clinton's mentor at Georgetown University, Professor Carroll Quigley, has candidly revealed that

> the powers of financial capitalism had another far-reaching aim, nothing less than to create a world system of financial control in private hands able to dominate the political system of each country and the economy of the world as a whole. This system was to be controlled in a feudalist fashion by the central banks of the world acting in concert, by secret agreements arrived at in frequent private meetings and conferences. The apex of the system was to be the Bank for International Settlements in Basle, Switzerland, a private bank owned and controlled by the world's central banks which were themselves private corporations. Each central bank ... sought to dominate its government by its ability to control Treasury loans, to manipulate foreign exchanges, to influence the level of economic activity in the country, and to influence cooperative politicians by subsequent economic rewards in the business world.[41]

In the following chapters, we shall describe the evolution of the mechanisms by which these goals have been achieved.

4. Central Banking and the Rise of the Money Power

It should be evident that any effort to alter the status quo must be informed by a thorough understanding of the mechanisms that have been used to consolidate power and wealth. In our modern era, the chief instrument by which that consolidation has been achieved is by *control of the machinery for creating money.* Money has consistently been abused by those who have had authority over it. In medieval times, it became common for princes and kings to recall and reissue the gold and silver coins that then served as money, each time enriching themselves by reducing the precious metal content of the new coins and forcing their subjects to accept them at the same nominal value as the old.

But it is only within the past three centuries that the machinery of money and banking has been refined to enable levels of control approaching the absolute to be wielded on a worldwide basis by a handful of individuals. In something resembling "the divine right of kings" they must imagine themselves to possess superior qualities that entitle them to their positions of privilege, dominance, and rulership. This privilege, they claim in private to be their legitimate reward for bringing order to the "unruly mob." Surely the most valuable and effective privilege for maintaining control and appropriating wealth in the modern era has been the privilege of controlling the machinery of money and banking. Meyer Amschel Rothschild, the patriarch and founder of the celebrated banking dynasty, is quoted as having said, "Give me the power to create a nation's money and I care not who makes the laws." And from whence does that power derive? It is the corruption of government that Hamilton spoke of. Make no mistake about it, government — of whatever shape or description — is a dispenser of privilege. It favours the few at the expense of the many and becomes ever more corrupt as it arrogates ever more power. This is the seed and soil from which central banking has sprung.

Central Banking, an Unholy Alliance

Imagine being able to borrow and spend as much money as you want and never having to pay any of it back. Imagine being able to write an IOU for each purchase you make and have someone else redeem it, or being able to write cheques against someone else's bank account. Imagine having the legal privilege to create virtually all of the nation's money by making a few bookkeeping entries and lending it out at interest. Shocking as it may seem, this is the nature of the monetary and financial regime that has spread around the world. But who holds these privileges and how are they exercised?

The Bank of England

That story begins with the founding of the Bank of England more than three hundred years ago. William III (William of Orange) and Mary II had ascended to the throne of England as co-rulers in 1689. William was at war with France (under Louis XIV) in what is known as the War of the League of Augsburg (1688–97). War is an expensive proposition, and William needed to raise money to finance it. Another William, the Scotsman William Patterson, provided the solution to the king's financial problem – "he proposed a loan of £1.2m to the government; in return the subscribers would be incorporated as The Governor and Company of the Bank of England with long term banking privileges including the issue of notes."[42] By 1708, the government had fallen more deeply into debt to the bank, and as a result the bank's privileges were extended – giving it a virtual monopoly in the issuance of banknotes.

That was the beginning of the unholy alliance between politics and finance that has enabled governments to spend without being limited by tax revenues, and has given bankers the privilege of creating credit money (originally, in the form of banknotes, now as "deposits") and lending it out at interest. The Bank of England became the prototype for central banks that were eventually to be established in virtually every country of the world.

Riegel provides this summary of the matter:

> Throughout the ages the devices of cunning men have turned money to their nefarious purposes. Money, beginning with private enterprise as a means of escaping the limitation of barter soon developed the cheat to exploit the honest trader who in an effort to protect himself turned to government for protection, only to find that now he had two thieves, the private money changer and the political plunderer working hand in glove against him. By this combination the money changer gained the prestige of political sanction through legislative license and the state secured a deceptive device for laying taxes upon the citizenry [by means of the hidden tax called inflation]. It was and remains a vicious alliance.[43]

Professor Quigley regarded "the founding of the Bank of England by William Paterson and his friends in 1694" as "one of the great dates in world history." Quigley observed that

> this organizational structure for creating means of payment out of nothing, which we call credit, was not invented by England but was developed by her to become one of her chief weapons in the victory over Napoleon in 1815. The emperor, as the last great mercantilist, could not see money in any but concrete terms, and was convinced that his efforts to fight wars on the basis of "sound money," by avoiding the creation of credit, would ultimately win him a victory by bankrupting England. He was wrong, although the lesson has had to be relearned by modern financiers in the twentieth century.[44]

Central Banking in the United States

No sooner had the colonies taken steps to sever their ties with Britain, than the élite forces set about replicating the Bank of England model in America. The first attempt in that direction had been made even prior to the end of the Revolutionary War with the chartering by Congress of the Bank of North America on the very last day of 1781. Wikipedia provides this account:

> Earlier, on April 30, 1781, Alexander Hamilton, then only twenty-three years old and still serving in the military, had sent [Finance Minister, Robert] Morris a letter. First, Hamilton revealed that he had recommended Morris for the position the previous summer when the constitution of the executive was being solidified. Second, he proceeded to lay out a proposal for a National Bank. Morris, who had corresponded with Hamilton previously (1780) on the subject of funding the war, immediately drafted a legislative proposal based on Hamilton's suggestion and submitted it to the Congress. Morris persuaded Congress to charter the Bank of North America, the first private commercial bank in the United States.[45]

As Murray Rothbard describes it, "This bank, headed by Morris himself [in an evident conflict of interest], ... was not only the first fractional reserve commercial bank in the US; it was to be a privately owned central bank, modeled after the Bank of England ... [The Bank] received the privilege from the government of its notes being receivable in all duties and taxes to all governments, at par with specie that is, gold and silver. In addition, no other banks were to be permitted to operate in the country. In return for its monopoly license to issue paper money, the bank would graciously lend most of its newly created money to the federal government to purchase public debt and be reimbursed by the hapless taxpayer."[46] The Bank of North America, despite its monopoly powers, did not fare well. By the end of 1783, it had ceased to function as a central bank and shifted its status by obtaining a state charter in Pennsylvania.

The First Bank of the United States
The next attempt came a few years later, after the Articles of Confederation had been replaced by the Constitution. Led by Alexander Hamilton, who had fought alongside George Washington in the

Revolutionary War and now served in his cabinet as Secretary of the Treasury, the élite interests proposed that a Bank of the United States be chartered to serve as the depository of federal government funds. The bank also, like the Bank of England, was to enjoy certain privileges. It would have the power to issue notes that would be acceptable by the government in payment of taxes. In 1791, Congress approved the charter and the bill was signed by President Washington. Thus, the first Bank of the United States came into being. It was a private corporation owned mainly by foreign, mostly British, interests. This bank lasted until 1811 when its twenty-year charter expired and the bill to renew it failed by one vote in Congress.

Andrew Jackson and the "Bank War"
The Second Bank of the United States, chartered in 1816, was essentially a replica of the first Bank of the United States. It also had a twenty year charter that was due to expire in 1836, at which time the bank's proponents expected that it would be renewed, but the election of Andrew Jackson as President in 1828 threw a spanner into that plan. In 1832, during Jackson's campaign for a second term, the bank became a major issue. Jackson argued that "The Bank of the United States is in itself a Government which has gradually increased in strength from the day of its establishment."[47] He said of the bankers, "You are a den of vipers and thieves. I intend to rout you out, and by the Eternal God, I will rout you out." He saw himself as a champion of the people against "a heartless monied aristocracy."[48] In his view, the "bank war" was a contest for rulership — would the United States be governed by the people through their elected president and representatives, or by an unelected financial élite through their central bank instrument?

Nicholas Biddle, then president of the bank, had lobbied Congress to pass a bill to recharter the bank early. The sentiments of the antibank forces were ably expressed by Thomas Hart Benton on the floor of the Senate:

> First: Mr President, I object to the renewal of the charter ... because I look upon the bank as an institution too great and powerful to be tolerated in a government of free and equal laws

... Secondly, I object ... because its tendencies are dangerous
and pernicious to the government and the people ... It tends to
aggravate the inequality of fortunes; to make the rich richer,
and the poor poorer; to multiply nabobs and paupers ... Thirdly,
I object ... on account of the exclusive privileges, and anti-
republican monopoly, which it gives to the stockholders.[49]

Despite such pleas as Benton's, Congress did pass the recharter bill —
but on November 24, 1832, Jackson vetoed it. While Jackson acknowledged in his veto message that "A bank of the United States is in many
respects convenient for the Government and useful to the people," he
argued that the bank *as constituted* was a privileged monopoly created
to make rich men "richer by act of Congress." The bank, he declared,
was "unauthorized by the Constitution, subversive of the rights of the
States, and dangerous to the liberties of the people."[50] In the penulti-
mate paragraph of his veto message, Jackson provided this inspiration
and challenge:

Experience should teach us wisdom. Most of the difficulties our
Government now encounters and most of the dangers which
impend over our Union have sprung from an abandonment of
the legitimate objects of Government by our national legislation, and the adoption of such principles as are embodied in
this act [to recharter the Bank]. Many of our rich men have
not been content with equal protection and equal benefits, but
have besought us to make them richer by act of Congress. By
attempting to gratify their desires we have in the results of
our legislation arrayed section against section, interest against
interest, and man against man, in a fearful commotion which
threatens to shake the foundations of our Union. It is time to
pause in our career to review our principles, and if possible
revive that devoted patriotism and spirit of compromise which
distinguished the sages of the Revolution and the fathers of
our Union. If we can not at once, in justice to interests vested
under improvident legislation, make our Government what it
ought to be, we can at least take a stand against all new grants

of monopolies and exclusive privileges, against any prostitution of our Government to the advancement of the few at the expense of the many, and in favour of compromise and gradual reform in our code of laws and system of political economy.[51]

Those words seem even more relevant today than they were when Jackson wrote them.

It was Jackson's intention to begin withdrawing the government's funds from the central bank in 1833, a feat that he was able to accomplish only after replacing two secretaries of the treasury who had refused to carry out his order. When Jackson appointed Roger B. Taney

GENERAL JACKSON SLAYING THE MANY HEADED MONSTER.

Figure 4.1 1836 Cartoon — The "Bank War" between Andrew Jackson and Nicholas Biddle. This 1836 cartoon is a satire of President Jackson's campaign to destroy the Second Bank of the United States, which is represented as a many headed snake, by use of his cane — which represents his veto of the recharter bill. The largest of the snake's heads is that of Nicholas Biddle, the bank's president.[52]

to the post, the instructions were carried out. Government funds were withdrawn from the bank and federal tax revenues were subsequently deposited in various state banks.

Biddle was outraged at Jackson's actions and retaliated by constricting credit throughout the country. He attempted to pressure Jackson to change his policies toward the bank by calling in loans and refusing to make new ones. This all but crashed the economy, causing widespread distress by depriving legitimate business of the credit money it needed to conduct normal operations. Arthur Schlesinger describes the situation thus: "The determination which enabled Jackson to resist the hysteria of panic came basically from the possession of an alternative policy of his own. Madison had surrendered to a corresponding, though less intense, pressure in 1816 [when he allowed the Second Bank of the United States to be chartered] because he had no constructive programme to offer. But, for Jackson, the emotions and ideas which underlay the hard-money case against the Bank were crystallizing into a coherent and concrete set of measures, designed to capture the government for 'the humble members of society,' as Hamilton's system had captured it for 'the rich and powerful.'"[53] Initially, the business community blamed Jackson for their distress, but they eventually came to realize that the fault lay with Biddle and the Second Bank.

Andrew Jackson is not the only American president to have warned against the money power. Thomas Jefferson said, "I sincerely believe ... that banking establishments are more dangerous than standing armies."[54] President James A. Garfield, who had previously been chairman of the Banking Committee in the House of Representatives, said, "Whoever controls the money in any country is master of all its legislation and commerce."[55]

The Free Banking Era
The demise of the Second Bank was followed by a period known as the "free banking" era (1837–63), during which the credit creation process was opened up to competition and oversight of banking activities devolved to the various states. While critics have pejoratively referred to this time as the era of "wildcat banking," a defensive statement has

come from no less a personality than former Federal Reserve Chairman Alan Greenspan, who said:

> Free banking meant free entry under the terms of a general law of incorporation rather than through a specific legislative act. The public, especially in New York, had become painfully aware that the restrictions on entry in the chartered system were producing a number of adverse effects. For one thing, in the absence of competition, access to bank credit was perceived to have become politicized — banks' boards of directors seemed to regard those who shared their political convictions as the most creditworthy borrowers, a view not unknown more recently in East Asia. In addition, because a bank charter promised monopoly profits, bank promoters were willing to pay handsomely for the privilege and legislators apparently eagerly accepted payment, often in the form of allocations of bank stock at below-market prices.
>
> While free banking was not actually as free as commonly perceived, it also was not nearly as unstable. The perception of the free banking era as an era of "wildcat" banking marked by financial instability and, in particular, by widespread significant losses to noteholders also turns out to be exaggerated. Recent scholarship has demonstrated that free bank failures were not as common and resulting losses to noteholders were not as severe as earlier historians had claimed.[56]

During that time, each bank issued its own currency notes and it was left to the market to evaluate their soundness. Fractional reserve banking prevailed and banknotes were still redeemable for specie (gold or silver). Typically, the farther a banknote strayed from its home territory, the more it would be discounted from face value — or sometimes completely refused as payment. The plethora of currencies in circulation gave rise to a large number of "note brokers," who made a profit by buying banknotes at a discount then presenting them at the issuing banks for redemption at par. The activities of the note brokers provided an important element of discipline to the issuing banks, since they had to be prepared to redeem their notes that were rapidly returning from the hinterlands. These brokers also published periodic directories called "banknote reporters," which listed the prevailing discounts on the notes of thousands of banks. This information was invaluable to merchants and other banks. Greenspan describes it thus:

> Throughout the free banking era the effectiveness of market prices for notes, and their associated impact on the cost of funds, imparted an increased market discipline, perhaps because technological change – the telegraph and the railroad – made monitoring of banks more effective and reduced the time required to send a note home for redemption. Between 1838 and 1860 the discounts on notes of new entrants diminished and discounts came to correspond more closely to objective measures of the riskiness of individual banks.[57]

In an unexpectedly friendly gesture toward free banking, Greenspan goes on to say,

> During the Civil War, today's bank structure was created by the Congress. It seems clear that a major, if not the major, motivation of the National Bank Act of 1863 was to assist in the financing of the Civil War. But the provisions of the act that incorporated key elements of free banking provide compelling evidence that contemporary observers did not regard free banking as a failure. These provisions included free entry and collateralized bank notes.[58]

As financial crises proliferate in our own time, economists would do well to make a careful study of the free banking period and to propose the reimplementation of those "key elements."

The Federal Reserve

The interests of international banking and finance might be delayed, but they were not to be defeated. From the time of the Civil War onward, they gradually resumed control and eventually managed to get a new central bank in the form of the Federal Reserve. The act to create the Fed was passed by Congress in 1913 – just before Christmas, when most representatives had already gone home for the holidays. The secret meetings and other events leading up to its passage are well told in a book, *The Creature From Jekyll Island*,[59] and in various other sources.[60] Rothbard offers this critical assessment: "The financial élites of this country, notably the Morgan, Rockefeller, and Kuhn, Loeb interests, were responsible for putting through the Federal Reserve System, as a governmentally created and sanctioned cartel device to enable the nation's banks to inflate the money supply in a coordinated fashion."[61]

President Woodrow Wilson, who ironically supported the creation of the Fed, also expressed dismay over the concentration of power in the hands of a financial élite. In his book, *The New Freedom,* Wilson said, "Some of the biggest men in the United States, in the field of commerce and manufacture, are afraid of somebody, are afraid of something. They know that there is a power somewhere so organized, so subtle, so watchful, so interlocked, so complete, so pervasive, that they had better not speak above their breath when they speak in condemnation of it." He made it clear that he understood the nature of that "power" saying,

> there has come about an extraordinary and very sinister concentration in the control of business in the country. However it has come about, it is more important still that the control of credit also has become dangerously centralized. It is the mere truth to say that the financial resources of the country are not at the command of those who do not submit to the direction and domination of small groups of capitalists who wish to keep the economic development of the country under their own eye and guidance. The great monopoly in this country is the monopoly of big credits. So long as that exists, our old variety and freedom and individual energy of development are out of the question. A great industrial nation is controlled by its system of credit. Our system of credit is privately concentrated. The growth of the nation, therefore, and all our activities are in the hands of a few men who, even if their action be honest and intended for the public interest, are necessarily concentrated upon the great undertakings in which their own money is involved and who

necessarily, by very reason of their own limitations, chill and check and destroy genuine economic freedom. This is the greatest question of all, and to this statesmen must address themselves with an earnest determination to serve the long future and the true liberties of men. This money trust, or, as it should be more properly called, this credit trust, ... is no myth; it is no imaginary thing.[62]

Congressman and 2008 presidential candidate Ron Paul has called for the abolition of the Federal Reserve. During a hearing before the House Financial Services Committee on February 11, 2004, Paul, referring to the Federal Reserve, suggested that "maybe there's too much power in the hands of those who control monetary policy? The power to create the financial bubbles. The power to maybe bring the bubble about. The power to change the value of the stock market within minutes. That to me is just an ominous power and challenges the whole concept of freedom and liberty and sound money." The then Fed Chairman, Alan Greenspan, appearing before that committee, responded, "Congressman, as I've said to you before, the problem you are eluding [sic] to is called the conversion of a commodity standard to fiat money. We have statutorily gone onto a fiat money standard and as a consequence of that *it is inevitable that the authority, which is the producer of the money supply, will have inordinate power* ... And the power that we have is all granted by you [the Congress]. We don't have any capability whatsoever to do anything without the agreement or even the acquiescence of the Congress of the United States."[63]

That, of course, is technically correct, but very few members of Congress have been willing to challenge the power of the Fed or even to exercise the most perfunctory degree of oversight. Most are beholden to the same interests that have created the Fed and the global money and banking regime.

Central Banking Spreads around the World

Central banking, with its inherent privileges and conflicts of interest, has spread around the world. Quigley has pointed out that, "In most countries the central bank was surrounded closely by the almost invisible private investment banking firms. These, like the planet Mercury, could hardly be seen in the dazzle emitted by the central bank which they, in fact, often dominated. Yet a close observer could hardly fail to notice the close *private* associations between these private, international bankers and the central bank itself."[64]

Although the Bank of England was the archetypal central bank, it was not necessarily by direct emulation that central banks were established in virtually every country. But there can be little doubt that it has been brought about by the same objectives, along with pressures from the international banking establishment. The same circumstances seem to have led to similar outcomes of collusion between the financial powers and the political powers. Professor Heinrich Rittershausen traces the development from private issuing banks to modern central banks through the following stages:[65]

1. The exclusive license to issue notes is granted to a bank as state privilege.
2. The state discovers that the bank is a source of credit.
3. The government tax offices begin to accept the still purely private notes in tax payments instead of metallic money.
4. The state needs money in times of emergencies [like wartime]. The bank cannot refuse large loans to the government [for deficit spending]. Economically, these loans are long term.
5. In this way the note issuance becomes excessive. Redemption (in metallic money) becomes impossible and therefore is abolished by law.
6. In anticipation of feared reactions of the public, i.e., discounting the notes or refusal of acceptance, the notes are given legal

tender* power, i.e., compulsory acceptance. By this means,
the notes lose their character as an issue of a private bank
currency note.

7.   Legal tender (forced acceptance of the notes) and repudiation
of note redemption make the metallic standard inoperable.
The measure of value now becomes the paper currency itself.
The automatic regulation of the note supply by market forces
comes to an end.[66]

Riegel warned us that, "In the exercise of the money power, under
the dictates of political expediency, the state is driven inevitably from
libertarian forms of democracy and republicanism to the autarchic
forms of fascism, socialism and communism." Ultimately, these three
come to look very much alike, and in recent decades we have seen this
tendency become ever more a reality, particularly in the United States.
This sad state of affairs is well documented by Chalmers Johnson in his
recently published *Blowback* trilogy.

---

* Author's note: Legal tender is a form of payment that must, by law, be accepted when offered in
settlement of a debt obligation. If a creditor refuses to accept payment of legal tender money by a
debtor, the courts will not support the creditor's claim against the debtor to collect through other means.
A further implication is that if both a precious metal coin and a debased paper currency note have legal
tender status, debtors will choose to pay using the paper notes, and the coins will go out of circulation.
This is the essence of "Gresham's Law." The nature and consequences of legal tender will be more fully
treated later in the book.

5. The New World Order

Benjamin Disraeli, twice British prime minister under Queen Victoria, once said that, "The world is governed by very different personages from what is imagined by those who are not behind the scenes." Those who are set before the public often do us the favour of boldly describing just what it is that might otherwise be hard to imagine. From Disraeli's revelation to the first President Bush's proclamation of an impending "new world order," many of the élites appear sufficiently comfortable with the use of their power that they need not always keep it strictly secret.[67]

The Power Behind the Central Banks

In the previous chapter we described the emergence of central banks and their role in making money an instrument for consolidating political control. Carroll Quigley helps us to understand the connection between central banks and the financial élite. He writes:

> It must not be felt that these heads of the world's chief central banks were themselves substantive powers in world finance. They were not. Rather, they were the technicians and agents of the dominant investment bankers of their own countries, who had raised them up and were perfectly capable of throwing them down. The substantive financial powers of the world were in the hands of these investment bankers (also called "international" or "merchant" bankers) who remained largely behind the scenes in their own unincorporated private banks. These formed a system of international cooperation and national dominance which was more private, more powerful, and more

secret than that of their agents in the central banks. This dominance of investment bankers was based on their control over
the flows of credit and investment funds in their own countries
and throughout the world. They could dominate the financial
and industrial systems of their own countries by their influence
over the flow of current funds through bank loans, the discount
rate, and the re-discounting of commercial debts; they could
dominate governments by their control over current government loans and the play of the international exchanges... In
this system the Rothschilds had been preeminent during much
of the nineteenth century, but, at the end of that century, they
were being replaced by J.P. Morgan whose central office was
in New York, although it was always operated as if it were in
London (where it had, indeed, originated as George Peabody
and Company in 1838). Old J.P. Morgan died in 1913, but was
succeeded by his son of the same name (who had been trained in
the London branch until 1901), while the chief decisions in the
firm were increasingly made by Thomas W. Lamont after 1924.[68]

Quigley tells us that these investment bankers differ from ordinary
bankers

in distinctive ways: (1) they were cosmopolitan and international; (2) they were close to governments and were particularly
concerned with questions of government debts; (3) their interests were almost exclusively in bonds and very rarely in goods,
since they admired liquidity; (4) they were, accordingly, fanati-
cal devotees of deflation;[69] (5) they were almost equally devoted
to secrecy and the secret use of financial influence in political
life. These bankers came to be called "international bankers"
and, more particularly, were known as "merchant bankers" in
England, "private bankers" in France, and "investment bankers"
in the United States. In all countries they carried on various
kinds of banking and exchange activities, but everywhere they
were sharply distinguishable from other more obvious kinds of
banks, such as savings banks or commercial banks.[70]

Quigley goes on to spotlight the increasingly obvious superficiality of differences between political parties and to demonstrate their subservience to the money power, saying, "To Morgan all political parties were simply organizations to be used, and the firm always was careful to keep a foot in all camps."[71] Quigley's description of the various organizations established to influence public policy and the particular individuals who founded, ran, and financed them becomes tedious in its detail — but it is the forest that we need to see and not the trees. Naturally, in the more than four decades since Quigley wrote his book, the names of the personages (and even some of the organizations) have changed, but the goals and general structure of this élite establishment remain the same. While Quigley seemed to think that the power of the Anglo-American establishment was on the wane, it seems clear that the trend toward greater élite control has continued, though with a more diverse composition. Among those organizations and groups that are prominent on the current scene in advancing the élitist agenda are the Council on Foreign Relations, the Trilateral Commission, the Bilderberg groups, and the banking companies and the families that control them.

It is a curious thing that Quigley, in his book, would so frankly expose the machinations of the élite "money masters" and their plans to gain total global control, while warmly supporting their purposes and goals. I agree with W. Cleon Skousen's assessment that, "The real value of *Tragedy and Hope* is not so much as a 'history of the world in our time' (as its subtitle suggests) but rather as a bold and boastful admission by Dr Quigley that there actually exists a relatively small but powerful group which has succeeded in acquiring a choke-hold on the affairs of practically the entire human race."[72]

A Merging of Interests

The politicization of money, banking, and finance (which prevails throughout the world today) has enabled the concentration of power and wealth in few hands — a situation that has been extremely damaging to societies, cultures, economies, democratic government, and the environment. National governments have arrogated to themselves virtually unlimited spending power, which enables them to channel wealth to favoured clients, to conduct wars on a massive scale, and to subvert democratic institutions and the popular will. The privileged private banking establishment has managed to monopolize everyone's credit, enabling the few to exploit the many through their partiality in allocating credit, by charging usury (disguised as "interest") and increasingly exorbitant fees, and by rewarding politicians for their service in promoting their interests.

These two, government and banking, have colluded to create a political money system that embodies a "debt imperative" that results in a "growth imperative," which forces environmental destruction and rends the social fabric while increasing the concentration of power and wealth. It creates economic and political instabilities that manifest in recurrent cycles of depression and inflation, domestic and international conflict, and social dislocation. (All of this will be addressed more fully in Chapter 6.)

The balance of power in this collusion has at some times tended toward greater power for politicians and government and less for the financial interests, while at other times it has tended in the opposite direction. Either way, autocratic government is the outcome. Now, these forces seem to be more unified than ever in pursuing their common agenda to disempower democratic government and to assume power around the globe. Within the past several decades, we have seen a massive shift of power toward the financial establishment as their friends in government have lobbied hard for, and won, "deregulation" of the financial industry, and under the guise of "free trade" have pushed forward a neocolonial agenda. In the United States, the controls and oversight bodies that were painstakingly built up following the Great Depression have been systematically hobbled or dismantled.

Wars, Internal and External

The past few decades have seen a diminished middle class in America, and government power has been increasingly turned against the people as a way of forestalling dissent and suppressing reaction against the growing inequities. In February 2008, the United States and Canada agreed to help each other to quell civil disturbances. The February 22 edition of the *Ottawa Citizen* ran a story under this headline: "Canada, US Agree to Use Each Other's Troops in Civil Emergencies." Here is part of that article:

> Canada and the US have signed an agreement that paves the way for the militaries from either nation to send troops across each other's borders during an emergency, but some are questioning why the Harper government has kept silent on the deal. Neither the Canadian government nor the Canadian Forces announced the new agreement, which was signed Feb. 14 in Texas. The US military's Northern Command, however, publicized the agreement with a statement outlining how its top officer, Gen. Gene Renuart, and Canadian Lt.-Gen. Marc Dumais, head of Canada Command, signed the plan, which allows the military from one nation to support the armed forces of the other nation during a civil emergency.[73]

I leave it to the reader to imagine what kind of civil emergency might require the United States, the most powerful nation on earth, to ask for help from abroad. If there was ever a time when such help was needed it was during the Katrina hurricane disaster of 2005, but offers of help from many nations were refused. Under the present monetary system, policy makers must choose between two distasteful outcomes. The only thing that can prevent cripplingly high food and fuel prices is a worldwide economic recession. In either case, and exacerbated by the hobbling of our civil rights and traditional outlets for expressions of dissent, the citizenry is sure to become ever more restive. The peaceful public demonstrations that were so common during the 1960s and 1970s are no longer tolerated. Police have become increasingly heavy-handed and brutal in their dealings with assemblies of significant numbers of people in public places. The 1999 "Battle of Seattle" seems to have marked a turning point. In that case an estimated crowd of 40,000 people assembled to protest the meeting of the World Trade Organization and its undemocratic approach to economic globalization. Police, clad in black riot gear, used pepper spray, tear gas, and rubber bullets to disperse the crowd. Subsequent demonstrations in Miami and elsewhere have been similarly met. Contrary to the expectations of most Americans, particularly those with liberal or leftist leanings, these sorts of abuses by the police have become increasingly frequent even in such "social democracies" as Denmark.[74]

With regard to wars, it is fairly well recognized that every war creates innumerable opportunities for profit, but the extreme magnitude of the resultant profits escapes general notice. The most recent war in Iraq seems to have taken profiteering to a new level with contractors like Blackwater, Halliburton, and KBR racking up obscene profits on contracts from their Bush administration allies. More important and obscure is the opportunity that war presents for further élite concentrations of power and wealth when the rebuilding begins. The vested interests of the financial élite will rarely lead them to be vocal opponents to war, and may in fact bias them toward favouring war, even if psychologically they delude themselves into thinking this is because the war is somehow necessary. Consider the devastation of Europe and Japan during World War II. Most of the destroyed properties had been owned free and clear by diverse individuals and companies beyond the influence and control of western banks. In order to rebuild the destroyed infrastructure, governments, individuals, and companies had to take on enormous debts. The bankers of the world were, of course, ready to work their alchemy of turning those debts into spendable cash. In this way, the usury net encompasses ever greater portions of the world's real wealth and the financial élite gain greater political and economic leverage.

Money Power, the Key Element in the New World Order

I have argued that control of money and exchange mechanisms is the key structural element that determines the distribution of power, and that it must be *the* main focus if any degree of community empowerment and self-determination is to be achieved. A money monopoly, whether in private hands or government controlled, is inimical to freedom and equity. As E.C. Riegel has expressed it:

> The money mechanism, under the concept borrowed from England, is a contrivance that is both political and private but is strictly neither. It is a hybrid, and its name is finance. Compounded from both political and private interests, it compromises both private enterprise and public service. It confounds students of money and causes them to take sides for either the banking end or the government end when in fact a plague should be put upon both their houses. Control over money should be denied to both government and banks. Finance is the evil genius that brings discredit upon both the state and private enterprise and raises the threat of fascism and communism.[75]

Since those words were written, the "powers of financial capitalism," as Carrol Quigley called them, have been hard at work to complete their plan "to create a world system of financial control in private hands able to dominate the political system of each country and the economy of the world as a whole."[76] Their control has now become almost total. Besides controlling the *creation* of money and its source allocation, they also have firm control over the *flow* of money through the banking and financial channels. In the name of financial security, the war on terror, and the war on drugs, it has become almost impossible for the individual to maintain any degree of financial privacy – while government and the inner sanctum of high finance become ever more opaque, enabling the well-connected and those at the top to launder and hide their ill-gotten gains. In today's world of greatly diluted civil protections, if you do something to displease the "masters," you may well find your name on a "no-fly list," have your bank and credit card accounts frozen, or be abducted in an "extraordinary rendition" from anywhere you might be in the world to some secret prison camp that could be anywhere else in the world. "But I've done nothing wrong," you say. Well, that depends on who defines "wrong." President George W. Bush, shortly after the destruction of the World Trade Center in New York in 2001, vowed to "rid the world of evildoers." In the aftermath, Congress has allowed the executive branch to assume all but dictatorial powers that have sharply curtailed government's respect for American traditions, the Bill of Rights, and limitations on government abuse of power that go all the way back to the Magna Carta (such as habeas corpus), and allowed it to define on an ad hoc basis what is good and what is bad, what is legal and what is not. How President Obama utilizes those powers is yet to be seen, but their existence in the first place is cause enough for alarm. The tools are already in place for him or some future president to use as they see fit.

Erosion of National Sovereignty

One element in the élite plan is to further reduce the amount of discretion that national governments, particularly in the Third World, have over their own economies and finances. The primary strategy thus far has been to encumber countries with debt that is supposed to be used for development projects; when they are unable to repay, the International Monetary Fund imposes "structural readjustment" programmes that favour western banks, wrest away control of national resources, and create hardships for the local population.

Now these countries are being asked to give up their own national currencies. Granted, most governments have abused the issuance of their national currencies, but the powers that be are asking them to adopt global currencies that have also been abused. Benn Steil, Director of International Economics at the Council on Foreign Relations, in an article titled, "The End of National Currency," says that "The world needs to abandon unwanted currencies, replacing them with dollars, euros, and multinational currencies as yet unborn."[77] The ostensible plan is to reduce global exchange media to three — one each for Europe, the Americas, and Asia. One might reasonably suppose that at a later stage, those three would be combined into one currency also under the control of the global banking élite. Already, some countries (such as Ecuador) have taken that advice and chosen to use the US dollar as their national medium of exchange. Federal Reserve notes are just as necessary in Quito as they are in New York.

Political consolidation is also on the agenda. There is increasing talk, for example, of a North American Union similar to the European Union. In another recent article from the Council on Foreign Relations, professor Robert Pastor suggests that, "It's time to integrate further with Canada and Mexico, not separate from them." This article is a follow-up to a report by a 2005 Council on Foreign Relations task force that Pastor co-chaired, which shows it to be more than just one man's opinion.[78]

So there we have a brief sketch of the power structure in today's world, how it came about, and how it is proceeding with its programme. We've revealed here only the barest tip of the iceberg, but it is perhaps enough to help a few escape from the delusional "matrix." With America's emergence in the twentieth century as the world's only superpower, and the global economic imperium advancing under the banner of "free trade," the plan referred to by Quigley has been realized to a very high degree. The new world order is upon us. The demands of our would-be masters will become increasingly onerous as we enter the final stages. One need not be a Christian, or even religious, to wonder at the fact that we are now very close to an oppressive global system of order and control based on economic exchange, a system that was amazingly foretold almost two thousand years ago:

> And he causeth all, both small and great, rich and poor, free and bond, to receive a mark in their right hand or in their foreheads:
> And that *no man might buy or sell,* save he that had the mark, or the name of the beast or the number of his name.
> — Revelation 13:16–17 (AV) [emphasis added]

6. Usury and the Engine of Destruction

The growth god is dead. The era of seemingly endless growth is, in fact, coming to an end. Shall we lament its passing and try to sustain it a little bit longer, shall we passively watch as our world crumbles into ashes, or shall we welcome this crisis as the opportunity we've been hoping for to create the kind of world we want to live in and leave for posterity? That is not to say that growth per se has been all bad. The enormous expansion of economic output throughout the industrial era has provided material benefits and more comfortable lives for a substantial portion of the world's people. Yet billions of others have been excluded and exploited in the process. Our current system condemns them to ongoing destitution and drives the overall economy to grow for growth's sake. Like cancer, much of the growth now is the wrong kind of growth, out of control and in the wrong places, generating ever greater disparities of power and wealth, wasting valuable resources, and producing side effects that are ultimately harmful to the earth's capacity to support life.

Monetary Stringency, Past and Present

In the era of Columbus and the Conquistadors, the world was obsessed with gold and silver. The Old World was ready for an explosion of commerce and trade but governments were deeply in debt and there was a general lack of one critical element — money. As long as people could see only precious metals as acceptable forms of payment (money), it became imperative that they acquire more of them. When Columbus embarked upon his historic voyages, that is mainly what he sought. Thus ensued the tragic genocidal conquest of the American natives from whom the world has gained so much. As Jack Weatherford describes it,

"The Europeans sought desperately for ways to increase the trickle of gold that flowed up so slowly from the Gold Coast [of Africa] to Europe, and they wanted to find ways to circumvent the numerous Muslim merchants who monopolized the trade at each stage."[79] The enormous amounts of gold and silver that were plundered from the Americas and shipped back to Europe provided the metal required for a tremendous expansion of the money supply – which, in turn, fueled a revolutionary economic expansion by facilitating exchange and encouraging a further specialization of labour.

Today, we face a similar dilemma, except it is not precious metal money we are obsessed with, but a different kind of money – interest-bearing, bank-created, debt-money – and it is not Muslim merchants who make it scarce and expensive, it is a global financial cartel headed by a few élite bankers, finance ministers, and wealthy speculators. The world is now stuck, as it was five hundred years ago, awaiting the creation of a more adequate, abundant, and inexpensive medium of exchange that will allow the world to make the transformational leap into a sustainable steady state economy, a restored global environment, and a life of freedom and dignity for all.

Increasing Instability

The recurrent disorder in the financial markets and the cascading failures of financial institutions should come as no surprise. It is not possible for humans to live sustainably on this earth under the present monetary regime. Why? The simple answer is, because money is credit created on the basis of loans made by banks *at interest*. Those who recognize the impossibility of perpetual exponential growth and who understand how compound interest is built into the global system of money and banking expect that there will be periodic "bubbles" and "busts," each of increasing amplitude until the system shakes itself apart.

Engineers call this phenomenon "positive feedback." Such a system cannot find equilibrium but eventually "explodes." Imagine a heating system in which the thermostat, sensing a rise in temperature, calls for more heat instead of less. Such is the nature of the debt-money system. The imposition of interest on the debt by which money is created causes debt to grow exponentially with the passage of time. It therefore demands that more debt be created to enable the payment of the interest due. Such is the *debt imperative* that gives rise to a *growth imperative*. Among other things, it prevents the emergence of a steady state economy because no amount of production and increase in business activity can satisfy the lenders' demands for repayment.

Is the final round at hand, or can the system be saved yet one more time? At this writing, the US government has just passed legislation empowering the treasury secretary to spend (initially) up to $700 billion at his own discretion, including the financing of bank mergers and the bailout of bankrupt financial institutions by buying enormous amounts of their uncollectable junk, including that held by foreign institutions. Besides the $700 billion that has been appropriated, it is likely that additional amounts will shortly be needed to keep the global banking system from disintegrating.

The Magic of Compound Interest

Here's a little thought experiment. Take a dollar bill and bury it in the ground. Leave it there for fifty years, and then dig it up. What do you have? Depending on the care you took in burying it, you have either a dollar bill or a wad of soggy paper fragments. In the best possible case, you can go out and spend that dollar, but it probably won't buy much given the prospect of continued inflation.

Now take another dollar bill and deposit it in a savings account at a bank. Leave it there for fifty years, then withdraw your money. What do you have? Assuming an interest rate of 6 percent per year, you have $18.42. Amazing, isn't it, how money can grow? Even more amazing, if the interest rate had been 10 percent, you would have $117.39. How can this be? Well, that's the magic of compound interest. By leaving the interest earnings in your account, you earn more interest on the interest.

This kind of growth is called *exponential* or *geometric*, as we discussed in Chapter 2. If you can wait a while longer, the growth becomes really astonishing. After two hundred years at 6 percent interest, for example, your single dollar will have grown to over $115,000 — at 10 percent interest, it will have grown to almost $190 *million*. These are shocking figures, but they are correct. Get a financial calculator and try it yourself. You see, anyone can become rich; all you have to do is lend a little money at interest — and wait. "I should live so long," you say. True enough. While these interest rates are pretty ordinary by contemporary standards, two hundred years is a long time for a natural person to wait — but it is not so long for a "legal person," like a corporation or a government. The government of the United States is more than two hundred years old, and it has been in debt for most of that time. Debts grow exponentially in exactly the same way. If you had borrowed a dollar instead of depositing a dollar, and never made any payments on the loan, your heirs would owe debts of these same colossal amounts. Which legacy would you prefer to leave them?

Now it's hard to criticize the taking of petty interest by individuals who need to save up for their education or retirement or to make some large purchase. Considering that in today's world the purchasing

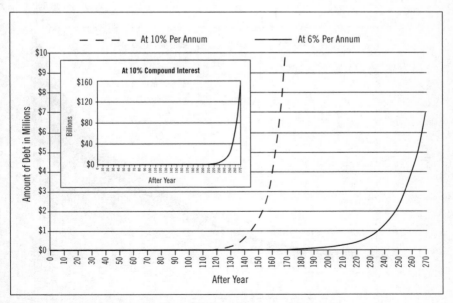

Figure 6.1 Growth of One Dollar of Debt at Compound Interest

power of money is continually being eaten up by inflation, one needs to have an additional return just to maintain the purchasing power of their savings. Such a return can be considered as compensation for loss. The original distinction between interest and usury was just that – interest was compensation for loss. And who can argue against the obvious fact that any investment that is denominated in terms of a national currency experiences a loss as time goes on? The loss in the purchasing power of virtually every national currency results from the abusive way in which it is issued and managed. Today's dollar, for example, is worth but a fraction of its value just a few decades ago. The new car that I purchased in 1965 for two thousand dollars would cost ten times that amount today, even accounting for changes in the performance and features in today's cars. The preservation of capital therefore requires a rate of return sufficient to offset the loss due to inflation. That is not to say that I advocate a perpetuation of debt

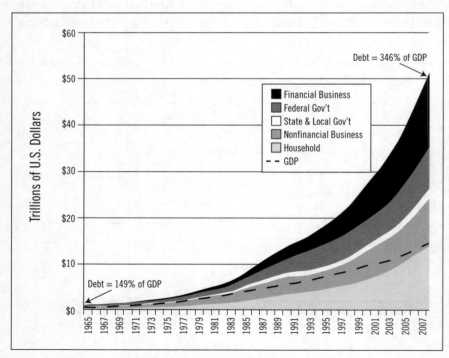

Figure 6.2 Actual Growth of Debt in the United States

financing. It is said that "the borrower is servant to the lender." The interests of each party in debt transaction are antagonistic toward one another. For this reason, we would be better off seeing a general shift away from debt financing, toward temporary equity financing that shares both the rewards and risks involved in any venture.

What's Wrong with the Global System of Money and Banking?

Adam Smith observed, more than two hundred years ago, that "When the division of labour has been once thoroughly established, it is but a very small part of a man's wants which the produce of his own labour can supply."[80] Since Smith's time the sources of those supplies have become ever more distant and impersonal. Consequently, we have come to be increasingly dependent upon devices like money and institutions like banks to help us in getting what we want and need from others through the marketplace. Those devices and institutions comprise what we will, for convenience, call "the money system."

It is a system that has been constructed over time, and because of its strategic importance has been an object of political contention. Today's centralized global money system (controlled as it is by a small élite class) is from the standpoint of equity, harmony, and sustainability, fundamentally flawed — and in my view, is a root cause of the mega-crisis confronting civilization. When that flawed money system is transcended, resolution of the other aspects of the mega-crisis will then become possible.

How Debt-Money Is Dysfunctional

The truly devastating thing about the dominant monetary system is that usury has been built into its very foundation, resulting in a *debt imperative* and the *growth imperative* that derives from it. This dual imperative creates a Hobbesian war of "all against all" as those in debt to the banks vie with one another in the market to capture enough money from an insufficient supply to repay their loans with interest. This not only causes gross inequities and social strife, but it also drives the destruction of our physical environment.

Chapter 9 will provide a thorough explanation of the nature and evolution of money, but for the moment we will focus on one essential fact, which is that *virtually all of the money throughout the world today is created by banks as debt*. The various national currencies that we are so familiar with, the paper money we pass from hand to hand, are merely physical representations of some of that debt – but most of the money exists not as paper notes but as bank account balances ("deposits"). Those who borrow from the banks are required to pay interest on that debt. But compound interest is an exponential growth function. That means *the debt grows simply with the passage of time*, not at a constant steady pace (linearly) but *at an accelerating rate (geometrically)*. This feature means that the debt growth must shortly outrun the increases in economic output needed to support it. Banks must continually expand their lending in order to avoid collapse of the global monetary and financial system, and to do so they must find additional bases for putting new money into circulation. Monetization of government debts seems to be their ultimate choice.[81]

Kevin Phillips points out in his book, *Bad Money*, that over the past few decades there has been a reversal in the American economy. While manufacturing has declined from about 25 percent to 13 percent of GDP, financial services have grown from 11 percent to 21 percent.[82] And what is the stock in trade of the financial services industry? Debt. By promoting, packaging, and marketing debt, the financial services industry has thrived while domestic manufacturing has been dismantled in favour of imports from abroad. Over only the past twenty years, total public and private debt in the United States has quadrupled to $43 trillion. The money problem can be summarized thus: *the way in which money is created by the banking system today causes a debt imperative, which drives a growth imperative – this forces destructive competition for the available supply of money, which is never sufficient to enable all debtors to pay what they owe*.

As borrowers compete with one another to try to meet their debt obligations in this game of financial "musical chairs," they are forced to expand their production, sales, and profits. They must take measures to enhance revenues and reduce costs by controlling both the markets in which they sell their products and those in which they buy their productive inputs, including labour. A major reason why corporations merge and consolidate and increase in size is so that they can exercise both greater political influence and greater market dominance. The result of all this is ever-increasing environmental despoliation and social degradation. The rise of the power of corporations in relation to national governments has exacerbated the problems because legal restraints upon huge transnational companies are being systematically eliminated by politicians who are "hired" to do their bidding.

Three Aspects of Money Dysfunction

Bank-created debt-money malfunctions in three primary ways. First is its artificial scarcity. There is never enough money to allow every debtor to pay what is owed to the banks. The debt grows simply with the passage of time but the supply of money to repay those loans *plus the interest* can only be maintained by the banks making additional loans to either current or new borrowers. These new loans have the same problem. Thus, debt continually mounts up, and businesses and individuals are forced to compete for markets and scarce money in a futile attempt to avoid defaulting on their debts. The system makes it certain that some *must* fail. Capital wealth becomes ever more concentrated in corporate conglomerates that must seek higher returns on their investments. They are driven to expand their markets and dominate economies, often enlisting the support of governments to apply military power both overtly and covertly to ensure the continued flow of low-priced raw materials, the availability of low-cost labour, and access to markets in which to sell their products.

Secondly, the requirement that interest be paid causes a net transfer of wealth from the debtor class to the moneyed class, or from producers to nonproducers. Besides the direct payment of interest on our own debts, we all pay the cost of interest that must be added at every stage of production to the price of everything we buy. It is easy to show statistically that lower-and middle-income households, because they are net debtors, pay much more interest than they receive; those in the highest income brackets, because they are net lenders, receive back more interest than they pay. Those who must earn their livelihood by selling their labour and talents in the market are kept at a disadvantage relative to those who live off returns from their capital.

Thirdly, the money created as bank credit is misallocated at its source. Much of it goes to finance government's deficit spending for weapons, military interventions, and transfer payments to corporate clients. The term "corporate welfare" has been used to describe not only direct government subsidies, but also "sweetheart contracts" to politically connected companies. Another large chunk is provided to the well-connected few who use it to finance such things as real estate developments, which are presumably well collateralized but are often supported by inflated land values and overblown prospects of profitability. Thus we find an abundance of hotels, resorts, and upscale residential construction but a chronic shortage of affordable housing.

This entire system favours authoritarian government, increasing concentrations of power and wealth, short-range planning, and the production of short-lived disposable junk over durable consumer products. That cannot continue. The global monopoly game is reaching its climax and coming to a close. As economist Michael Hudson concludes, "The economy has reached its debt limit and is entering its insolvency phase. We are not in a cycle but the end of an era. The old world of debt pyramiding to a fraudulent degree cannot be restored."[83]

Moral Arguments, Laws, and Practical Solutions

Three major world religions – Judaism, Christianity, and Islam – all inveigh against the practice of usury. Volumes have been written about the morality or immorality of usury, the distinction between usury and interest, and the practical necessities of allowing it to enable industry and commerce to flourish. There has been no lack of arguments, well thought out and eloquently expressed, and legal statutes restricting the practice prevailed for more than a millennium. It is John Calvin

(1509–64) who has been, depending on one's point of view, either credited or blamed for the eventual relaxing of the moral and legal rigidities, arguing that "if all usury is condemned tighter fetters are imposed on the conscience than the Lord himself would wish." At the same time he warned that, "if you yield in the least, with that pretext, very many will at once seize upon unlicensed freedom, which can then be restrained by no moderation or restriction." Calvin has certainly been proven right in the latter regard. Citing the changed conditions from the time of Moses and the Prophets, Calvin asserted, "Therefore usury is not wholly forbidden among us unless it be repugnant both to Justice and to Charity."[84] And there lies the crux of the matter, as all considerations of justice and charity have been swept aside. Over time financial dealings have become ever more impersonal, economics has been separated from religion, and ethics has been separated from economics. Moral arguments have failed to hold sway, legal prohibitions have (rightly or wrongly) been totally obliterated, and usurious lending (even in its most oppressive form) has come to be part of the financial landscape. The "train of civilization" needs to be decoupled from the engine of destruction that is our present politicized system of money, banking, and finance. But if that is to be achieved, the problem needs to be framed not only in moral or ethical terms, but especially in practical terms.

Keys to Transcendence

We have discerned the patterns of action and relationships that have brought us to this point of mega-crisis, and now it is imperative that people effectively address it – not by opposing what is, or reverting to past primitive forms, but by reenvisioning and reinvention. There are "leverage points" at which the application of small forces can produce massive effects. My intensive and wide-ranging research has convinced me that a primary leverage point is the process of economic exchange, and the device we call "money."

When the system spins out of control what will come out of the chaos? When the dollar crashes, the financial and political élite class will certainly try to orchestrate a new global monetary regime based on the same old mechanisms for centralizing power and concentrating wealth in their own hands, seeking to complete the new (feudal) world order that has been building for the past three hundred years. Indeed, some observers are arguing that we are experiencing the equivalent of a controlled demolition of the global financial system as part of the plan to grab control of ever more of the world's resources.[85]

But the way is open for us to realize another possibility, which is the emergence of a decentralized, democratic, and sustainable system of exchange — as well as more equitable methods of finance and investment, which can provide the solid foundation needed for a different kind of new world order.

Exchange and Finance — Two Distinct Credit Functions

In achieving that, there are two basic questions that need to be addressed, one relating to the exchange function, the other relating to the finance function. Both of these involve the use of credit. The exchange function has need of short-term credit that bridges the gap between the delivery of goods to market and the sale of those goods. It is this credit, and only this credit, that should be embodied in modern money. Money, then, becomes a virtual representation of real value in the form of goods and services that is ready to be bought and consumed. The question is, "What is the proper basis upon which money should be issued? The principle that applies to proper operation of the exchange function is this: money should be created on the basis of goods and services that are already in the market, or shortly to arrive there. This is the essence of what is called "the real bills doctrine."[86]

The finance function has need of long-term credit that enables "capital formation," i.e., it provides the means by which production capability can be renewed or increased. The question here is, "How shall capital formation be financed?" The applicable principle in this case is that long-term uses of credit should be matched to long-term sources of credit. The logical conclusion is that investments should be matched to savings. To use a simplified concrete analogy, we might say that

Two Distinct Kinds of Credit		
	Exchange Credit	Finance Credit
Duration	Short term	Long term
Purpose	To facilitate exchange	To fund capital development
Relationship to money	Newly created money	Reallocation of existing money from savers to entrepreneurs

the seed that has been saved from the previous harvest is invested in producing a new crop. A corollary to this is that new money should *not* be created to finance capital formation. Why? Because money creation should be matched to goods and services that are in the market *now*, but capital investments deliver goods and services to market *later*. If more money is put into the economy but more goods are not, the value of a currency will be diluted. Under legal tender, that shows up as rising prices.

In practice today, these principles are commonly violated by banks. Banks provide both functions by making loans, and make little distinction between them. As banks of issue, they create money; as depositories, they reallocate funds from savers to investors. But as Ralph Borsodi observed, "Most [present-day money] is 'backed' by loans which should never be made — loans made to monetize the debts of government; loans made to finance war and the military-industrial complex, monetize the securities of giant corporations which should not exist at all, and to finance speculations in securities, commodities, and land."[87]

All of those improper bases of issue are not only inflationary (when a currency is given legal tender status), but also are preferential toward the centres of power and wealth and against the interests of legitimate business, tending to create ever greater monopolies and divisions among the classes. In today's world, credit is the substance of money and the means of payment. Precious metals no longer play a monetary role. But credit is monopolized by a banking cartel that keeps it scarce. As Riegel put it, "The political money system starves productive enterprise but finances lavishly the destructive activities of war."[88]

The most damaging aspect of the political money system, as described earlier, is the fact that the debts owed to banks and subject to compound interest grow with the mere passage of time, but the money needed to pay those debts does not. Additional money comes into circulation only as the banks make additional loans. This is the engine of destruction that injures not only the debtor, but also the entire society and the physical environment. The solution for the exchange function under the old paradigm would be the creation of money by the discounting of "real bills."

On the other hand, a new paradigm approach to the exchange function, which will be described in detail in later chapters, is to provide *interest-free credit* to producers within the process of *mutual credit clearing.* That is the process of offsetting purchases against sales within an association of merchants, manufacturers, and workers. It will eventually include everyone who buys and sells, or makes and receives disbursements of any kind. The costs of operating such credit clearing exchanges can be managed by small fees applied to each transaction.

The solution for the finance function would seem to lie mainly in making a shift from debt financing to *temporary* equity financing. Whereas debt makes borrowers and lenders antagonistic toward one another, equity (being shared ownership) tends to harmonize the interests of the user of capital with those of the provider of capital in that both the rewards and the risks are shared. But to make a permanent sale of one's future fortune for the sake of a temporary financial need is in most cases odious, hence the need that such investment claims be temporary. There are, to be sure, cases in which permanent equity shares might be appropriate, but these need not concern us here.

The solutions we propose here are based on private, voluntary initiative. So long as the right of contract and freedom of association are preserved, there is a chance that the "great leap forward" in exchange and finance can be made. We need not reopen the political debate about what constitutes usury, nor lobby for the restoration of usury laws, for these and other political solutions have receded far beyond our present grasp. But once these proposed approaches begin to gain a foothold, the distinction between usury and interest and debates about what levels of interest are justified will become moot. The problem of how to transcend the engine of destruction will have been elevated to a plane on which we may converge toward a solution.

I have only outlined a rough sketch of these ideas in this chapter. The remainder of the book will provide essential background and further elucidation that will enable a deeper understanding. For the moment it suffices to say that the most urgent need is for the implementation of new exchange systems (money systems) that do *not* force perpetual economic growth. Such exchange systems are a prerequisite for achieving the emergence of a steady state economy that can provide to every member of the human family the material benefits needed for a dignified and fulfilling life, while at the same time nurturing the natural systems that support all life on our planet. Along with the elimination of the growth imperative from the exchange function, it is also necessary to shift the finance function away from interest-bearing debt contracts toward equity investments that harmonize stakeholder interests. Economic development efforts must inevitably change their emphasis from quantitative to qualitative. Instead of aiming for ever greater quantities of output and consumption, the object should be to improve the quality of life — not only for a few, but for everyone. The prescriptions offered in the later chapters of this book are intended to accomplish those objectives.

7. The Nature and Cause of Inflation

Most bankers and politicians talk about inflation as if it were some mysterious natural phenomenon. The truth is that the only real mystery about inflation is why we allow it to continue. Most of the confusion about inflation comes from the failure to distinguish between cause and effect. Let us be clear, a general increase in the price level is the effect; inflation is the cause.

What Is Inflation?

Despite the morass of confusion that prevails even within the halls of ivy, there have been a few economists who have put the spotlight exactly where it belongs. Yale economist Irving Fisher, speaking of inflation and deflation as far back as 1928, maintained that "the extreme variability of money [meaning its purchasing power] is chiefly man-made, due to government finance, especially war finance, as well as to banking policies and legislation."[89] He further acknowledged that "we may notice that the worst examples of inflation have come from unbalanced government budgets. As we have seen, when a government cannot make both ends meet, it pays its bills by manufacturing the money needed."[90] More recently, and more emphatically, famed economist Milton Friedman has maintained that "inflation is always and everywhere a monetary phenomenon." Labour, with its supposed "excessive wage demands," is often blamed for inflation, but labour is a convenient scapegoat used to deflect attention from the real culprits.

The prices of individual commodities may increase because of changing conditions that affect their supply or demand. A widespread drought or crop failure, for example, might cause an increase in the price of food commodities — but this "dearness" is a different phenomenon, and it is unlikely that it would cause a general rise in all prices (unless it were a basic input to production, like petroleum).

It is common for pundits and academics to explain inflation as "too much money chasing too few goods." But that does not really explain it because it neglects to say how "too much money" comes into existence.

Who Has the Power to Inflate?

Inflation is simply *the improper issuance of money into the economy,* but how is that accomplished and who might be responsible?[91] These are the possible inflators of money.

- Private counterfeiters
- Central banks
- Commercial banks
- Central governments

A legitimate issuer of currency knows that his currency is a credit instrument representing a claim against his current and future production. It is his intention to accept his currency back at some later time as payment for his own goods and services that he offers for sale in the market. Everybody knows that currency buys goods and services, but most fail to also recognize that goods and services buy currency. Just as the issuer "sold" his currency at the point of issuance in return for goods and services, so he must later buy his currency back by selling his own goods and services. This cycle of issuance and redemption completes the demands of reciprocity, which is the fundamental purpose of money.

In coming to understand inflation, the matter may be made clear if we first consider the private counterfeiter. Private counterfeiters have the power to inflate the money supply to the extent that their counterfeit bears an adequate resemblance to official currency, and so long as they are able to avoid being caught by the authorities. The private counterfeiter prints notes that he then spends in the marketplace, receiving valuable goods and services from unsuspecting vendors. The counterfeiter is a cheat and a thief because he has no intention of reciprocating by accepting back his notes in payment for anything. For him, the issuance of his (bogus) currency is a one-way street. Any kind of issuance that expands the total supply of money without expanding the amount of goods and services available in the market is inflationary, but the damage done by counterfeiters is generally insignificant in comparison with the *official* currency debasement that has become so prevalent.

Central banks also have power to inflate the money supply. They do it under colour of law[92] by monetizing various kinds of long-term obligations, especially the bonds of the federal government. This is accomplished by what the Federal Reserve calls "open market operations," whereby the Fed buys US government bonds in the open market. Since the Fed has the power to create from nothing the funds with which to pay for these purchases, money is added to the existing supply. Just as in the case of the counterfeiter, such an expenditure puts no additional goods or services into the market. Even worse, that newly created money then goes into the banking system where it becomes additional "reserves" that enable the banks collectively to lend many times that amount of money into circulation. That is why this kind of money, created by the Fed, is called "high powered money."

Improper Basis of Issue by Banks Is Inflationary

As pointed out earlier, the vast majority of money is created by commercial banks by the process of lending it into circulation. They have the power to make loans (issue money) on either a proper basis or an improper basis. It is not the amount of money per se that causes inflation, but the basis upon which it is created. Loans made on an improper basis have the effect of inflating the money supply. What would be an improper basis?

An improper basis is any loan that does not put goods or services into the market either immediately or in the very near term. Commercial banks play a dual role. They act both as "depositories" and as "banks

of issue." In their role of *depository*, banks lend out depositors' funds
(your savings and mine) to those who have need of them. That may
be for either consumption or the creation of new productive capacity (capital formation). As *banks for issue*, they create new deposits
(money) on the basis of short-term commercial bills that accompany
the delivery of goods to market. That's the way it is supposed to work.

   In practice, however, banks these days make little distinction between
these two roles and they commonly create deposits (money) by making
loans to finance both the flow of goods and services into the market
as well as making loans that take them out of the market. When a
bank makes a loan for the purpose of financing consumer purchases
or for investment in long-term productive assets, those newly created
deposits are inflationary – because they deliver goods and services to
the marketplace only in the distant future, or not at all. Improper bases
of issue, then, include the purchase by banks of government bonds in
excess of time deposits held by savers, as well as loans that finance
market speculation.

Government Deficits and Inflation

Finally, we need to consider how governments inflate the money
supply. In some countries governments spend their currency directly
into circulation. The "greenbacks" that were spent into circulation by
the United States government during the Civil War are one historical
example. Such issuance is inflationary if it exceeds the short-term tax
and other revenues of the government. In countries like the United
States, the government does not inflate the money supply directly,
but instead accomplishes it in collusion with the central bank and
the banking system. When the Federal Reserve or a commercial bank
buys government bonds as described above, money is added to the
economy on an improper basis. The purchase of government bonds
does not bring any additional goods or services into the market. Ron
Paul has on many occasions reminded his colleagues in Congress how
this collusion works. In 1997, he told them this:

The Congress will spend too much because there is tremendous pressure to spend on all these good things we do; all the welfare programmes, and all the military expenditures to police the world and build bases around the world ... lo and behold, there is not enough money to borrow and not enough tax money to go around, so they have to have one more vehicle, and that is the creation of money out of thin air, and this is what they do. They send the Treasury bills or the bonds to the Federal Reserve, and with a computer they can turn a switch and create a billion or $10 billion in a single day and that debases the currency. It diminishes the value of the money and alters interest rates and causes so much mischief that, if people are concerned about the economy or their standard of living or rising costs of living, this is the source of the problem ... Why do we allow the Government to counterfeit the money and make it worthless all the time?[93]

Figure 7.1 Watering the Milk (Drawing by Dennis Pacheco)

In response to inflation, vendors (including workers and professionals who sell their labour services) will raise their prices (if they have sufficient market power to do so) as the only way they have of compensating for the malfeasance of the government and banking sectors.

The process of inflation can be likened to a farmer adding water to his milk. Suppose the farmer were to divert half his milk production to his own use, leaving only half of the amount that he formerly delivered to his customers. With only half as much milk to sell now, he would have to leave many of his former customers to go without. In order to avoid a loss of income, a dishonest farmer might simply add water to the remaining milk to deceive his customers into believing that they were receiving just as much milk as before. If that process were extended little by little, with more and more water being added to less and less milk, it might go undetected. Thus there would be the appearance that customers would have the same amount of milk while they slowly starve to death. So it is with the creation of "money" that adds no value to the economy.

The German Hyperinflation – A Classic Case

Probably the most notorious case of hyperinflation was the one perpetrated by the Weimar government in Germany following World War I. At the beginning of the war the exchange rate of the German mark to the US dollar stood at 4.2 to 1 (one mark was worth about 24 cents). By the end of 1922 the mark had fallen to 1,500 to 1, and by the end of November 1923 it had fallen to an astounding 4,200,000,000,000 to 1.[94] The folklore about the incident includes images of people taking wheelbarrows full of German currency to bakeries to buy a loaf of bread. Robert Hetzel describes the situation this way:

> In 1913, total currency in Germany amounted to just 6 billion marks. In November 1923 in Berlin, a loaf of bread cost 428 billion marks and a kilogram of butter almost 6,000 billion marks. From the end of World War I until 1924, the price level rose almost one trillionfold. The economic cause of this

Hyperinflation was the monetization of public and private debt by Germany's central bank, the Reichsbank. The political cause lay in the inability of a fragile democracy to impose the taxes necessary to pay war reparations... Unable to cover its expenditures through explicit taxes, the German government ran deficits exceeding 50 percent of its expenditures from 1919 through 1923. Reichsbank purchases of government debt made the printing press the ultimate source for funding these deficits."[95]

The political circumstances of the German hyperinflation, while they cannot justify it, help us to understand why it occurred. A defeated Germany was forced to accept punishing terms under the Treaty of Versailles. These terms included the payment of reparations, the amounts of which were impossibly huge for an economy weakened by the war and stripped of some of its most valuable and productive resources. Even though a policy of inflation is ultimately self-defeating for a government, it is seen by politicians as being politically expedient. The then head of the German central bank himself maintained that, "So long as the reparations burden remains, there is no other means to procure the necessary means for the Reich than the discounting of Reich Treasury notes at the Reichsbank."[96] In other words, the central bank created out of thin air the money needed to buy the government's debt instruments.

With the accelerating rates of currency debasement and increasing prices of goods, employers paid their workers daily — then several times a day. Cash would be handed over to family members so that it could be quickly spent before prices in the shops increased further. In the absence of a reliable currency, people increasingly reverted to barter — refusing to accept money for the things they had to sell to stay alive. Pensioners and others whose incomes were fixed saw their purchasing power evaporate into nothingness. The middle class was ruined as their savings and financial investments became worthless. "The poor became even poorer and the winter of 1923 meant that many lived in freezing conditions burning furniture to get some heat. The very rich suffered least because they had sufficient contacts to get

Figure 7.2 A 100 Million Mark Note of Weimar Germany This is a photo of an actual note that has been carried for decades in the wallet of a German friend Johann Rennberger, now aged 88, who fought in World War II and was held prisoner by the Russians. (Photo by Theo Megalli)

food etc. Most of the very rich were land owners and could produce food on their own estates."[97]

As the value of a currency continues to plummet, people naturally turn to more stable means of value reckoning. To protect the real value of their transactions they may express prices in some more stable currency unit, like the dollar, or some useful commodity. Hetzel reports that,

> The actual breakdown of German economic life came about because of interventions by the German government to maintain the paper mark as the medium of exchange. Holtfrerich writes of hyperinflation Germany, "The economy had already largely turned over to a foreign, hard-currency standard ... The crisis arose out of the reluctance of the Reich to permit business to employ foreign means of payment in domestic transactions as desired; indeed the Reich could not permit the practice ... as long as inflation remained as a 'tax' source."[98]

Ulrich von Beckerath provides an interesting anecdote relating to this. In a letter to one Dr Runge, dated July 5, 1949, Beckerath mentions a meeting that took place in 1923 between Hans Luther, then minister of food and agriculture, and Herr Petersen, the mayor of the city of Hamburg. Beckerath said,

> I do not know if you know what the currency meeting of Luther and Mayor Petersen in 1923 in Hamburg was about. Petersen had created a gold currency in Hamburg, and the wages of the Hamburg citizens were paid in gold marks. Luther went there horrified and tried to browbeat Petersen; he even talked about high treason, about the Reich army marching in, about having him arrested, etc. However, Luther had picked the wrong man to bully. Petersen announced that he would accept civil war. A city of 1 million can raise 100,000 armed defenders, he told him, and as for the arrest talk, Luther should be glad that Petersen was not inclined to have him arrested on the spot by his Hamburg police. He did not look as if he were joking, and he was also a man who did not issue idle threats. Luther returned to Berlin with his tail between his legs, and shortly thereafter the Reich's printing press was shut down.[99]

How the Inflation Was Ended

Luther, however, should not be seen as the villain of the piece, for it is he who is credited with later saving the day by introducing the Rentenmark, as Beckerath explains.

> Luther was attacked as partly responsible for the monetary crisis in Germany. But the crisis was due to circumstances not created by Luther. Where Luther was really unfettered, he not only proved to be of the greatest service to the German economy but also to the world economy ... When in 1923 the German mark had fallen to a millionth part of a millionth part; when the social

and political order was on the point of dissolving, Luther, who was then Minister of Finance, introduced the Rentenmark which saved Germany and thereby averted serious complications for Europe and the world. The Rentenmark offers an example of a gold-less gold currency being established in the course of a few days. It is well worth therefore a retrospective examination.[100]

What did Beckerath mean by a "gold-less gold currency"? Simply that the currency was denominated in gold units, but was not redeemable in gold. Then what was it that enabled the Rentenmark to maintain its value relative to gold? It was this set of provisions:

- the Rentenmark was acceptable by all tax offices *at face value* in payment of taxes;
- there was no legal compulsion for anyone else to accept it, thus it was made to stand on its own merits in the marketplace and might legally pass at a discount from face value in private transactions;
- the amount issued was modest in relation to the tax revenues that supported it.

Figure 7.3 A One Rentenmark Note Dated January 30, 1937

There were other provisions that were intended to support the value of the Rentenmark, but these, according to Beckerath, proved to be unnecessary. Beckerath maintains that, "The new currency could scarcely have been better devised; and if some foreign Finance Minister should ever be placed in a similar predicament, he would be well advised to study the German Rentenbank Act." Bearing this in mind, we shall revisit the story of the Rentenmark in Chapter 19 where we will offer some advice to governments.

At about the same time as the issuance of the Rentenmark, the official currency (the reichsmark) was revalued and pegged to gold. According to Hetzel,

> The November 1923 stabilization programme committed Germany to exchange 1,392 reichsmarks for a pound of gold. However, German economic stability then became dependent upon the stability of the international gold standard. Starting in 1928, the deflationary monetary policies of two of the largest adherents to the gold standard, France and the United States, forced deflation and economic depression on Germany. Short-run salvation led to longer-run doom.[101]

Hyperinflations always end in the utter worthlessness of the currency and the destruction of the monetary unit. Eventually a new unit is declared and a new currency issued. Obviously, the German authorities felt that monetization of the debt was the only politically feasible option. To be sure, there were pressures from many sides, but the bottom line is that only the monetary authority can cause inflation and only the monetary authority can stop it. The piper must be paid; the only question is, who will be made to foot the bill? Inflation is a tax imposed by underhanded means. Under a policy of inflation it is the pensioners and all who have fixed dollar claims, like bank accounts and bonds, who are made to pay this "hidden tax." The middle class bears the greatest burden as the purchasing power of their savings evaporates. Whether the monetization of government debt is carried out by the government directly or indirectly by a private central bank, the result is the same.

Once inflation reaches a certain level, it begins to create behavioral effects that exacerbate the problem. Rising prices produce a psychology that tends to cause further price increases. As people lose confidence in the stability of money's purchasing power, they try to spend it as quickly as they can before prices rise further. Vendors, seeing their shelves being quickly cleared, raise their prices more – causing ever-greater demand for goods, causing further price increases. Money becomes a "hot potato." As it continues to lose value, nobody wants to hold money or financial claims that are denominated in the monetary unit; they seek to convert it quickly into goods that will maintain their value.

Professor Heinrich Rittershausen, in his book *The Central Bank*, explains that, "During extreme inflation, 'businessmen go into commodities,' during deflation 'they go out of commodities'."[102] In the first instance, inflation, they become less liquid, preferring to hold commodities instead of depreciating money. Thus other sectors of the economy become more liquid, i.e., there is more money in the hands of consumers and an increased rate of circulation – because in a runaway inflation no one wants to hold large amounts of money. With this hoarding of commodities, there is a decreased supply of commodities in the market even while the money supply is being inflated – adding a further pressure to drive prices upward.

In the case of deflation, the money supply is being restricted by the monetary authorities so that it is insufficient to enable the available goods and services to be purchased except at reduced prices, often at less than their cost of production. In that case "cash is king," and businessmen will prefer to hold money until prices bottom out.

Similarly, at the end of an inflation, merchants again begin selling commodities for the new money, which they will want to hold onto – thus tending to drive commodity prices further downward.

As we said before, without legal tender laws and forced circulation of a currency, such dishonest and disruptive actions cannot be sustained by any government. After Germany's defeat in World War II, inflation was again becoming a problem. In an editorial he wrote to the *Freie Gewerkschaft* [*Free Union*], dated December 10, 1945, Beckerath wrote,

Clear insight into these circumstances would give workers the
ability to cope with inflation, precisely as they ultimately coped
with it in 1923, namely by rejecting – in spite of all prohibitions – the money issued by the government, in this way forcing the government to change the monetary standard or by
simply forcing a change from their employers. Essentially, that
change was the transition from the paper mark to the "Gold
reckoning standard."[103]

There have been numerous other cases of hyperinflation, some even
worse than the German inflation just described. These include Hungary
following World War II and Yugoslavia between 1993 and 1995, in

*Figure 7.4 A Five Hundred Billion Dinar Note of Yugoslavia (Photo courtesy Juan Carlos.
Creative Commons Attribution 3.0)*

what is described to be the "worst hyperinflation in history." According to Professor Thayer Watkins, "Between October 1, 1993 and January 24, 1995 prices increased by 5 quadrillion percent. That's a 5 with 15 zeroes after it."[104]

Currently the government of Zimbabwe is abusing its money, economy, and citizens through currency inflation and draconian legal measures aimed at preventing people from protecting themselves. According to a March 2008 Voice of America report:

> The Zimbabwean government has made it illegal for citizens to hold more than Z$500 million in cash, currently equivalent to just over 20 US dollars. A recently introduced statutory instrument says anyone found in possession of more than this sum can be charged with unlawful hoarding. Companies are barred from settling bills over Z$250 million, about US$10, with cash. In recent days the exchange rate against the US dollar has soared to Z$24 million. The decree was issued in an effort to regain control over the money supply and to put what Reserve Bank Governor Gideon Gono calls "cash barons" out of business. He coined the phrase to describe large operators on the country's bustling parallel markets in foreign exchange and most essential commodities.[105]

Such measures of legal compulsion are typically employed by governments as they try to force others to suffer the burden of their profligate spending and fiscal mismanagement through official abuse of the money power.

Constraints upon Debasement of the Money

Are there any constraints upon the ability of these various entities to inflate? Gold convertibility of paper currency, while not an ideal approach, in the past did apply some discipline upon the overall volume of credit money (notes and deposits) creation, but that has long since been eliminated. It did not, however, force banks to conform to the requirements for proper issuance. That can probably be achieved only by the subjection of their currency to free market forces, i.e., the elimination of the legal tender privilege, about which there will be more in Chapter 19.

Recall that Irving Fisher mentioned three factors that underlie inflation: government finance, banking policies, and legislation. Each of these plays a role. We have seen that the first of these comes down to deficit spending and the accumulation of ever more government debt. We have seen that banking policies enable the creation of money on the basis of that debt (monetization), and on the basis of loans made to finance long-term assets or speculation. These add to the money supply without putting additional goods or services into the market. The third factor is the legislation that prevents the debased money from being refused or discounted in the market, i.e., legal tender laws. Such laws require that official money be accepted in payment of "all debts, public and private," and that it be accepted at face value. The truth is that without legal tender, there can be no sustained inflation of the money.

Responding to Inflation

In the face of official currency debasement, people are not entirely powerless. In a 1948 letter to Henry Meulen, author of the book *Free Banking*, Beckerath wrote,

> I may remind you of one of the greatest revolutions in history: The revolt of the German people against the government's "exclusive currency" in the years 1922 and 1923. Every day new thousands declined the notes of the Reichsbank and accepted other kinds of money or money-substitutes. If at that time a programmeme of Free Banking had been known to the public, thousands of Free Bankers would have replaced the Reichsbank, the crisis of 1930/32 would not have occurred, Hitlerism would have been impossible, no war would have happened, Germany's towns would still stand, I would still have my 3,000 books, you

would still have your library – probably with a second copy of Greene's "Mutual Banking" – a terrible loss – and we would correspond upon details of Free Banking in Germany.[106]

Among these "other kinds of money and money substitutes" are private or semiofficial claims on real value – typically goods and services, including telephone, gas, and electric utilities as well as various kinds of transport services. In a letter to a Mr Walker, dated June 4, 1954, Beckerath referred to a very effective currency alternative to the inflated government currency of the time. This was the issuance of "German railway money by the Railway Minister Öser ...in the years 1923 and 1924 amounting to several hundred million RM put in circulation, and thereby (in my opinion) Germany was saved." Walter Zander wrote about the superiority of such service-based currencies in his article "Railway Money and Unemployment," observing that when a business acquires what it needs by borrowing money, it promises to deliver

something [money] at a fixed date which at the time of the promise it only hoped to obtain. Whether its hope will materialize, is uncertain. The undertaking to pay at maturity contains therefore a speculative element, which is particularly hazardous in times of depression. It is therefore obvious that the Railway must be extremely circumspect in making credit purchases, i.e., in promising to pay at a later date with resources which have yet to be secured. *But the Railway may promise something else, namely, to transport commodities and persons, that is, to fulfill its function as a Railway. There is nothing speculative about that.* The means required for this, rolling stock and other plant, are available... The capacity of the Railway to act as a carrier is at any rate unquestionable.[107] [emphasis added]

Zander also mentions that a form of railway money had been issued a century earlier. When the Leipzig Dresden Railway was established, one third of the company's capital (500,000 thaler) was in the form of "railway money certificates" that remained in circulation for forty years.

The actual value of every currency, whether issued by a government or a private entity, is established by there being, to quote John Zube,

> a short-term continuous demand for it, be it coercively and wrongly, via compulsory taxes or tributes, or via the debt payment foundation of the private economy, where, e.g., department stores or shop associations issue their own currency and it is accepted because it has "shop foundation" as Rittershausen calls it, i.e., the local shops accept it as ready money — and must do so, because it amounts to their own IOUs.[108]

Unlike public legal tender currencies, the acceptance of private currencies in the market is voluntary. This makes private currencies self-regulating in that the issuers themselves will manage their issuance in such a way as to avoid having it discounted or refused in the market.

8. The Separation of Money and State

Money needs to be depoliticized, and the time has come for the separation of money and state to be accomplished.

Some will argue that money and state have already been separated, since the central bank in the United States, the Federal Reserve, is a privately owned corporation that operates independently of the US government. But that separation is more apparent than real. In reality, the federal government and the central bank are both controlled by a small group of powerful men (mostly), and they work together in ways that are detrimental to the common good. The collusive arrangement between them, following the pattern that was instituted more than three hundred years ago with the founding of the Bank of England, is the pattern that prevails today in virtually every country of the world, regardless of whether the central bank is privately owned or government owned.

Under this arrangement, the banking cartel gets the privilege of creating money as debt and charging interest on it, while the central government gets to spend as much as it wants without regard to its limited tax revenues or the popular will. Does anyone really believe that the US government, for instance, will ever repay its accumulated debt that now amounts to more than $10.8 trillion? That's more than $35,000 for each man, woman, and child in the United States, not counting the full extent of the ongoing bailouts and stimulus spending being enacted as this book is finalized in February 2009, nor the massive amounts of government guarantees that are not reported as part of the debt.

Through legal tender laws and banking regulations, governments endow their respective central bank currencies with the full support of the government, and give the banking establishment the privilege to effectively monopolize everyone's credit and lend it out at interest. While the central government of the United States is precluded from directly monetizing its debts, that same result is achieved indirectly through the banking system. When government borrows money to finance its budget deficits, it sells its bonds on the open market. It is not only the portion which is bought by the Fed that gets monetized, but also the bonds that are bought by the commercial banks. This debt monetization process has the same effect as spending counterfeit money into the economy.

When it comes to financing its operations, government can look either to its current tax revenues or to its future tax revenues. If current tax revenues are deficient, as they almost always seem to be, government must borrow. When government borrows in order to finance its deficits it would appear that it is choosing to tax us later instead of taxing us now. Ordinarily, money borrowed must eventually be repaid out of future revenues. That means there must be eventual budget surpluses sufficient to offset the current budget deficits. But budget surpluses have been few and far between, so governments and central banks together have conjured up another possibility – monetization of the debt and legally enforced circulation of debased currency by means of legal tender laws.

It should be obvious by now that the debts of the central government will never be repaid. As described in the previous chapter, it is like the farmer adding water to his milk. The part of the debt that is monetized adds "empty dollars" to the money supply, dollars that are not matched by additional goods and services going to market. The part of the debt that is *not* monetized by the banking system is acquired by individuals and institutions who allocate our collective savings to be spent by the government. The situation is very much like the following: Suppose you are regularly putting money aside into a shoe box to save up for your college education, but your drug-addicted parent is regularly taking that money out and replacing it with their IOUs. Will that suffice to get you through college? Only if your parent changes their ways and repays what they owe you. Our government is the wayward parent. It has been taking real value out of the economy and providing empty promises in return. Will it ever reform itself and start paying back its debt? Judging from past experience, that will never happen. What then is the likely prospect?

Fiscally irresponsible government has only two choices: it must either eventually default on its debt repayments — acknowledging that its bonds, bills, and notes are worthless — or it must continue to monetize more and more of its debt. For a country like the United States which constitutes the world's biggest market and whose currency serves as the global reserve currency for foreign governments and investors, the former course is unthinkable. That leaves continued monetization, continued bailouts, and inflation. According to official figures, inflation rates in the United States for the past several years have been modest — in the range 3 percent — but at other times they have been much higher. Furthermore, these figures do not seem to reflect the true cost of living. The most common measure of inflation, the Consumer Price Index, has been widely criticized in this regard. In any case, the cumulative effect over time of government debt has been an enormous decline in the purchasing power of the dollar. The prospects are for that decline to accelerate as the budget deficits and trade deficits continue to mount up. On the global scene, the dollar has already lost a major part of its value and is beginning to lose its status as the preferred global reserve currency.

Under the central banking regime that prevails in virtually every country around the world, money has been politicized. The collusion between politicians and international bankers enables governments to extract wealth from the economy by deficit spending, and banks to extract wealth by charging interest on money as they create it by making loans. These two parasitic elements take wealth away from productive members of society and lavish it on military adventures, international intrigues, wasteful boondoggles, and financial finaglers. The truth of the matter is that central banks have one overriding function — *to manage the effects of the parasitic drain,* to decide who will pay the price and who will feel the pain. They can either (1) restrict credit in the private sector, thus causing recessions, bankruptcies, and unemployment; or (2) they can expand credit and inflate the money supply by monetizing debts (either public or private) that are ultimately uncollectable.

The Separation of Church and State — A Comparison

A useful parallel can be drawn between the necessary *separation of money and state* and the recently established *separation of church and state*. While controversy still persists over the constitutional mandate and the exact meaning of the latter phrase, there is general agreement on the point that each individual should have the freedom to practice whatever religion they might choose, and that the government should not favour any particular religious organization by granting it special recognition, privilege, or financial support.

Inspired most likely by the writings of John Locke, the idea of the separation of church and state was championed by Thomas Jefferson and James Madison, first in the Virginia Statute of Religious Freedom and later in the United States Constitution. Religious establishments, having been long accustomed to enjoying legal privileges from governments around the world, were reluctant to give them up. Even in the context of late eighteenth century America, there was serious dispute over the allowable extent of religious freedom. Jefferson's Virginia Statute of Religious Freedom was by no means an easy sell, and was bitterly opposed. It was eventually passed in 1786 after the assembly had made significant deletions to Jefferson's original draft.[109]

It is instructive to read the original with the deleted clauses (in bold).

> **Well aware that the opinions and belief of men depend not on their own will, but follow involuntarily the evidence proposed to their minds; that** Almighty God hath created the mind free, **and manifested his supreme will that free it shall remain by making it altogether insusceptible of restraint;** that all attempts to influence it by temporal punishments ... tend only to beget habits of hypocrisy and meanness, and are a departure from the plan of the holy author of our religion, who being lord both of body and mind, yet chose not to propagate it by coercions on either, as was in his Almighty power to do, **but to extend it by its influence on reason alone;** that the impious presumption of legislators ... [who] have assumed dominion over the faith of others ... hath established and maintained

false religions over the greatest part of the world; ... **that the opinions of men are not the object of civil government, nor under its jurisdiction;** ... and finally, that truth is great and will prevail if left to herself; that she is the proper and sufficient antagonist to error, and has nothing to fear from the conflict unless by human interposition disarmed of her natural weapons, free argument and debate; errors ceasing to be dangerous when it is permitted freely to contradict them.

The object of these efforts was, in Madison's words, to "extinguished forever the ambitious hope of making laws for the human mind." Having spent considerable amounts of time in countries that still have an official religion, I have observed firsthand some of the "habits of hypocrisy and meanness" referred to in that statute.

The United States is recognized as the first country to completely disestablish its government from any religion. This separation was explicitly stated in the Bill of Rights of the US Constitution that was ratified by the colonies in 1791.[110] The First Amendment states, "Congress shall make no law respecting an establishment of religion, or prohibiting the free exercise thereof; or abridging the freedom of speech, or of the press; or the right of the people peaceably to assemble, and to petition the Government for a redress of grievances."

The pertinent "religion clauses" in that amendment (1) preclude Congress from passing any law that would establish a particular religion, i.e., require citizens to observe particular religious practices or support (financially) any particular church or other religious association; and (2) preclude Congress from prohibiting the free exercise of the religion of one's choice. James Madison, principal architect of the Bill of Rights, said that "practical distinction between Religion and Civil Government is essential to the purity of both."[111] Similarly, I argue that the practical distinction between *money* and civil government is essential to the purity of both.

The Disestablishment of Monetary "Religion"

As I have maintained throughout, the fundamental purpose of money is to facilitate the voluntary exchange of objects of material value between independent persons. The long-established rights of contract and voluntary association argue in favour of the free selection of such facilitating mechanisms that buyers and sellers judge to best serve their mutual interests. To grant "legal tender" status to any particular brand of money, or to support by legislation any particular banking establishment or cartel, is akin to making a law respecting an establishment of religion. *There should be no monopoly of credit, no central authority with exclusive power to issue money, and no forced circulation of any currency.* The credit power must be decentralized, and every currency must be made to make its way in the marketplace on it own merits. Robert Somers, writing in 1873 about the superior system of Scottish banking, clearly posed the matter, saying:

> The question betwixt a central and a plural issue is in reality a question whether banking is to be confined to the great capitalists, or to a few of the greatest towns, and to the high commerce of nations, or opened up to all classes of people and made to embrace the industry, savings and interests of the many. *The tendency of a State or central form of issue is to aristocratize banking.* The effect of a plural issue is to popularize this powerful lever both of moral and material improvement. The one seems, therefore, as comfortable as the other is counter to the social tendencies of the age, and to that ever-advancing impulse to raise, enrich, refine and brighten the whole body of a people, which is the crowning glory of all civilization.[112] [emphasis added]

The fact that the establishment of monetary and banking privilege has become general throughout the world is not sufficient reason for its continuance. On the contrary, the evils that have been spawned by such collusion between political power and financial power are far worse even than those that arose historically from the collusion between political power and religious power.

Two Meanings of "Dollar"

Because of general legal tender laws, the "dollar" has come to have two meanings — (1) as a medium of exchange or payment (a currency) and (2) as the standard of value measurement or pricing unit. Any alternative currency or credit system must eventually decouple from both "dollars," but the more urgent need, by far, is decoupling from the official dollar currency as a means of payment. This means the independent creation of credits or currencies outside of the conventional banking system.

As I've pointed out in my previous books, a community currency that is issued on the basis of payment of a national currency (e.g., a local currency that is sold for dollars), amounts to a "gift certificate" or localized "traveler's cheque."[113] It amounts to prepayment for the goods or services offered by the merchants that agree to accept the currency. As such, it substitutes a local, limited-use currency for a national, universal currency. That approach provides some limited utility in encouraging the holder of the currency to buy locally, but the option of redeeming the currency back into dollars without significant penalty raises the question of how many times it will mediate local trades before being redeemed and leaking back to the outside world. Most importantly, that sort of issuance requires that someone have dollars in order for the community currency to come into existence. No dollars; no community currency.

Delinking from the Dollar as a Payment Medium

To truly empower a community, a currency must be issued on the basis of goods and services changing hands, i.e., it should be "spent into circulation" by local business entities and individuals who are able to redeem it later by providing goods or services that are in

everyday demand by local consumers. Such a currency amounts
to a credit instrument or IOU of the issuer, an IOU that is voluntarily accepted by some other provider of goods and services (like
an employee or supplier), then circulated and eventually redeemed
– not in cash, but "in kind" by the original issuer, as depicted in
Figure 8.1. In this way, community members "monetize" the value
of their own production, just as banks monetize the value of collateral assets when they make a loan – except in this case, monetization is done by the community members themselves based on their
own values and criteria, without the "help" or involvement of any
government, bank, or ordinary financial institution, and without the
need to have any official money to begin with. That is what I mean
when I talk about liberating the exchange process, or restoring the

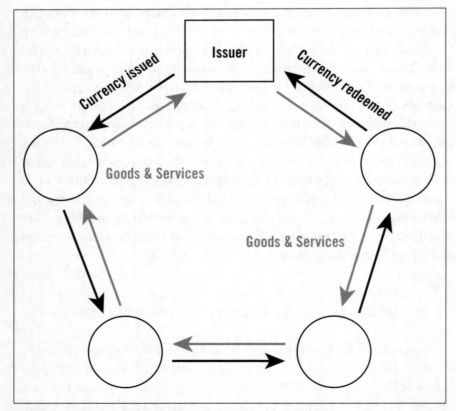

Figure 8.1 The Currency Issuance, Circulation, and Redemption Circuit

"credit commons"* and bringing it under local control. In this way, the community gains a measure of independence from the supply of official money (dollars, euros, yen) and the policies and decisions of the central bank and the banking cartel. This is the primary mission that needs to be accomplished if we are to transcend the destructive effects of the global monetary and banking regime, devolve power to the local level, and build sustainable economic democracies.

Delinking from the Dollar as a Measure of Value

With regard to the second meaning, the dollar as a measure of value, we need to understand that a standard becomes established by common usage. We in the United States are accustomed to valuing things in dollar units. We know from our everyday shopping experiences what the value of the dollar unit is in terms of the things we buy and in terms of our own earning power. Any new "language of value" will have to be translated into the dollar language that we already understand. How we measure value is a separate question from how we create our own payment media. In the process of monetizing local production as described above, we can choose to give our credit unit any name we wish − be it a *val*, an *acorn*, or a *cru* − but it makes sense to *initially* define the value of that unit as being equivalent to that of the national currency unit.

In an alternative exchange system, like a mutual credit clearing exchange, large credit balances will not be held for very long. Therefore even though the debasement of the dollar unit through monetization of government debt continues, defining our unit as being equivalent to the official unit (the dollar) will result in only slight losses for individual users of the exchange or community currency, and not a loss for the users collectively. It is only when the rates of inflation become

---

* The concept of the "commons" is an ancient one referring to a resource for which there is open access to anyone within a community or geographic area, as opposed to private property or government-owned "public" property. Legal rules or social customs may govern some aspects of the use of the shared resource, but these rules or customs do not prevent people from gaining access to the resource in the first place. In the case of money, our collective credit which supports the money and banking system has been privatized and appropriated to serve the interests of a small élite class.

large (generally meaning double digit), or we begin to hold *long-term* claims denominated in our own new value unit, that we will urgently need to define our unit in concrete, objective terms to avoid following the dollar or other political currencies into the abyss of worthlessness.

Stable Value Reckoning

The US dollar was originally defined as a specified weight of fine silver, then later a specified weight of gold, but those objective definitions were obliterated by laws that made paper currency legal tender. So now the value of the *dollar unit of measure of value* depends entirely upon the value of the *dollar currency*, but the value of the dollar currency is continually declining as more of it is issued on an improper basis, particularly on the basis of government debts that will never be repaid and that bring no concomitant goods and services into the market.

In the previous chapter, we described at some length the hyperinflation of the German mark following World War I. It is difficult for people who have not lived through that kind of experience to appreciate what it means or to understand what it takes to avoid it. It was only by defining the mark in concrete, physical terms (in that case, gold) that the German people were able to end that nightmare. Britain, the United States, and the European Union have thus far seen only moderate rates of inflation – so people have been inured to it, accepting it as a natural part of the economic landscape. Neither have they developed the necessary skepticism against legal tender currencies and their issuing agencies. Goods and services and wages are still priced in legal tender currencies, so under these conditions it makes sense to talk about changes in the price of gold or silver or other commodities. But we need to shift our thinking to regard not that these commodities have a legal tender money price, but rather the other way round. We need to think of the currency having a price in terms of silver or gold or other commodities.

Applying that reasoning to the present day United States, we would say that the price of silver or gold should not be reckoned in Federal Reserve "dollars," but that Federal Reserve dollars should be reckoned in, say, silver dollars. The simplest way to do that is to use the original definition of the US dollar, which was 371.25 grains of fine silver. If there are 480 grains in a troy ounce, and the market price of silver is $16.50 per troy ounce (as it was on June 13, 2008) then a Federal Reserve dollar would be worth about 7.8 (silver dollar) cents. For most of 2005, silver traded at around $7 per ounce, making the Federal Reserve dollar worth about 18.5 (silver dollar) cents at that time. That means the Federal Reserve paper dollar has lost almost 58 percent of its previous value in just three years time based on a silver standard.

A stable value unit will eventually need to be defined in terms of some commodity or group of commodities that are commonly traded. Such a definition will then provide the "Rosetta stone" that can enable us to relate, from day to day and minute to minute, our own new value unit to the old dollar language. That process is explained in my first book, *Money and Debt: A Solution to the Global Crisis,* Part III and Appendices.[114] An abridged description is also provided in Appendix B of this volume.

Toward Freedom of Exchange

The separation of money and state implies greater freedom of people to choose which currencies they will use and to create their own. Buyers and sellers, who are the affected parties in a transaction, should be able to choose the particular credit instrument (money) that enables their reciprocal exchange. Here are the basic principles that underlie a system of free exchange.

- Buyers and sellers should be free to use any payment medium that is mutually agreeable to them, including the issuance and acceptance of their own currencies.
- Only the issuer of a currency should be obliged to accept it as payment, and must always accept it at face value ("at par").
- There should be no forced circulation of any currency. *Legal tender* should obligate government only, and should not apply to transactions between private parties.

- Governments should give *legal tender* status only to their
  own currencies that they spend directly into circulation,
  and should not grant privileged status to the currency of
  any particular issuer.
- Government currencies should be denominated in
  objective units against which the market may evaluate
  them, and governments should oblige themselves to
  accept their currencies at par regardless of the market rate
  (discount).

As John Zube puts it, "Currency cannot be acceptable unless it is
rejectable." The freedom to use, refuse, or discount a currency is essential to its acceptability.

9. The Evolution of Money — From Commodity Money to Credit Money

It was in a dusty old bookshop close to the British Museum in London that I discovered a slim volume that was to complete for me the picture of how money has evolved over time. I had been traveling in Europe and the United Kingdom in the summer of 2001 with my then partner, Donna, partly to attend conferences in Germany and England, partly to spend time with friends and cohorts, and partly to do a bit of touring. It was actually Donna who discovered the book in the basement stacks and brought it to me, saying "what about this one?" The book was *The Meaning of Money* by Hartley Withers.[115] Although I had already been engaged in intensive research into the subjects of money and banking for more than twenty years, and had written three books of my own on the subject, I had not previously heard of Withers. It was evident that Withers must have been, in his day, a recognized authority on the subject and that his book must have served for a long time as a leading text. I surmised that from the fact that the volume I held in my hands was the seventh edition, published in 1947, of a work that was first published in 1909. Reading Withers crystallized my understanding of the double transformation that money had undergone during the previous three hundred years, an understanding that allowed a clearer comprehension of the nature and significance of the changes that have taken place and that prepares the ground from which to launch the next great improvement in the exchange process.

What We Don't Know Is Hurting Us

Money is clouded in mystery and there are few who really understand it. It is not that it is so difficult to understand, but because it is made to seem that way by financial journalists, bankers, and monetary economists who speak an obscure language, indulge in superficial speculations about markets and policy changes, and behave as if the wizards of Wall Street were possessed of some superior form of intelligence. This discourages most people from even trying to understand money. But what we don't know can hurt us, and it is this general ignorance that is at the root of much of the present misery in the world. As John Adams, the second president of the United States, expressed it in a letter to Thomas Jefferson, "All the perplexities, confusions and distresses in America arise not from defects in the Constitution or Confederation, not from want of honour or virtue, as much as from downright ignorance of the nature of coin, credit and circulation." That is probably even more true in our present day than it was in the late eighteenth century.

Money is a human contrivance created to serve particular purposes, primarily to facilitate the exchange of goods and services. In this chapter, we will dispel the mystery by telling the story of money in a way that clearly distinguishes the various kinds of money and reveals their essential nature. We will explain the transformational stages through which money (or more accurately, the exchange process) has passed, and in the following chapter how it is once again being transformed. Subsequent chapters will describe the more efficient and equitable exchange mechanisms that are now emerging, and will suggest how they might be further perfected. For this, we need not speculate about the distant past, nor seek to uncover the obscure origins of money in ancient societies. It will suffice to examine how money and banking have evolved together over the past three hundred years.

Kinds of Economic Interaction

To begin with, it is necessary to realize the precise role that money is intended to play. To do that, we must distinguish among the various modes by which real economic value changes hands. These are as follows:

- Gifts
- Involuntary transfers
- Reciprocal exchange

In the case of a gift, if it is truly a gift, something of value is transferred without any particular expectation of the giver receiving anything in return. In the case of involuntary transfers (such as theft, robbery, extortion, or taxes) some form of force or threat is applied to coerce the transfer of value from one person or entity to another. In reciprocal exchange, two parties voluntarily agree to exchange one value for another. Each, ostensibly, values the thing received more than the thing surrendered, so both are enriched by the bargain.

It is within the realm of reciprocal exchange that money plays its fundamental role as a *medium of exchange* or means of payment. Any feature of a monetary system that subverts reciprocity is dishonest and destructive to the intended outcome of mutual benefit among those who use money.

The Ladder of Economic Civilization

The key to understanding money lies in being able to distinguish between its mere *forms* on the one hand, and its true *essence* on the other. We often hear that money evolved from gold and silver coin, to paper money, to "chequebook money." But that does not really tell the story. Such a progression confuses money's forms with its essences. What we really need to know is the value basis of money in each of its historical manifestations. Paper is not the essence of paper money, but only the carrier of information. The nature of that information is what we shall describe shortly.

The process of reciprocal exchange has, over the centuries, evolved through numerous stages of what Withers has called "the ladder of economic civilization." It is extremely instructive to trace this evolution and to realize how money has repeatedly been transformed. Here, in sum, are the steps, each of which will be discussed in turn.

- Barter trade
- Commodity money
- Symbolic money
- Credit money
- Credit clearing

The First Evolutionary Step — Barter to Commodity Money

The first evolutionary step in the process of reciprocal exchange was from simple barter to commodity money. Barter is the most primitive form of reciprocal exchange. Barter involves only two people, each of which has something the other wants. However, if Jones wants something from Smith, but has nothing that Smith wants, there can be no barter trade. So barter depends upon the "double coincidence" of wants and needs. Money, in its most fundamental role, enables traders to transcend this barter limitation. Money bridges the gap in both space and time, acting as a "placeholder" that enables the need of a buyer to be met wherever and whenever the needed good or service may be found. This requires the agreement of the seller to defer satisfaction and to find his needed goods or services elsewhere. Thus, the first evolutionary step in reciprocal exchange came when traders began to use as an exchange medium some useful commodity that was in general demand and could be easily passed along in payment to other sellers.

Commodity Money

The most primitive type of money, then, is commodity money. Commodity money carries value in itself and can fulfill all of the classical functions attributed to money. It is at once a payment medium, a measure of value, and a store of value. Throughout history, a wide variety of commodities has served as money including cattle, tobacco, grains, nails, shells, hides, and (of course) metals — especially the so-called precious metals, gold and silver. I may personally have no use for tobacco, but if there are many others who want it, I will accept it in payment for the things I sell because I know that I can use it later to pay for something I want. So some commodities acquired "exchange value" as well as "use value." But by using commodities as money, the transaction essentially remained a barter trade of one thing for another.

Because they are durable, portable, and easy to divide into smaller amounts (fungible), certain metals (notably silver and gold) became commodities of choice for mediating the exchange of all other goods and services. Eventually, these metals were struck (minted) into pieces (coins) of certified weight and purity (fineness) as a way of obviating the need for sellers to weigh and assay in the market the metal that was offered as payment. The certification may have been made by some trusted person or entity. There are many examples of private coinage, but more often coinage was claimed as a prerogative of the local political authority, a prince or a king, because there were good profits to be made from it. Official certification, if it could be relied upon, increased the convenience of using metallic money and reduced the cost of evaluating it. But over time, it became common for the certifying authority — the prince, the king, or the government — to abuse its authority by forcing people to accept inferior coinage.

The first coins to be minted date from antiquity. In modern times, every civilized country has minted and circulated a variety of gold or silver coins. When the constitution for the United States was written, it simply recognized the monetary standard that had already been established by popular usage. That happened to be the Spanish milled "dollar." Spanish dollars were silver coins that circulated widely throughout the American colonies. This fact was acknowledged by

Thomas Jefferson in his treatise *Notes on the Establishment of a Money Unit, and of a Coinage for the United States*. Jefferson stated that "The unit or dollar is a known coin and the most familiar of all to the mind of the people. It is already adopted from south to north."[116]

These Spanish dollar coins, however, were not uniform in weight or fineness. Dollar coins issued at different times varied slightly from one another. To complete the task of defining the monetary unit for the United States in a way that would not disturb commerce, a committee was commissioned to survey the money stock and assay a representative sampling of Spanish dollar coins so that the American dollar would closely approximate those coins already in circulation. This was easily accomplished and it was quickly settled that the United States dollar should be defined as a silver coin containing 371.25 grains of fine silver.[117] Coins were subsequently minted according to that specification along with gold coins valued in dollars. As the country developed, various expedients were implemented to make money more abundant. These measures, unfortunately, were also used to concentrate economic and political power into fewer hands, as we have already described.

Symbolic Money

The simplest form of symbolic money is the "warehouse receipt" or "claim cheque" for goods on deposit somewhere. A prime example is the grain bank receipts that have been issued at various times and places. In ancient Egypt, as in some African countries today, a farmer might bring his grain crop to a central warehouse and receive receipts for his grain. These receipts might then be exchanged in payment for other goods and services — and when issued in conveniently small denominations, might serve as a general medium of exchange within the region. The holder of the paper notes then has the option of presenting the notes at the warehouse and obtaining the grain they represent.

Paper notes that are redeemable for gold or silver coins are another example of a symbolic currency. The general acceptability of symbolic money derives from the fact that it can be redeemed by the holder on demand for the amount of the commodity that it represents. The shift from direct exchange of commodities to the exchange of notes or tokens representing claims to commodities was a sort of half-step that prepared the way for the next evolutionary step. Figure 9.1 depicts the process of creating symbolic money on the basis of deposits of gold.

The Second Evolutionary Step – From Commodity Money to Credit Money

The second evolutionary step, what I call *the great monetary transformation*, was the shift from metallic money (commodity money) and "claim cheque" money (symbolic money) to *credit money*. This transformational development provided a major leap forward in the potential efficacy of exchange media – but unfortunately, it also opened the door for greater abuse. The failure to distinguish between the different kinds of paper money that came into circulation caused much confusion and enabled subtle forms of cheating to proliferate, as we will explain. For now, let us just say that the important question to be answered with regard to any piece of paper currency is "what does the paper represent?" Not all paper is created equal.

Credit money initially took the form of paper banknotes issued independently by various banks; later on, it took the form of bank "depos-

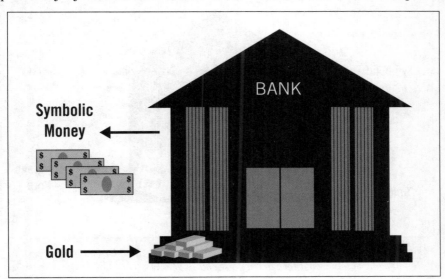

Figure 9.1 Bank Notes Issued as Symbolic Money The first bank notes were symbolic money. They were warehouse receipts for gold or silver on deposit.

its" against which cheques could be drawn, i.e., what have been called *demand deposits* or, in Europe, *sight deposits*. In either case, whether it takes the form of paper notes or demand deposits, credit money is essentially a promise to pay – what we call an IOU. By Withers's account, the introduction of the banknote was the first step in the development of the machinery for "manufacturing credit." As he describes it, "Some ingenious goldsmith conceived the epoch-making notion of giving notes not only to those who had deposited metal, but to those who came to borrow it, and so founded modern banking."[118] Withers's view of credit money is one of "mutual indebtedness" between the banker and his customer. The customer would give the banker his promissory note or mortgage (the customer's debt to the banker) in return for the banker's notes (the banker's debt to the customer), which also carried a promise to pay gold. This process is depicted in Figure 9.2.

But did that "ingenious goldsmith" intend to revolutionize money, or was he perpetrating a fraud? The prevalent mindset, at that time, considered money to be gold or silver, and banknotes to be merely claim cheques (symbolic money) for gold or silver held on deposit.

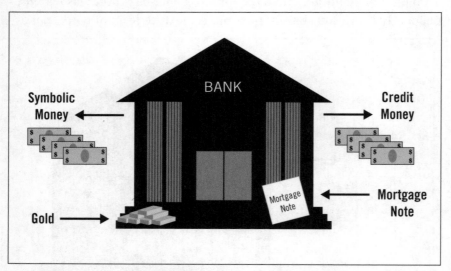

Figure 9.2 Bank Creation of Both Symbolic Money and Credit Money Banks issued two different kinds of money but they did not distinguish between them, and few people realized it. The same identical bank notes were issued to represent both symbolic money and credit money.

When the banker issued notes in amounts greater than the amount of metal in his vault and made all notes redeemable on demand for metal, the stage was set for trouble.

Two Distinct Kinds of Money — Fractional Reserve Banking

This situation became problematic because now there were two different kinds of paper money being issued into circulation, the one a "claim cheque" for gold on deposit and the other a credit instrument issued on the basis of a promise to pay and backed by some other form of collateral assets such as merchandise inventories or real property, *yet both were redeemable for gold*. This "fractional reserve system," as it came to be known, was problematic from the start. Whenever people, for any reason, lost confidence in a bank or began to have doubts about the bank's ability to redeem their notes, there would be a "bank run." Those who got there first got the gold. When a bank's stores of gold were exhausted, it would have to close its doors, sometimes never to reopen. At times, when there was sagging confidence in the banking system as a whole, bank panics became generalized and widespread. Many perfectly sound banks were put out of business because their supply of gold was inadequate to redeem any substantial portion of their issue of banknotes. In the classic film *It's a Wonderful Life*,[119] actor Jimmy Stewart dramatically explains to the people how their money resides not in the bank's vault but in the homes and businesses of their neighbours, perfectly sound collateral the value of which would eventually become liquid again as people repaid their loans.

Those who have decried the issuance of *paper* money have had good reason to do so, but they have also failed to recognize that it is not the paper that is problematic; it is what the paper represents. Paper money that is *properly issued* on the basis of sound collateral can be a perfectly sound and legitimate medium of exchange. It cannot be too greatly stressed that, as we have already shown, one of the most fundamental problems with paper money historically was the fact that *both* symbolic paper and credit paper were made redeemable for gold. But that problem was compounded by another, more fundamental error – the frequent issuance of paper money on an improper basis, often featuring collateral having questionable value. Such worthless collateral, which might be a promissory note, was (like a fraudulent cheque) often referred to as a "kite."

It is important to realize that those who would have us revert to commodity money like gold and silver do so because they see no other way of imposing discipline upon the powers that have gained control over the process of money creation and allocation, namely bankers and politicians. But by understanding the fundamental nature of modern money *as credit*, it becomes possible to liberate and perfect it, and to avoid throwing out the more evolved credit money "baby" with the "bath water" of perverse centralization of power.

Another aspect of the money problem was, and is, the manipulation of the supply of credit money by the banking interests operating under the aegis of central governments. By first making credit abundant, then restricting its supply, they can induce people and businesses to borrow and then force them into bankruptcy and foreclosure. The "subprime" mortgage crisis that developed during 2007 and 2008 is a conspicuous example of this. That crisis developed out of the prior inordinate expansion of credit by the banking system on the basis of inflated real estate values. The banks created the real estate "bubble" by lending on (initially) easy terms and low interest rates to unqualified borrowers. Later, when higher interest rates kicked in, many were unable to pay.

Redeemability Abandoned

Eventually, the redeemability feature of money was abandoned. In stages, silver and gold were officially demonetized. Now virtually all of the money in circulation is credit money, created by banks when they make loans. This money exists not as banknotes, but in the form of "deposits" in bank accounts. We see then that the problem of the scarcity of conventional money, which at first consisted of gold and silver, was alleviated by the introduction of a new kind of payment medium – credit. This credit was manifested on one side of the bank's ledger (asset) as the borrower's promissory note, and on the other side (liability) as paper currency notes, which were the banker's IOU, as depicted in Figure 9.3. Giving those early bankers the benefit of the doubt, one can argue that it was first necessary for the community to develop sufficient confidence in this form of money to accept it as a form of payment, and that making the new (credit) money redeemable for the old (gold) money was necessary to building that sort of confidence. Others will argue that making both kinds of money redeemable caused more harm than good to the credibility of paper money generally.

Be that as it may, the evolutionary step from metallic (commodity) money to credit money was accompanied by much confusion, abuse, and discomfort. The problem stemmed, as we've said, from the concurrent circulation of two different kinds of money and the general failure to distinguish between them. Was a paper banknote merely a claim cheque for gold held on deposit in the bank's vault, or was it money in itself, a credit instrument backed by some other form of value (a lien against physical inventories of goods, a mortgage on a farm or factory, etc.)?

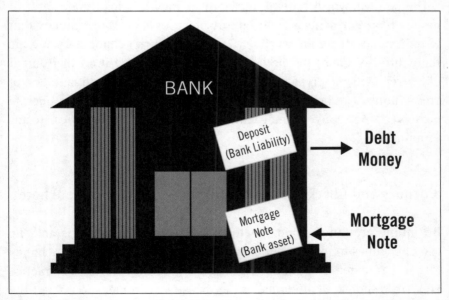

Figure 9.3 The Creation of Bank "Debt Money" as Deposits Banks now issue only debt money, not as notes, but in the form of bank "deposits" when a "loan" is granted.

The problems that arose from the concurrent circulation of both symbolic money and credit money might have been avoided if a clear distinction between them had been made from the beginning and the redeemability feature had been explicitly limited. This, in fact, was proven by the operation of Scottish banks during the early part of the nineteenth century. During that period, notes issued by the Scottish banks gave the banks the option of delaying gold redemption for a certain period of time according to the availability of gold. These banks became known for their strength and stability, and their notes were readily accepted at face value despite this "gold option clause." Banknotes issued on the basis of valuable assets (proper collateral) have proven to be just as sound and acceptable an exchange medium as precious metal coins, without their physical quantity limitations and inconvenience of their transfer. The redeemability feature was carried over during the period when it was thought that public confidence required it. History has shown that redeemability could be readily dispensed with, and credit money has become universally acceptable in its own right.

The point is worth reiterating: credit money is a legitimate form of money that represents a great improvement over symbolic money that is redeemable for gold or silver. Under the current monetary regime the control of credit by the banking cartel has made it an instrument of power causing great social harm. Nonetheless, the advantages of credit money can be more fully realized as we develop ways to liberate ourselves from conventional banking institutions and political forms of money.

Cheques and Checkable Deposits Displace the Use of Banknotes

Beginning around the mid-nineteenth century, bank deposits and the use of cheques to make payments came to predominate over the hand-to-hand transfer of banknotes. Withers describes how this practice arose in response to attempts by the British government to restrict the issuance of banknotes representing credit money and to maintain the note-issuing monopoly in the hands of the Bank of England. In an attempt to address the frequent abuses by issuing banks, which caused recurrent bank failures, the British Parliament passed the Bank Act of 1844. This act prohibited all banks except the Bank of England from issuing banknotes and required that any subsequent issuance of notes by the Bank of England must be based only on metal, not on securities. It was an attempt to make the bank note "a mere bullion certificate,"[120] i.e., a warehouse receipt for gold held on deposit. While the intention of this law may have been good, the effects could have been extremely problematic for trade and industry because it restricted the supply of exchange media.

Withers points out that,

> If the apparent intentions of the Act of 1844 had been carried out, the subsequent enormous development of English trade, if it had been possible at all, must have been accompanied by the heaping up of a vast amount of gold in the Bank's vaults. But its intentions were evaded by the commercial community, which had already accepted the advantages of a currency based on mutual indebtedness between itself and the banks [credit money]. The commercial community ceased to circulate bank-notes under the new restrictions, developing the use for daily cash transactions of a credit instrument which had already acquired some popularity, namely, a draft or bill on its bankers payable on demand and now commonly called a cheque. The drawing of cheques was not in any way limited by the Act of 1844, and the cheque was in many ways a more convenient form of currency than the bank-note ... The use of the cheque, however, involves the element of belief to a much greater extent than that of the bank-note.[121]

Thus we see another instance in which "necessity is the mother of invention." Since a cheque is not money but merely an order to pay money, anyone who accepts a cheque must first ascertain the credibility of both the drawer of the cheque and the bank upon which it is drawn. Does the drawer of the cheque actually have an account with the stated bank, and is that account not overdrawn? Does the bank on which the cheque is drawn actually exist, and is it solvent? Despite these risks, and despite the fact that cheques were not legal tender, their use became ever more popular. In Withers' words, "the cheque has had to fight its way to its present supremacy without this advantage [of legal tender status], and to drive gold and notes out of circulation ...in spite of the fact that they were legal tender and it was not. This it was enabled to do by its safety and convenience and the power of the drawer to hedge it about with restrictions."[122]

The convenience of the cheque is obvious to those of us who grew up using it, but considering the risks described above, what makes it safe, and what are the restrictions that Withers speaks of? First off, it can be legally negotiated (cashed or deposited) only by the payee. Unlike banknotes (which anyone can spend) a cheque, if it is lost or stolen, cannot easily be cashed or spent by the finder or thief. In addition, it can be made out for the exact amount due and after it is cancelled it is returned to the drawer to serve as a record and receipt for payment.

Gold Versus Credit Money — A Comparison

Many monetary reformers today still believe that money, to be sound, must be fully backed by gold or silver and be redeemable on demand. But this would be a step backward to a more primitive medium of exchange, and would unnecessarily throttle the exchange process. The limited supply of whatever commodities might serve as money would limit the amount of trading that could take place with disastrous consequences for the economy. The reasons for this will become clear as we proceed. The answer to the abusive issuance and circulation of credit money lies not in turning back the clock and reverting to more primitive forms, but in perfecting the superior form, credit money, within the arena of free competition. The biggest challenge then is to find ways of transcending the political money system that has gained a virtual monopoly on credit worldwide.

The general lack of understanding of the real nature of money and the proper basis for credit money has often caused the political debate to run askew, leading many well-intended reformers to inadvertently restrict the supply of exchange media in an attempt to remedy abusive banking practices. Such was the case during the Jackson era (roughly, the second third of the nineteenth century). In the "Bank War" that we described in Chapter 4, President Andrew Jackson rightly put an end to the extreme privilege and power of the Second Bank of the United States, but at the same time he also adopted a restrictive "hard money" policy. Fortunately, the proliferation of banks and the easy availability of credit during this "free banking" period, while sometimes flawed, enabled a great expansion of industry and commerce.

The real argument is not between gold versus paper, but between *commodity* money versus *credit* money. To posit the argument as between specie and paper misses the point by confusing the physical manifestation or form of money with the substance of money. It is the *basis of issue* of money that is all-important. Paper money can represent a "claim cheque" or "warehouse receipt" for gold on deposit (symbolic money), or it can represent the value inherent in particular collateral assets against which credit is monetized (credit money). Under the original fractional reserve banking system, these two were confused and intermingled, making trouble inevitable. So long as both claim cheque money and credit money were redeemable for specie one could expect periodic bank runs and panics.

The supply of commodities like gold and silver is limited by natural factors, and the cost of increasing such supply (by the process of mining, refining, and coining – or even by taking it as plunder) is very great. Furthermore, it is destructive to the environment. How does it make sense to dig gold out of one hole (a mine) only to bury it again in another (a vault)? Gold has very little use value aside from ornamentation – its desirability derives primarily from its historical "exchange value." In times of financial uncertainty, gold may serve as an effective *savings medium* by hedging against the effects of inflation of legal tender currency. It can also provide portability of wealth for refugees, as well as some measure of financial privacy. Gold might serve to define a measure of value, but it will not return as a primary payment medium unless there is a major breakdown of civilization. The expansion of credit, on the other hand, can be achieved at very low cost, and its quantity is limited only by the collective capacity to produce and the aggregate value of the goods and services that people wish to exchange. *By enabling every producer to create — within reasonable limits — the credit money needed to satisfy their needs for goods and services, it is possible to have a flexible-yet-sound means of facilitating exchange.*

How Credit Money Malfunctions

A multitude of problems derive from abuse of the credit creation function. The great leap forward that credit money represented was, and still is, perverted by a financial regime that centralizes power and concentrates wealth. The monopolistic control over credit, exercised through a banking cartel armed with government-granted privilege, allows wealth to be extracted from producer clients and, despite the trappings of democracy, the control of governments to be maintained in the hands of a few. Credit is allocated on a biased basis to favoured clients, including central governments, which distorts both the system of economic rewards and the exercise of political power. Under this regime, the people's own credit is privatized and "loaned" back to them at interest. The enormous benefits that credit money makes possible can be realized only if credit is created democratically on a proper value basis by the people themselves. What that basis should be and how it should be done will be addressed subsequently.

10. The Third Evolutionary Stage —
The Emergence of Credit Clearing

Let us begin by summarizing the evolutionary steps that were described in the previous chapter:

1. the circulation of *gold and silver coins* gave way to paper banknotes redeemable for gold or silver coins;
2. this gave way to *irredeemable banknotes* supported by a lien against various other collateral assets (some valuable and others not) and government obligations (bonds);
3. this gave way to *cheque deposits*, similarly created on the basis of various kinds of loans made by banks (including their purchase of government securities).

Banks and the Credit Clearing Process

The use of deposits and cheques actually represented the introduction of the clearing process within the banking system. As Withers pointed out, the creation of money as "deposits" (account balances) rather than banknotes enabled the banks to circumvent government's limitations on their issuance of banknotes. Money became abstract, and the role of banks became primarily (1) the vetting of requests for credit and (2) the clearing of credit among the various depositor's accounts.

Think about this scenario. You receive your salary from your employer in the form of an automatic electronic transfer from your employer's bank account to your bank account. You then go shopping and use your debit card to transfer the price of your purchases from your account to the merchant's account. You might also go online and make a payment on your credit card balance, transferring an amount from your bank account to the account of the credit card company. Where is the money in all of this? Each of these transactions merely increased or decreased the numbers in your account and the accounts of those with whom you do business. Money is no longer substantial. Money is merely an accounting system, a way of "keeping score" in the economic "game" of give and take. Your purchases have been indirectly paid for with your sales, the services or labour you provided to your employer.

In actuality, everyone is both a buyer and a seller. When you sell, your account balance increases; when you buy, it decreases. The bank's role in this is to provide the accounting necessary to offset (clear) your purchases against your sales. But banks still prefer to act as if money is a *thing* that they can lend out, so they can charge interest on it. Your bank account is not allowed to have a negative balance unless you have an "overdraft privilege." In that case, if you *do* overdraw your account, the negative balance will be offset by the bank making an automatic deposit to your account. Where does that "deposit" come from? The bank creates it.

As we described in the previous chapter, banks more typically create deposits by preauthorization. They do this by taking your loan application, evaluating your credit history and the value of any collateral assets. If your application is approved, a "deposit" is created and credited to your account. This process is called "monetization." It transforms the value of illiquid assets, like a house or other collateral assets (or even just your signature), into liquid or spendable form, i.e., "deposits" that are now called money. Banks call this practice "making a loan," even though nothing is loaned.

A Confusion of Language

The word "deposit," along with other terminology in banking and finance, is anachronistic – something that has been carried over from the days when commodity money, like gold and silver, was actually *deposited* in a bank. The words may be the same, but the meanings are entirely different. Think of the way we speak about the things we do every day, like "driving" a car. You don't actually "drive" a car. A car is a machine; you "operate" it. The word *drive* has been carried over from a different time and a different mode of transport. It comes from a time when one would *drive* a team of horses or mules pulling a wagon. The process, skills, and responses involved in driving a team are quite different from those involved in "driving" a car. The experience of driving a wagon team probably bears a greater resemblance to dog training or coaching a football team than it does to operating a motor vehicle.

Likewise, in the realm of money and banking, such anachronisms include the words *deposit, reserve, redemption,* and *credit.* When money took the form of silver or gold, a deposit was just that, an amount of silver or gold left in the care of a banker. The paper banknotes that the depositor received amounted to deposit receipts. But now, *money is merely numbers in an accounting system,* and the balance (number) in your account on a bank ledger, while still referred to as a deposit, simply shows your current score or *credit* in the economic game. The perpetuation of this dysfunctional system is aided by the confusion that persists over the process of money creation. If we have not made it clear before, let us explicitly state that banks have two fundamental roles. They are at once "depositories" and also "banks of issue" — that is, they accept deposits of existing money, and they also create new money by making loans. A further quote of Quigley's may aid in clarifying this point. He says that, "with typical bankers' ambiguity," banks use the same term, "deposits," to refer to things that arise from

> two entirely different kinds of relationships: (1) "lodged deposits," which were real claims left by a depositor in a bank, on which the depositor might receive interest since such deposits were debts owed by the bank to the depositor; and (2) "created deposits," which were claims *created by the bank out of nothing as loans from the bank to "depositors"* who had to pay interest on them since they represented debt from them to the bank. In both cases, of course, cheques could be drawn against such deposits to make payments to third parties, which is why both

were called by the same name. *Both form part of the money supply.*[123] [emphasis added]

Particle or Wave? Thing or Relationship?

Here's an analogy that may be helpful. Scientists have two distinct ways of explaining the phenomenon of light. Light can be described as either a particle or as a wave that propagates through some medium. Money can likewise be described as either a thing or an account balance based on a relationship agreement. We can speak of credit as a thing, especially when it manifests in the form of a currency note or voucher, but its essence is more easily understood as a fluctuating number.

The process called "clearing" is the simplest and most efficient mechanism for mediating reciprocal exchange, and represents the next (perhaps the ultimate) step in the evolution of reciprocal exchange. The possibilities of credit clearing have long been recognized but are still far from being fully realized. As early as 1914, Hugo Bilgram and L.E. Levy noted that, "If there were no money, any system of crediting sellers and debiting buyers would be fully competent to accomplish the work now performed by money."[124] It is the creation and operation of such systems that is crucial to the advancement and sustainability of civilization.

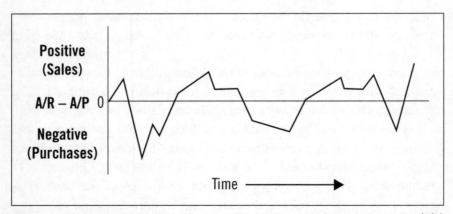

Figure 10.1 Money Viewed as a Wave Ongoing difference between Accounts Receivable (A/R), and Accounts Payable (A/P)

Clearing is simply the process of accounting that offsets debits (resulting from purchases) against credits (resulting from sales). When you sell something, your account balance is credited (increased); when you buy something, your account balance is debited (decreased). It's that simple. In effect, *the things you sell pay for the things you buy.* This will be explained more fully in Chapter 12, which elaborates credit clearing principles and illustrates them by means of a simple example, but for now we'll just outline the basic process.

Consider a typical small enterprise; let's call it the Alpha Company that does business on "open account" with a group of both customers and suppliers. That means it extends credit to customers and receives credit from suppliers. When Alpha Company makes a sale, it has money coming to it. In accounting terms, a sale gives rise to an *account receivable* (A/R). Similarly, when Alpha Company makes a purchase, it owes money to someone else. In accounting terms, a purchase gives rise to an *account payable* (A/P). Figure 10.1 depicts the process of clearing, which can be thought of as the "wave" nature of money. When Alpha Company has made sales that total an amount greater than its purchases within the group, it has a positive clearing balance; when its purchases are greater than its sales within its group, it has a negative clearing balance. Over time, its balance will fluctuate, at some times being positive and sometimes negative.

Clearing through Banks Versus Mutual Credit Clearing

Now consider two possibilities. First consider the use of conventional money and banking to clear accounts among a group of companies that trade with one another, then compare that with clearing accounts independently and directly. Figure 10.2 on page 120 depicts the conventional payment process using bank credit money that has been borrowed into circulation, while Figure 10.3 on page 121 shows the direct clearing process that uses no bank credit for the following hypothetical case. Suppose that Alpha owes Bravo $100, Bravo owes Charlie $100, Charlie owes Delta $100, and Delta owes Alpha $100. In the conventional process, one or more of the companies must borrow money from a bank in order for them to pay what they owe to each other. In the simplest scenario (Figure 10.2), Alpha borrows $100 from the bank to pay Bravo, who then uses that money to pay Charlie, who then uses it to pay Delta, who then uses it to pay Alpha. Everyone has now been paid – including Alpha, which can now repay the bank. But in addition to the $100 principal, Alpha must also pay the bank some amount of interest. In sum, each company used a third-party credit instrument (the bank's liability in the form of banknotes or bank deposits) to pay the others what was owed. But interest must be paid for the use of this bank-authorized credit (money). Herein lies the

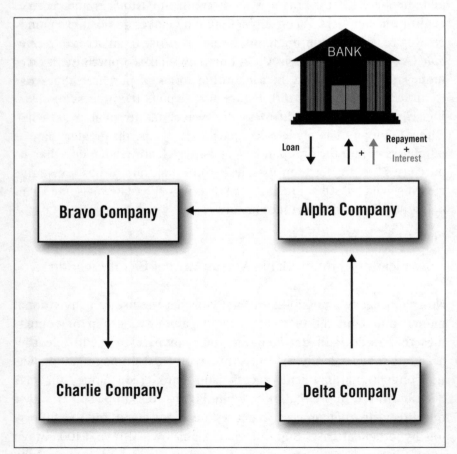

Figure 10.2 Conventional Payment Process Using Bank Credit Money. Bank credit used to clear debts among companies.Interest must be paid on credit borrowed from a bank.

greatest flaw in the debt-money system. When the bank made the loan, it created the principle amount, but not the amount of the interest. In order for Alpha to pay back the principle, plus the interest, it must compete in the market to capture enough money to pay the interest. If it succeeds, that will leave a deficiency of money in some other similar circuit. There is never enough money in circulation at any given time for all borrowers to pay what they owe to the banks. This is like a game of "musical chairs" in which there must be some losers.

Why can't these companies pay one another using their own credit without the involvement of a bank? Indeed, they can, and this is portrayed in Figure 10.3. As in the previous scenario, each owes an amount to another. But now, suppose Bravo is willing to accept Alpha's self-issued credit instrument (IOU) in payment, and each of the other companies in turn is also willing to accept Alpha's IOU. Alpha Company writes an IOU and uses it to pay Bravo, Bravo then passes Alpha's IOU on to Charlie in payment for what it owes, then Charlie passes it on to Delta to pay its debt, and Delta finally returns Alpha's IOU to Alpha

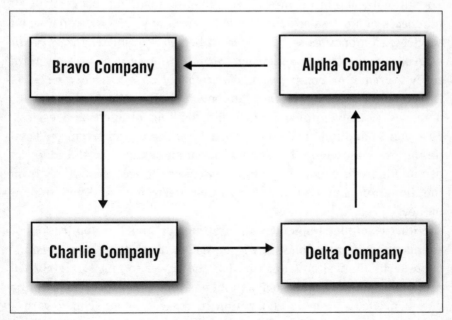

Figure 10.3 Credit Clearing Process Without Bank Credit. Mutual credit used to clear debts among companies. No interest payment required.

in payment for its debt. Now all debts have been paid, no money was borrowed, and no interest was paid. In practice, there is no need for anyone to literally write an IOU because the companies simply agree to buy and sell among themselves without using conventional money and to settle their accounts using the clearing process. They simply keep a ledger in which each company's purchases from one company are paid for by making sales to another company. Each company's account is allowed to be negative to some extent for some period of time. This is a credit clearing circle in which all of the participants agree to give each other a line of credit, which is typically – and should be – interest-free. This is an organized way of extending the usual business practice of selling on "open account," i.e., selling to customers on credit.

Direct Credit Clearing Makes Conventional Money and Banking Obsolete

The ultimate step in reciprocal exchange then is the direct clearing of purchases against sales. Goods and services pay for other goods and services, so money as we've known it becomes obsolete. *Direct credit clearing among buyers and sellers obviates the need to use any third party currency or credit instrument (money) as a payment medium.* Direct credit clearing is the "gunpowder" that makes the "castle" defences of conventional money and banking obsolete and useless. Just as the adoption of cheques allowed traders to circumvent the legal limitations imposed on the issuance of banknotes, so does the adoption of mutual credit clearing circles allow traders to free themselves from the limitations imposed by monopolized bank-credit and government money.

With the proper implementation strategies and the application of sound financial principles, direct mutual credit clearing is an unstoppable technological advance that has the power to ameliorate myriad economic, political, and social problems and establish a solid foundation needed to enable civilization to make a major leap toward a harmonious, sustainable way of living.

The necessary steps in achieving that transformation are:

1. to organize mutual credit clearing exchanges that transcend the privileged creation of conventional cheque bank accounts and the monetization of government debts;
2. to network those circles together into a worldwide payment system based upon a web of trust; and eventually
3. to define and utilize a nonpolitical, concrete standard of value and unit of account that cannot be manipulated to the advantage of any particular bank, cartel, government, or individual.

Various approaches to achieving that programme are described in subsequent chapters, but let us conclude by summarizing the benefits of direct credit clearing.

- There need never be any shortage of credit within a trading community to enable all legitimate trades to occur.
- Credit allocation is determined on a democratic and decentralized basis by the participants themselves according to their own rules and levels of trust in one another.
- Participants can save huge amounts in avoided interest costs and bank transaction fees.
- Participants can avoid the adverse effects of outside factors like the inflation of political currencies, restrictive credit policies of banks, and global economic and financial instabilities.

11. Solving the Money Problem

The Basis of Monetary Dysfunction

We have shown in previous chapters how money has been politicized and how the control over its creation and allocation has become, as I call it, "the keystone in the arch of power." The inherent dysfunctions of the present monetary regime derive mainly from three things.

1. Legal tender status for central bank-created currency.
2. The monopolization of credit by the banking cartel.
3. The lack of an operational measure of value and unit of account that is independent of political currencies.

We have seen how the powers of the central bank and legal tender status for official currency enable national governments to spend beyond their means, allow banks to reap inordinate profits while deciding how money power shall be distributed, and give a small élite group the ability to control political and economic affairs worldwide. Such a state of affairs is both destructive and unsustainable. Solving "the money problem" is a fundamental necessity in solving the other critical problems facing civilization. How might we go about doing it?

Reform or Transcendence?

Among those who have recognized that our money system is problematic there are, on the one hand, those who seek to reform money and banking through political means, and on the other, those who seek to transcend it by private initiative and the creative application of new technologies and methods. These two approaches are quite at odds with one another. Why? Because the reform approach accepts as given the sociopolitical foundations of the present monetary regime and adheres to the erroneous belief that money should be the exclusive province of government.

Reformers have proposed new legislation that would take the money power away from international bankers and give it to national governments. They have even managed to succeed in getting a few politicians to sponsor a bill or two calling for the government to spend money directly into circulation as President Lincoln did with "greenbacks" during the Civil War. But that approach unwittingly perpetuates the money problem. It fails to recognize the insidious nature of élite power, and that the fundamental problem with the present political money system is the monopolization of credit (money) per se, and not who happens to be the owner of that monopoly.

Benn Steil is the Director of International Economics at the Council on Foreign Relations. He acknowledges that governments cannot be trusted with the money power and will not act to remedy the situation, saying, "In the nineteenth century, governments spent less than ten percent of national income in a given year. Today, they routinely spend half or more, and so *they would never subordinate spending to the stringent requirements of sustaining a commodity-based monetary system*"[125] [emphasis added]. By commodity-based monetary system, he means one in which the value of the currency is measured in relation to gold or some other commodity. His statement makes it clear that there will be no end to deficit spending and no end to inflation. Yet he advises governments of less-developed countries to surrender their money creation power and adopt the dollar, or euro, or proposed pan-Asian currency – a move that seems to be from the frying pan into the fire.

Given the fact that national politics has come so completely under the control of the élite interests, and given the collusive arrangement that has aligned the political interests with the global financial interests, the political approach would seem to have little chance of solving anything. But reformers have done some good in educating the public about the money problem by making it once again a political issue. Ron Paul's 2008 presidential campaign has been well worthwhile on that basis alone, but what we really need for government to do is not to take control of the money monopoly, but to end it. In raising this point, I hope not to drive a divisive wedge between would-be allies, but to promote a deeper understanding between "reformers" and "transformers" so that they might be brought into alignment toward a common, more fundamental goal. If that goal is "empowerment of the people," then we must explore every possibility and exploit every opportunity, but we should choose to apply our resources to actions that promise the biggest payoff and have the potential to effect timely change. Buckminster Fuller has argued that "All who are really dedicated to the earliest possible attainment of economic and physical success for all humanity – and thereby realistically to eliminate war – will have to shift their efforts from the political arena to participate in the design revolution."[126]

The approaches advocated in this book are of that sort, and an important element of the "design revolution" is education. I agree with Riegel when he says that,

> The greatest enemy of mankind is ignorance of the inherent money power in all of us. When the realization of this comes to man he will, like Samson, push down the walls of his prison ... Finance which is the creature of the unholy wedlock between banker and state cannot be solved by either partner dominating or consuming the other. The only solution lies in the people denying the power of both over industry, and their assertion of their own money power.[127]

Thus we have called for the separation of money and state, but since the people do not control their government, we believe that separation can only be achieved as the people assert their money power. But, what is this "money power" that Riegel urges us to assert, and how can it be done? That will be explained in the remainder of the book.

Emerging Exchange Alternatives

The most graceful and promising approach to empowering ourselves and our communities is through voluntary, entrepreneurial activities that can liberate the exchange process and reclaim the credit commons. While we may not be able to do much in the short-run to change the legal privilege of political currencies or bank-created credit money, we can reduce our dependence upon them. The way to do that is by taking control of our own credit, and organizing independent means for allocating it directly to those individuals and businesses that we trust and wish to support. Riegel reminds us that "there is no constitutional or statutory barrier to the inauguration of a private enterprise, non-debt, non-interest, mutual money system."[128] Only popular control of credit and competition in currencies can transcend the money problem. As Ulrich von Beckerath has observed, "extension of exchange transactions without State money is in reality the beginning of a new system of settling accounts, indeed the beginning of a new economic order." A new economic order is precisely what is needed at this point in history.

While in the past, credit was more decentralized and private currencies were not uncommon, the emergence of independent credit-based exchange alternatives is still in the early stages of development. It may be compared perhaps to the state of development of aviation in the early twentieth century. In drawing that analogy, we might ask: why were the Wright brothers successful in achieving manned powered flight when so many others had failed? It seems clear to me that it is because their approach was both diligent and systematic. They learned all they could about the principles of flight by reading what others had already learned, by making careful observation of the phenomenon of flight in nature, and by conducting well-designed experiments. Clayton Christensen makes a similar observation with regard to innovation in general, saying that

> the ancients who attempted to fly by strapping feathered wings to their arms and flapping with all their might as they leapt from high places invariably failed. Despite their dreams and hard work, they were fighting against some very powerful

forces of nature. No one could be strong enough to win this fight. Flight became possible only after people came to understand the relevant natural laws and principles that defined how the world worked: the law of gravity, Bernoulli's principle, and the concepts of lift, drag, and resistance. When people then designed flying systems that recognized or harnessed the power of these laws and principles rather than fighting them, they were finally able to fly to heights and distances that were previously unimaginable.[129]

The same applies to innovation in exchange systems. In order to optimize exchange system designs and develop effective implementation strategies, it is necessary to study both the history of money and to understand the theory of money; to observe social dynamics, markets, and networks; to examine the systems that already exist; and to design our experiments to be unambiguous in their answers. What has and has not worked in the past? Who has proposed promising solutions that have not yet been adequately tested or demonstrated? How, where, and under what circumstances can those proposed solutions be adapted to today's conditions? What are the factors that favour such innovations, and what are the market elements that are likely to oppose them?

In supporting the "freedom approaches" advocated by Riegel, I have considered what can be done by private, voluntary initiative – by associations of businesses, by grassroots organizations, by nonprofits and NGOs, and even by municipal and provincial governments. Thanks to some brilliant thinkers who have preceded us, we now have an adequate understanding of the principles needed to design exchange mechanisms that are sound, effective, and economical – but more importantly that are honest, fair, and empowering. And thanks to the new computerized telecommunications technologies, we now have the tools and the infrastructure that are necessary to easily implement these designs.

When I tell people that my work involves the design and implementation of systems for trading without the use of money, they almost invariably respond with, "Oh, barter." That evidently is because barter is the only exchange alternative they have ever heard of. I then have to explain that, no, barter is not what I'm talking about, that barter is very inefficient and limited in its possible scope, and that there are indeed other possibilities — like nongovernmental currencies and credit clearing exchanges. In Chapters 9 and 10, I described in some detail how the reciprocal exchange process has evolved from simple barter to different kinds of money — commodity money, symbolic money, and credit money. And while all of these forms are called "money," they each have distinctly different characteristics — and now, with direct credit clearing, we have the potential to create effective exchange systems that transcend money completely.

The keys to transcending the monetary confusion, and liberating the exchange process, lie in accomplishing the following:

1. the separation of the various functions that money is supposed to serve,
2. the democratization and decentralization of the exchange process, and,
3. the definition and use of an objective, concrete, international standard unit of account.

Separating the Functions of Money

Anyone who has ever taken a course in economics has learned that money is basically three things: (1) a medium of exchange, (2) a store of value, and (3) a measure of value. But as I have pointed out before, those are three *functions*; they do not describe the *essence* of money. The essence of modern money is credit. While commodity money can serve all three functions, credit money should not. These three functions are mutually contradictory. If money is a medium of exchange, it needs to be spent, but if it is a store of value, it should be held. And if money is a credit instrument, there should be some way of assigning a value to it using some objective measure of value. A currency should not itself be the measure of value. What we need is to segregate these three functions in order to optimize and restore honest dealing to the reciprocal exchange process.

Having studied monetary history and theory with a distinct bias toward promoting social justice, economic equity, and personal freedom, I believe that there is nothing more practical than a good theory. Let us look at the subject afresh with the objective of defining a set of instruments and processes that will better achieve each function. In a highly developed, interdependent, and interactive society, the problem boils down to answering three fundamental questions.

1. What can best serve the purpose of mediating economic exchange, i.e., what can be used as a payment medium to settle accounts?
2. What is the best way to "store" value and provide financing for capital formation?
3. What is the best way to measure economic values, i.e., how shall we define a unit of account that can be used to specify contractual obligations and to price the items of value offered in commerce?

When commodities, like gold and silver coins, served as money, they could, and did, accomplish all of the described functions. But we don't use commodity money anymore; we use credit money. Credit money is two evolutionary steps beyond commodity money, as I described in Chapter 9. We have now learned enough about credit and the exchange process to invent more perfect forms of reciprocal exchange based on credit. The problem of economic exchange involves the first and the third of the above questions: how to make payments and how to measure the value of goods and services being exchanged.

Money should serve only to facilitate the exchange of goods and services. We will use the term money to mean only a medium of exchange or means of payment. As such, money should be created as "turnover credit" that accompanies the delivery of goods and services to the market. In that way, it provides the payment media needed for those goods and services to be bought from the market by consumers. We have already introduced that concept in Chapter 6 and shall say more about it in Chapter 14. As it becomes more generally recognized that money is merely an information system, myriad competing payment media will emerge and the use of the catch-all term *money* will diminish in favour of more specific terms that better describe each monetary function. Equitable and efficient exchange mechanisms, free from political manipulation, will become the norm. These will include both private and public community currencies, business-to-business trade exchanges, and mutual credit clearing circles. Uniform measures of value will be adopted enabling these to interact and providing ever more efficient and convenient payment processes.

Back to Commodity Money?

The so-called gold standard of the past did manage to impose a measure of fiscal discipline upon government issuers of currency, but the inevitable inclination of nation states toward armed conflict made it impossible to sustain. That standard has been obliterated by legal tender laws imposed to accommodate the economic demands of centralized power. There is no chance that governments will again submit to the harness of an objective measure of value. If there is to be a monetary role for gold or silver or any other commodity, it will be in private exchange systems; however, as we have argued in Chapter 7, while precious metals might serve as an objective measure of value, they should not be relied upon to be the payment media because of their limited supply.

They might also serve as a store of value since commodities in general can help to preserve wealth in times of inflation and financial chaos. Commodity monies are useful for impersonal exchange transactions. They also provide portability of wealth and can be useful when people are displaced by natural disasters, political strife, and war. But under more normal conditions, economies require exchange media whose supply is flexible enough to grow or shrink in accordance with the volume of trade that is required. We should remember that ultimately our best security is not in cold sterile commodities, but in our relationships with one other and in our networks of trust and mutual support. These can provide the basis for credit money. The purpose of every complementary currency should be to empower people to monetize the value that they themselves create, to exchange their goods and services according to their own values, ideals, and objectives, and to reduce their dependence upon exploitative systems of money and finance. We shall explain later how mutual credit clearing, augmented by credit vouchers or notes, will ultimately provide a much more flexible, effective, and efficient system for exchange. As local credit clearing associations proliferate, they will inevitably be networked together into federations that will span the globe, providing exchange media that are locally controlled yet globally useful.

Like most people, I have no gold or silver. What I do have to offer to the market is goods and services. You are likely in a similar position with your own goods and services ready to sell. In the end, we each pay for the things we buy with the things we sell. In other words, goods and services buy other goods and services; money is just an intermediary device to assist that process. The problem then becomes, how do we transcend the barter limitation – the "double coincidence" of wants or needs? Sure, we can use some commodities that are in general demand as an intermediary, like gold or silver – or as was common in early postwar Europe, cigarettes, Hershey bars, and nylon stockings. But it is much more efficient to simply sell to one another on credit, and then spend our credits to requisition whatever we may want from others in the market. The supply of any chosen commodity is limited and most of the gold and silver is closely held by those who run the dominant system – the central governments and central banks. They, to a large extent, control the prices we must pay for those commodities. But credits can be created as needed at minimal cost so all desirable trades can take place. To be sure, credit money has been badly abused. The banking monopoly has perverted it into usury-debt-money. The answer is not to discard credit money, but to perfect it through the establishment of mutual credit clearing networks and independent private and community currencies. This will not only liberate the exchange process but also will help to knit a new social fabric to replace that which has been eroded by the dominant system.

The Unit of Account Versus the Unit of Currency

One thing that almost everyone seems to have difficulty with is distinguishing between units of measure, on the one hand, and the things being measured, on the other. Accordingly, one hears talk about the shortage of money being analogous to a "shortage of inches" – an obvious absurdity. Of course, there can never be a shortage of any units of measure, but there can be a shortage of the things being measured in those units. Thus, in building a house there is never any shortage of inches or pounds or other units, but there may be a shortage of lumber (which is measured in inches and feet or metres) or nails (which are measured by weight, pounds or kilograms).

Certainly, the shortage of official money is one of its most serious defects, but solving the money shortage requires a proper understanding of the concepts of money and exchange and the reasons that cause the shortage in the first place. In Chapter 8 we spoke about the need for separation of money and state and showed that this confusion between the units of measure of value and the number of monetary units of credit available for making payments derives from legal tender laws that give the word "dollar" two distinct meanings. People generally fail to make this distinction between the unit of account and the currency unit because in today's world the currency unit *is* the unit of account, but this has not always been the case – nor does it adequately serve the public interest.

As we have stated repeatedly, *every piece of currency is a credit obligation* – an IOU of a particular issuer, be it a government, a bank, a merchandising corporation, or some other entity. People generally think of currency as paper money, but currency may take other forms as well. Besides circulating paper notes, currency can also take the form of bank balances ("deposits") or smart card balances. But regardless of the form a currency may take, its essential nature remains the same – it is a credit obligation, an IOU. It is a fundamental necessity to be able to evaluate every credit instrument in terms of something of real value.

The Measurement of Value

The various value standards that have been used or proposed can be classified as follows:

1. a currency standard (an existing currency unit, like the US dollar or UK pound sterling);
2. a commodity standard (a specified weight of some commodity, like silver or gold);
3. an energy standard (a specified amount of energy, such as a kilowatt hour of electricity);
4. a labour standard (a statistical unit of labour productivity);
5. an index standard (a composite group − "market basket" − of basic commodities).

A complete discussion and evaluation of these various proposals is beyond the scope of this book, but we will briefly consider the most promising possibilities.

The "measure of value" or "unit of account" function has not historically been well served by any currency. Government- or bank-issued fiat currencies, the type that are almost universal today, are especially unreliable measures of value because they are undefined and subject to gross manipulation by governments and central banks. Being undefined, the purchasing power of these IOUs is determined by the monetary policies of the issuer, rather than by actual productivity relationships or supplies of goods. The politicization of money has inhibited the widespread adoption of better alternatives. While political currencies might appropriately be used in the settlement of accounts, they need not and *should not* be used in defining the value of goods and services to be exchanged.

Dr Walter Zander proposed "the introduction of unambiguously determined gold units of account as a monetary basis." Failing government action in this direction, he pointed out a way in which private merchants and businesses have successfully protected themselves from official monetary malfeasance and consequent general price increases:

Even if, however, no State were for the moment ready to proceed along this line, there remains the possibility of finding a way out of the monetary chaos through private initiative or at least to prepare the way for this. When in the eighteenth century the national monetary units, because of alleged State needs, continually fluctuated and when it was therefore impossible to rely on the value of currencies for a measurable time even, Hamburg merchants, more particularly, discovered a way out. By founding the famous Hamburger Girobank, they, following the centuries' old Chinese Tael system, *made themselves independent of the debased State coinage by adopting as the basis of all their accounts an unminted definite weight of silver in the place of State money.* This weight, called *Mark Banko*, constituted an unchangeable unit of calculation, which came to be of the greatest service economically for the whole of Northern Europe.[130] [emphasis added]

Proper Relationship Between Commodities (Gold/Silver) and Credit

Gold/silver is concrete and enduring;
Credit is insubstantial and transient.

Gold/silver is impersonal;
Credit is personal.

A sublime whole emerges when each assumes its proper role.

Gold/silver becomes a measure;
While credit becomes the quantity measured.

Giving credit implies the quality of trust in a relationship;
The quantity of credit measured in gold describes the limits
   of that trust.

Payment is a definite conclusive act, limited in time and
   involving two parties;
Clearing is an ongoing process of continuing relationship,
   extending over time and involving multiple parties.

That unit did not require the minting of any coins or that payments be made in silver. The Mark Banco was merely a way to measure the value of things exchanged. Payment could still be rendered in any agreeable currency or through credit clearing. Such a silver unit of valuation could easily be utilized again. Free people can voluntarily choose to use their own accounting unit in dealings among themselves. A particular weight of silver or gold would be better than an undefined, manipulated currency unit, like the dollar or the euro. In times past, each bank issued its own currency notes independently. These notes, denominated in dollar units, promised redemption in silver dollars – thus they were accepted as payment for various goods and services to the extent of the value of the silver promised. When an issuing bank was not known to the seller of goods, or he had doubts about the bank's solvency, its notes could be refused or discounted (accepted at less than face value). When paper notes of the government or central bank, denominated in dollars, were forced to circulate at par, that commodity standard was obliterated.

When the global financial crisis reaches the acute stage, we can be sure that the international banking establishment will come forward to offer their own "solution." You can be sure it will be one more step in the wrong direction toward further centralization of control over credit, meaning further disempowerment of the people. We need to be ready with true liberating solutions. Benn Steil and the Council on Foreign Relations are already making the pitch for greater centralization. Steil argues that countries wanting to develop their economies have no alternative but to utilize the international financial system, and is calling for them to give up monetary nationalism and "replace [their] national currencies with the dollar or the euro or, in the case of Asia, collabourate to produce a new multinational currency over a comparably large and economically diversified area."[131]

The justification for such a proposal is that national governments have abused the issuance of their currencies. That is indisputable, but abuse has been almost universal. The élite groups that manage the dollar and the euro are no exception. They simply have a larger flock to fleece. It is also true that a common unit of measure of value would be of great benefit to the world, but that can be accomplished without using a common currency or trusting a self-appointed financial élite to manage their currencies in the public interest. Remember, any currency is a credit instrument. The dollar currency is a credit obligation of the Federal Reserve, the euro currency is a credit obligation of the European central bank, the British pound is a credit obligation of the Bank of England. These are all third party credit instruments. If the seller of goods is the "first party" and the buyer is the "second party," then the payment media they have traditionally used have been the IOUs of some "third party," namely a central bank or government.

Private and community currencies provide alternative "third party" credit instruments that may be used as payment media. These can help empower local communities and associations of *prosumers,** but the best solution, in my opinion, will be *to use no third party credit instrument at all*. Rather, buyers and sellers can use their own credit within an extensive (eventually global) network of locally controlled credit clearing exchanges that will use an independent objective unit of account. That unit might be a specified weight of silver, and what better weight specification than the silver content of the US dollar as defined in the original 1792 coinage act of the US Congress. The dollar was then defined as being 371.25 grains of fine silver. That unit should appeal to widely diverse political and economic viewpoints both in the United States as well as internationally. (Among some Islamists, the silver dirham consisting of 2.975 grams of fine silver is being promoted, along with a gold dinar. The state government of Kelantan in Malaysia has commissioned the production of a gold dinar coin composed of 4.25 grams of 22-carat gold.)

A silver coin minted to that specification, though not really necessary, would be useful in establishing that standard as a value measure. It need not be used in daily commerce as a payment medium, but it will no doubt be traded in sufficient volume to establish its benchmark value on a daily basis relative to political currencies like the Federal Reserve dollar, the euro, and the yen. In retrospect, the issuers in recent years of the private "Silver Liberty" or "Liberty dollar" might have

---

*Futurist Alvin Toffler is widely credited with coining the term prosumer, which combines the words producer and consumer.

been more effective in achieving their basic objective, and encountered
less harassment by the federal government, if

1. their silver coins had been designed to look less like the silver
    coins historically issued by the United States Mint,
2. they had avoided using the word "dollar" and the dollar sign
    ($) on the coins, and
3. they had called the coin by a different name and denominated
    it in some other unique unit, say a "liber."

As I said at the Gold Dinar Conference in Malaysia in July 2007,
precious metals might serve as *workable interim standards*,[132] but my
preference would be for a unit that is defined not in terms of any single
commodity, but in terms of an assortment of basic commodities. (See
Appendix B on how a multicommodity, objective value standard works).
Such a unit would be preferable because the value of a single commodity is subject to all the forces that determine its supply and demand in
the market. A unit that is defined on the basis of a "market basket" of
commodities will tend to be more stable over time because the price
fluctuations of the various commodities tend to average each other out.

In any case, using a silver or gold unit of account does not mean that
payment must be made in silver or gold, or that paper notes and ledger
credits should be redeemable for silver or gold. Neither would a "market
basket" unit need to be backed up by commodities held for redemption. Rather, if a dollar is defined as so much silver, and I owe you one
hundred dollars, that does not necessarily mean that you can demand
payment in silver. It just means that I owe you one hundred dollars
worth of *something*, and that worth is determined by the current value
of silver relative to all other goods and services and currencies that
might be used as payment. We need not revert to commodity money or
symbolic (redeemable) money as a means of payment in order to have
an honest money system. Credit money can be perfectly sound if properly issued on the basis of an adequate value foundation, like goods
in the shops or on their way to market. But since credit money is an
IOU the market must be free to refuse it or discount it. Only the issuer
should be compelled to accept his own currency at face value (par)

because that is his promise, and his alone. Again, goods and services pay for other goods and services. We just need an honest measure, and the freedom to judge for ourselves the value of not just goods and services, but also anything we might use as a medium of exchange.

Confusion Caused by Legal Tender Laws

We've described how legal tender laws have obliterated objective definitions of the monetary units by making it illegal to discount inferior paper currencies from their face value, so that now the dollar (and every other political currency) has two meanings — first as a means of payment or medium of exchange, and also as a measure of value or unit of account. Walter Zander described this disastrous confusion as follows:

> *Whatever the monetary system of a country, it is essential that the measure of value should be clearly and unequivocally determined.* Thus, where there is a gold currency, a silver currency, or an index currency, the value should be measured by gold, silver and the index respectively. This basis of measuring economic values, and therefore of any monetary system, is destroyed when in the case of gold or silver currency the notes of the bank of issue are made *legal tender, for this compels everybody to accept these notes in payment regardless of their real value.* Compulsory acceptance renders it even impossible to measure the notes by the unit of value within the country. Indeed, *it establishes a legal fiction on the basis of which note and unit of value are identical.* For this reason, the names of the units of value — *e.g.*, the terms dollar, mark, pound — become ambiguous in that they mean now a fixed weight of gold, and then the note of a bank of issue. Accordingly, the measure of value, on the unambiguity of which everything depends, comes to have two definitions. This renders impossible any real measurement and thus the whole monetary system is falsified.[133] [emphasis added]

Concrete definition of the monetary unit acted as a brake to limit the abuses by banks and governments in their issuing of paper currency notes or creating deposits. As already described in Chapter 7, the motivation that underlies every legal tender law is the wish of governments and their central bank cohorts to escape the consequences of their irresponsible financial manipulations. National currencies should be legal tender only for payments made to the government issuer and not for private transactions. Government should be required to accept at face value for payment of taxes or any other dues whatever bills, notes, or other instruments it may issue into circulation. Over the past century, the monetary units in the United States and throughout the world have been transformed from ones defined in terms of gold or silver to ones that are abstract. A shift has been made from an objective *commodity standard* to a *currency standard*, and this has occurred without any proper legal or constitutional foundation.

The store of value function will be taken up in Chapter 20.

12. Credit Clearing, the "UnMoney"

In Chapter 10 we explained that the highest stage in the evolution of reciprocal exchange is "credit clearing." This is a process that, when applied on a wide scale directly to transactions between buyers and sellers, makes money as we know it obsolete. A thorough understanding of the clearing process is imperative, so it will be further explained in this chapter. While the clearing process is most commonly associated with banks, it is an ancient process said to date from at least the Middle Ages. It is said to have been used among participants in the periodic commercial trading fairs that were common during medieval times. As we will show, clearing is a process that can be used to offset claims among not only groups of banks, but also among any entities that have financial claims against one another. Most significantly, it is a process that may be applied among buyers and sellers of goods and services to directly offset their respective claims without the use of intervening banks or conventional currencies.

What Is Credit Clearing?

The term "clearing" refers to the process by which claims among a group of participants are netted-out or offset against one another. The clearing process has long been used by banks to settle claims arising from cheques drawn on one other. They have accomplished this by means of *clearing houses*, which are established in every significant urban community. A clearing house is defined as "an association of commercial banks, brokerage houses, central banks or other institutions established to settle simultaneously the claims of its members to one another."[134]

Since the credit clearing process has been highly developed within the banking sector, it is illuminating to review a bit of history about how it developed, and how it was managed in earlier times. Here is an account of clearing from *The Illustrated Columbia Encyclopedia*:

> Before the introduction of clearinghouses each bank periodically sent runners to other banks. The clearinghouse instead holds meetings of representatives of all banks in a given area to adjust claims. The New York Clearing House, for example, clears five times daily. Each bank sends a delivery clerk and a settling clerk to the house; they bring with them bundles of cheques and other obligations due their banks from other banks, each bank being represented by a separate package. Lists of these obligations are handed to an inspector before clearing begins; the total of the lists is the total amount to be settled that day. When clearing begins, each delivery clerk passes from one desk to another, depositing on each his bank's claims upon the bank represented at that desk. When a settling clerk at any one desk has received all his packages, he draws up a statement of the demands made upon his bank, as shown by the totals of the packages. He sends this to the manager of the clearinghouse, along with the total that his bank is owed. When all settling clerks have done this, the accounts are examined and proved, and the manager certifies the amounts that each bank owes to and is entitled to receive from the other banks. A settlement in cash or credit is then made or received by each bank. *Thus settlements are effected without the transfer of cash or by the transfer of a much smaller amount than would otherwise be needed.* All packages of claims are accepted at the clearinghouse desks without examination; they are later carried back to the banks receiving them and are there examined. If any claims are found invalid, the banks concerned rectify the error without using the clearinghouse.[135] [emphasis added]

According to Ulrich von Beckerath, a legend has it that the runners themselves, meeting in a central coffee shop, really invented the clearing house in London "to save their legs." Their bosses merely sanctioned their practice once they came to understand it.[136]

By means of the clearing process, banks collectively clear millions of cheques a day. With the advent of modern computers and communications technologies, the detailed procedures have changed, but the essential process remains the same. Indeed, these technologies enable clearing to be a continuous and instantaneous process, and the clearing house has morphed into a computer network. The cheques and other claims that are now processed electronically may add up to enormous sums in monetary terms, but when they are netted out against one another the amounts owed by and to each bank will typically end up being very small relative to the total amount of claims that have been processed.

A Simple Example of Clearing among Banks

In order to fully explain this accounting concept, let us take it down to the level of individual bank accounts and trace the movement of claims through the banking system. We will consider several possibilities starting with the simplest case. Consider a transaction in which Amy buys a piece of artwork from Andrew for $100, and pays for it by writing a cheque drawn on her checking account at Alpha Bank. Suppose, too, that Andrew also has a checking account at Alpha Bank. When Andrew deposits the cheque into his account at Alpha Bank, it is strictly an internal matter for Alpha Bank – which credits Andrew's account (increases his balance) and debits Amy's account (decreases her balance) by the same amount (in this case, $100). The total amount of deposits held by Alpha Bank does not change as a result of this transaction.

Next, consider another transaction in which Amy buys a bicycle from Brandon for $200. Again, she pays by writing a cheque drawn on her checking account at Alpha Bank. Now Brandon happens to have his account at Bravo Bank, so when he deposits Amy's cheque into his account, that creates an obligation between the two banks. Bravo Bank will at some point present Amy's cheque to Alpha Bank and funds must be transferred from Alpha Bank to Bravo Bank.

Next, consider that Alpha and Bravo are the only banks in a town, and that each day there are many such transactions. As account holders of the two banks write cheques to one another, each cheque represents funds that must be transferred from one bank to the other. Suppose depositors of Alpha Bank write cheques to depositors of Bravo Bank amounting to $1,500,000, while depositors of Bravo Bank write cheques to depositors of Alpha Bank totaling $1,450,000. After all the cheques have been cleared, Alpha Bank will owe Bravo Bank the net difference between the two amounts, $50,000. Note that the total amount of business transacted between depositors of the two banks amounted to $2,950,000, but only $50,000 had to be transferred at the end of the day from one bank to the other.

The greater the number of banks involved in the clearing process, the more complex the accounting becomes, but the basic process remains

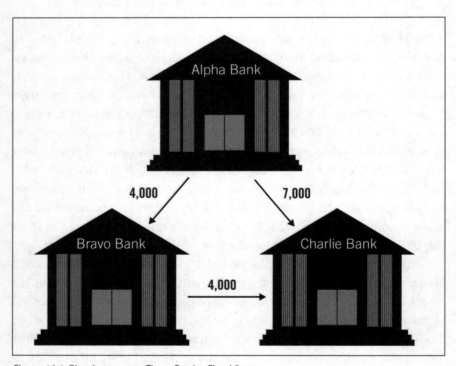

Figure 12.1 Clearing among Three Banks, First View

the same. Consider next an example involving three banks — Alpha, Bravo, and Charlie. Suppose that after all cheques have been tallied, the balances are these:

Alpha owes Bravo	$43,000
Bravo owes Alpha	$39,000
Alpha owes Charlie	$51,000
Charlie owes Alpha	$44,000
Bravo owes Charlie	$61,000
Charlie owes Bravo	$57,000

The *net* balances show that Alpha owes Bravo $4,000 ($43,000 – $39,000), Alpha owes Charlie $7,000 ($51,000 – $44,000), and Bravo owes Charlie $4,000 ($61,000 – $57,000). If each were to pay the

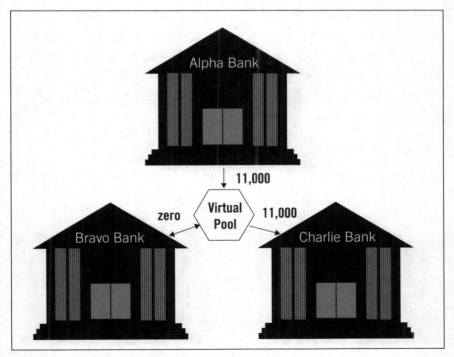

Figure 12.2 Clearing among Three Banks, Second View

others what is owed, Alpha would pay Bravo $4,000, Alpha would pay Charlie $7,000, and Bravo would pay Charlie $4,000. This is shown in the diagram in Figure 12.1.

However, in the clearing process each participant effectively pays into or takes out of a virtual "pool." In this case, Alpha puts in $11,000, Bravo puts in nothing and takes out nothing, and Charlie takes out $11,000. This is depicted in Figure 12.2.

The important point to understand is that in multiparty clearing *what you owe to one party can be cleared or netted against what some other party owes to you*. In effect, your debtors (those who owe you) pay your creditors (those whom you owe). So in our example, Bravo's debt to Charlie was, in effect, paid by Alpha. This is depicted in Figure 12.3.

Note, too, that the net transfer of funds required to settle all accounts was only $11,000 even though total exchanges among the three banks

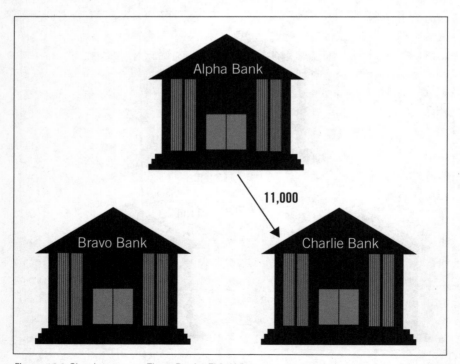

Figure 12.3 Clearing among Three Banks, Third View

of $295,000 were transacted. The total transactions might easily have
been in the millions, and the net amount might just as easily have
come out to an even smaller number, even zero. Sometimes a particular bank will be a net recipient of funds, at other times it will be a net
payer of funds − but over the long run each bank's settlement amounts
should average out near zero. A bank whose settlement balances are
chronically negative might soon become insolvent.

Settlement of Accounts

As shown above, at any given point in the clearing process, some
accounts will be negative (will owe) and some will be positive (will be
owed). Traditionally, these balances have been settled by the payment
of some form of money − originally precious metal coins or bullion,
and later banknotes and paper currencies issued by governments and
central banks. These days, money consists almost entirely of credit
represented as bank account balances and settlement is made by
transferring deposits. In the case of clearing accounts among banks,
settlement is made by transferring deposits held by central banks on
behalf of their member banks. A central bank can be thought of as the
bankers' bank that provides the service of multilateral clearing (even
though that is not its fundamental purpose, as we discussed in previous chapters).

Mutual Credit Clearing Systems as Clearing Houses

The clearing process need not be restricted to banks; it can be applied
directly to transactions between buyers and sellers of goods and services.
The LETS[137] systems (local exchange trading) that have proliferated in
communities around the world use the credit clearing process, as do
commercial trade exchanges. Credit clearing systems are, in essence,
clearing houses − but their members are businesses and individuals
instead of banks. There is, however, no absolute requirement for settlement. Balances, if they are not excessive, can simply be carried over

from one period to the next in the expectation that in the long run each account balance will fluctuate not too widely around zero.

In a traditional clearing process, each member has some amount of tangible resources that are used to settle account deficits. Obviously, a long string of deficits would soon deplete one's resources. The settlement feature provided a check on any member's ability to draw excessively from the system. If a mutual credit or LETS system has no provision for settlement, what is there to prevent a member from repeatedly buying more than they sell and becoming a chronic debtor? There must obviously be some limit on the debit balance that a member is allowed to carry. The questions of how those maximum balances should be determined and what their amounts should be are of primary importance in the design of a credit clearing system.

Direct Credit Clearing — A Simple Illustration Using Four Accounts and Ten Transactions

The fact is that goods and services pay for other goods and services, whether we use money as an intermediate payment medium or not. Ultimately, it is your sales that pay for your purchases. Direct credit clearing makes the use of *any* third party credit instrument (money) unnecessary. We still need a measure of value or pricing unit, but there is no need to use Federal Reserve notes or bank-created deposits or any other political currency as the payment medium.

A credit clearing association is based on an arrangement in which a group of traders, each of whom is both a buyer and a seller, agree to allocate to one another sufficient credit to facilitate their transactions among one another. The rest is merely bookkeeping. In such a system, the total amount of credit outstanding at any point in time can be thought of as the money supply within the system. That amount is determined by adding up the sum of *either* the positive balances or the negative balances. These two sums, of course, are merely two ways of looking at the same quantity — the total amount of credit that members have allocated to one another. As such, they must always be equal to one another.

To show how direct credit clearing between buyers and sellers works, it may be helpful to examine an example involving a small set of transactions among only a few participants. Table 12.1 shows ten hypothetical transactions among four participants. The associated bar charts show, as each transaction is processed, the cumulative total volume of transactions cleared (Figure 12.4), and the total credits outstanding, which can be thought of as the money supply (Figure 12.5). It can be seen from the chart in Figure 12.5 that the "money supply" need not be an ever-increasing number. Note how the money supply fluctuates up and down, decreasing as credit balances are spent and as debit (negative) balances are reduced when sales are made by those who had a negative balance. What does this mean for the quantity theory of money? Clearly, the quantity of money in a credit clearing system is self-adjusting in accordance with the trading needs of the associated members, and does not play the same crucial role as in a commodity money system where the money supply is relatively inflexible.

The fact is that present-day banking is itself mainly a credit clearing process in which additions and subtractions are made to the bank customers' account balances. However, banks perpetuate the myth that money is a "thing" to be lent. If a client's balance is allowed to be negative (by means of an overdraft privilege), the bank considers that to be a "loan" and will charge interest on it. Has the bank loaned anything? Not really. What they have done is to allocate some of *our collective credit* to the "borrower." For this they claim the right to charge interest.

It is clear from the example just discussed that any group of traders can organize to allocate their own collective credit among themselves – according to their own criteria, and interest-free. Such systems can avoid the dysfunctions inherent in conventional money and banking, and open the way to more harmonious and mutually beneficial trading relationships when done on a large enough scale that includes a sufficiently broad range of goods and services, spanning all levels of the supply chain from retail, to wholesale, to manufacturing, to basic commodities.

Table 12-1 Credit Clearing

Transaction Number	Buyer	Seller	Amount	Amy			Brad		
				Sales	Purchases	Balance	Sales	Purchases	Balance
1	Amy	Brad	200		-200	-200	200		200
2	Doris	Amy	200	200		0			200
3	Brad	Carl	300			0		-300	-100
4	Carl	Doris	200			0			-100
5	Carl	Brad	100			0	100		0
6	Doris	Amy	300	300		300			0
7	Brad	Doris	200			300		-200	-200
8	Amy	Brad	100		-100	200	100		-100
9	Amy	Doris	100		-100	100			-100
10	Amy	Brad	100		-100	0	100		0
Totals				500	-500		500	-500	

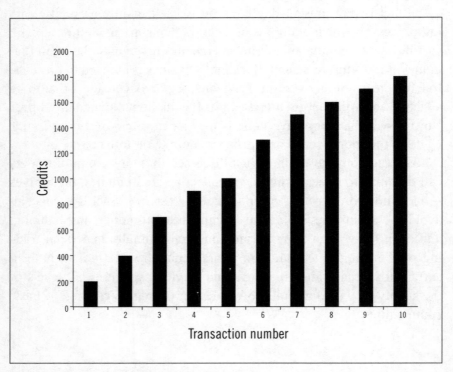

Figure 12.4 Total Amount of Transactions Cleared

	Carl			Doris		Total Amount Cleared — System	Money Supply
Sales	Purchases	Balance	Sales	Purchases	Balance		
		0			0	200	200
		0		-200	-200	400	200
300		300			-200	700	300
	-200	100	200		0	900	100
	-100	0			0	1000	0
		0		-300	-300	1300	300
		0	200		-100	1500	300
		0			-100	1600	200
		0	100		0	1700	100
		0			0	1800	0
300	-300		500	-500			

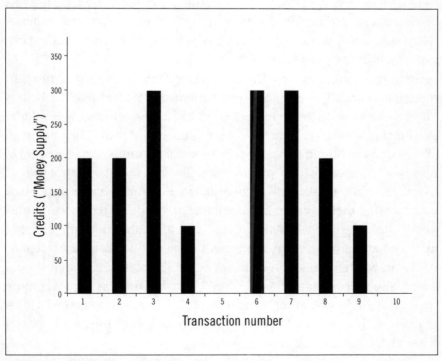

Figure 12.5 Total Credits Outstanding at Each Stage ("Money Supply")

Balance Limits and Settlement

In pure credit clearing there is a continual flow through each account. As described previously, account balances fluctuate up and down, being sometimes negative and sometimes positive. An account balance increases when a sale is made and decreases when a purchase is made. It is possible that some account balances may always be negative. That is not a problem so long as the account is actively trading and the negative balance does not exceed some appropriate limit. What is a reasonable basis for deciding that limit? We needn't stretch our imaginations too far in deciding about that. Just as banks use your income as a measure of your ability to repay a loan, it is reasonable to set maximum debit balances based on the amount of revenue flowing through an account – in other words, the maximum line of credit on any account should be decided on the basis of the amount of that member's sales of goods and services averaged over some recent time period. Past experience in conventional money and banking has provided a rule of thumb that may be useful here. It says that a negative account balance should not exceed an amount equivalent to about three months' average sales.[138]

Some have suggested that it is necessary that accounts be brought to zero periodically – i.e., that they periodically be "settled." If there is an agreement to settle accounts periodically, that settlement would be presumably a cash settlement, although the transfer of other financial claims or assets could serve as well. To settle accounts, those who have negative balances would put in enough cash to zero their account balances, while those with positive balances would draw out enough cash to bring their account balances to zero. While periodic cash settlement might be used initially to build confidence in credit clearing as a viable alternative payment method, even that degree of dependence on conventional money is not a functional necessity and should eventually be eliminated. As the credit clearing process becomes more familiar, people will come to realize that a properly managed clearing system can be relied upon to mediate their exchange transactions without the need for cash settlement.

Alternatively, accounts might be settled by the transfer of some privately or cooperatively issued local currencies, or some other financial claims like mutual fund shares or shares in real estate. But I consider settlement to be analogous to training wheels on a bicycle. Training wheels serve to provide initial support and to build confidence until the rider learns how to balance and control the bicycle. But at some point it becomes clear that they are not needed – and, in fact, constitute an encumbrance to effective operation. So it is with settlement. Clearing is a dynamic process in which only very minor adjustments are needed to maintain balance and stability. In a properly designed and managed credit clearing system, settlement may be dispensed with so long as there is active trading through each account and adequate provisions are made to prevent or cure defaults.

Providing Surety of Contract

At the same time, we should not be overly sanguine about people's behavior where money and material wealth are concerned. The fundamental requirement in any payment system is to assure *reciprocity*. Reciprocal exchange means that a participant must put as much value into the economy (by making sales) as they take out of the economy (by making purchases). Gifts and charity should be provided for by other means apart from the clearing system.

So long as there are competing exchange systems, including conventional banks and money, some provisions must be made to assure that participants in a credit clearing association do not drop out without first settling their balances. This can be achieved in a variety of ways. The most direct way is to require the pledge of some "collateral" or valuable assets as surety of contract, assets that would be forfeited in case of default. On this, we can take a hint from the Swiss WIR Bank. WIR, the largest and most successful mutual credit clearing system to date, has for more than seventy years been providing credit clearing services to small- and medium-sized businesses throughout Switzerland. WIR requires that account balances be secured, typically by the pledge of real estate (usually in the form of a second mortgage on the member's home). The value of such collateral should be used only to assure that a member lives up to his or her agreement and should not be the basis for setting debit limits on the account. Those limits, as we have said, should be based on the volume of sales made by that account.

Another possible approach is *coresponsibility*. In that case, each member would join not as an individual but as part of an *affinity group*, in which each member of the group shares the risk of default by any other member in their group. Such exposure would assure the development of solid "communities of interest" based on high trust levels, and would require responsible participation in all relevant decisions, such as the admission to membership in the affinity group and the setting of debit limits on individual accounts. This might at first seem an onerous burden, but it is essentially what occurs with group insurance. In that case, each claim is paid for by the other members of the group by way of the premiums they pay for the insurance. It is also the case with conventional political currencies. Those of us who operate in the dollar economy, for example, are coresponsible for satisfying all dollar claims held by others. The coresponsibility feature has been used effectively in the realm of microlending and has probably been a major factor in the success of the Grameen Bank and other microcredit systems that are modeled after it.[139]

An Insurance Fund

Despite the above measures, it is possible that some small amount of defaults may still occur. Those losses to the association can eventually be covered by an insurance pool or "reserve for bad debts," something that is typical in any well-run business. The clearing system must have revenues sufficient to cover all of its operating costs, including the cost of "bad debts." Such revenues should be obtained on a "fee for services" basis. Charging a small percentage fee on each amount cleared should provide ample revenues to support a clearing system operating at even a modest scale. These charges will be debited to the members' accounts and credited to the administration account within the ledger of accounts so that the system will always be in balance.

To sum up, a mutual credit clearing union can reclaim a part of the credit commons from monopoly control, enabling members to act independently of the banks in allocating their credit and conducting business and trading. The computing and communications technologies that are available today make the process of direct credit clearing between buyers and sellers entirely feasible, and at the appropriate scale extremely economical. Such systems can with relative ease be implemented at all levels of the economy, from the local to the global, and there are already available a number of software platforms that provide the required functionality for operating such networks. The main obstacles that are likely to be encountered are political ones, as vested interests try to maintain their privilege and prevent the emergence of competition. It therefore behooves us to act quickly in the establishment and proliferation of alternative exchange mechanisms so that they will achieve widespread patronage and support sufficient to resist those attempts.

13. The State of the Alternative Exchange Movement

Exchange alternatives are not entirely new. Indeed, in times past, there were many different exchange media that circulated simultaneously – and for a time, each bank was responsible for the issuance and redemption of their own banknotes. There are also numerous historical precedents for nonbank currencies – such as the 1930s Great Depression–era scrip issues, and the mutual credit clearing system that was organized in Switzerland as the WIR Economic Circle Cooperative (since renamed WIR Bank). There are entire catalogues that list the many kinds of privately issued scrip, vouchers, notes, and coupons that have circulated as payment media. Some of these have been described in my earlier books.[140]

The current wave of innovation and implementation of exchange alternatives dates from around the early 1970s with the advent of commercial "barter" exchanges (properly called "trade exchanges"). This was followed a few years later by the grassroots emergence of mutual credit clearing associations (LETS), Time Dollars, and various local currencies. From that time onward, we have seen a rapid proliferation, all over the world, of these kinds of exchange alternatives – they now number in the thousands. There has been growing global recognition and considerable journalistic coverage of these alternatives – with articles appearing in mainstream publications like the *New York Times*, the *Wall Street Journal, Time.com, The Guardian*, and more than a little coverage on TV and radio. The commercial (business-to-business) side of the movement also continues to grow, developing better standards of practice and becoming ever more sophisticated.

In addition, a new and growing wave of activist energy has been directed toward making money once again a political issue, with the objective of changing the dominant national monetary and financial systems. In this, there has been particular emphasis on the matters of usury and interest, metallic money, and the gold standard. Ron Paul's candidacy during the 2008 presidential campaign has been particularly significant in raising this issue in the United States, while in the United Kingdom similar efforts by various groups and Members of Parliament to raise awareness have been ongoing for many years. While prior efforts to reform the dominant monetary and banking system through the political process have been wholly unsuccessful, the issues they raise have relevance and need to be considered in the design of private, free-market exchange options.

Two Currents of Alternative Exchange

There are two distinct "currents" in the present movement toward alternative exchange and noncash payment mechanisms. They are:

1. the grassroots, noncommercial, community-oriented currencies and mutual credit systems; and,
2. the commercial, business-to-business trade exchanges.

Encouraging as these developments might be, none of the grassroots alternatives, with a couple of notable exceptions, has managed to become a significant economic factor; the commercial segment of the movement, while having achieved a measure of success, has barely begun to realize its enormous market potential. Both have been limited by some serious design deficiencies and various other factors that will be discussed in the following chapters. Many local currencies and LETS have been launched with a flourish of enthusiasm only to fall back into oblivion. The typical pattern is initial enthusiasm by the organizing group and rapid growth in participation, followed by volunteer burnout and a slow, steady decline in both trading volume and number of participants. A system may be formally declared defunct, but more often it simply limps along in the background with little trading and a much diminished participant base, then eventually fades away. Even well-designed systems can experience the same pattern of decline, as I can attest from personal experience.

The Tucson Experience

By the time I arrived in Tucson, Arizona, at the end of 1989, a mutual credit clearing system – called LETSonora – had already been launched. Working in conjunction with a small group of other community-minded people, LETSonora was started by David Koressel, a social entrepreneur who also happened to be a professional accountant. Having read the article about LETS systems that had appeared in the *Whole Earth Review*[141] (which I had coauthored with Michael Linton), they were inspired to give it a try. I soon joined the core team and helped to run the system until it finally ground to a halt around 1993. During that time, despite considerable inputs of volunteer labour, the membership never grew beyond about forty members and the monthly trading volume never exceeded more than a few hundred dollars.

A few years later, I began a series of discussions with some local activists with the intention of introducing them to the possibilities of using in-kind donations from local merchants to back the issuance of vouchers that might be used to support local nonprofit groups, vouchers that could also circulate as a supplemental local currency.[142] This was to be a type of arrangement that Michael Linton and Ernie Yacub refer to as "community way." This did not interest the people I was talking to, but they *were* interested in starting a mutual credit clearing system. I cautioned them about the difficulties and risks, describing to them my earlier experience with LETSonora, but they were enthusiastic and eager to try it – arguing that it wouldn't take much work to set up a ledger of accounts and that conditions might now be right for it to achieve critical mass. I agreed to act as an advisor, but made it clear that I would not be involved in the administration. Thus was launched Tucson Traders.

It was easy to create a set of accounts to keep track of trades among the twenty or so initial members. It started with a notebook and a pencil. The notebook contained a page for each account holder, on which their trades could be recorded and which would show their running account balance. Each page looked something like the table in Figure 13.1.

It was decided that the accounting unit would be called a Tucson Token (TT), with each token having a value equivalent to one US dollar.

It was also decided that, in the absence of any data upon which to decide initial lines of credit, each and every account would be allowed up to 200 tokens, i.e., an account balance could be negative to a limit of minus 200.

As the word got out among the various activist and nonprofit networks, the membership grew quickly – eventually reaching a peak of more than two hundred participants, which included a handful of progressive businesses. Trading fairs and potluck dinners were held regularly, and for a while they attracted a sizeable crowd of enthusiastic traders. A directory and a newsletter were also produced. Along with the growth in membership, the workload of recording the transactions also grew. The notebook ledger was shortly replaced with a computerized set of accounts. Still, the work of recording transactions became too much for the volunteer administrators. It was then decided that the administrative burden could be greatly reduced by eliminating the need to record each and every transaction. This would be accomplished by allowing each member to draw out paper currency notes against their line of credit. Thus someone who already had a debit (negative) balance of, say, 75 tokens would be allowed to draw paper notes to the extent of 125 tokens against her account. Members of Tucson Traders could then pay each other by passing the paper TT notes from hand to hand, in just the same way as we do with regular cash transactions. A few local artists volunteered to design the notes, and a local printer volunteered to print up a supply. There was a big party at which the notes were distributed, and at that point the tokens that originated as ledger credits began their life as a circulating paper currency. There was a formal agreement that, if anyone wished to leave the system, they would first settle any outstanding negative balance – either in tokens or in cash.

As the novelty wore off, people lost interest in potlucks and trading fairs, and with the membership scattered all over town, the inconvenience factor began to take its toll. Despite the reduced workload that accompanied the shift to circulating paper notes, the volunteer core grew tired and less enthusiastic. Administrative personnel changed several times, but the downward spiral continued. By the fourth or fifth year, trading using Tucson Tokens had virtually stopped.

MUTUAL CREDIT CLEARING EXCHANGE
ACCOUNT RECORD

Member Name: **Michael J.**   Number: **017**

Date	Provider	Recipient	Item Description	Transaction Amount	Account Balance
					0.00
May 2	011	Self	Garden veggies	- 12.	- 12.00
May 8	Self	019	Bike repair	+ 14	+ 2.00
May 11	004	Self	Dental services	- 50.	- 48.00
May 14	Self	008	Used bike	+ 30	- 18.00

Instructions:

All accounts begin with a balance of zero.

When you make a sale, provider is "self;" transaction amount is positive.

When you make a purchase, recipient is "self;" transaction amount is negative.

Update your balance by making the appropriate addition or subtraction from the previous balance.

Figure 13.1 A Typical Mutual Credit Account Page

This story typifies the experience of grassroots complementary currencies and mutual credit clearing systems as they have thus far developed. New ones continue to pop up and a few vintage systems are still functioning. One high profile case that has attracted an astonishing amount of worldwide media attention was the 2007 launch of the Berkshares currency in western Massachusetts. That is not a credit clearing system, but a local currency that (for the moment at least) is sold for cash.

It is important to recognize that, even though Tucson Traders did not achieve sustainability as a mutual credit clearing system, there were significant positive outcomes. In the words of permaculture design consultant Dan Dorsey, who had been a core group member, we who worked together on the project still refer to Tucson Traders fondly — as a wonderful and useful experiment and model that will be valuable when economic times really get tough. We also refer to the great connections and friends we made, which went beyond just the money exchange and trading. I still have friends today that I met through TT, who I might not have met otherwise ... I use Tucson Traders as an excellent local case history of using Permaculture design principles to put together what we call in Permaculture an "invisible structure" — those structures that have a big impact on our lives but aren't necessarily visible like sun angles and water cisterns.[143]

Why Exchange Alternatives Fail to Thrive

There is much to be learned from these experiences if we are willing to accept their hard lessons. Here we will consider the grassroots initiatives. The limitations and possible improvements to commercial trade exchanges will be addressed in Chapter 15.

The pertinent questions are:

- What are the main factors responsible for this pattern of decline?
- Why have complementary currencies and credit clearing options remained a fringe phenomenon and not been widely adopted?
- How can mutual credit and community currency systems be made to sustain themselves and to thrive?

There are two fundamental reasons why exchange alternatives fail to thrive. These are

1. failure of reciprocity and
2. inadequate scale and scope of operation.

Failure of Reciprocity

Any payment system exists for the purpose of facilitating *reciprocal exchange*, which can be roughly described as "getting as much as you give, and giving as much as you get." Whether it be a currency or a credit clearing system, anything that interferes with its ability to fulfill reciprocity (or creates doubt regarding its ability to assure reciprocity) will work against its adoption and continued patronage. Failures of reciprocity can stem either from *system design flaws* or from *management issues*.

System design flaws include:

- Improper basis of issue of credits or currency
- Inadequate account limits, i.e., overissuance of credits or currency in relation to an issuer's productivity and the demand for their goods or services
- Lack of a clear agreement between issuers and users of credits or currency

Management issues include:

- Lack of accountability and transparency
- Inadequate management procedures and controls
- Overreliance upon volunteer administrators
- Failure to respond to internal or external threats

Inadequate Scale and Scope of Operation

There are several aspects to the problem of scale and scope, which can be summarized as follows:

- Failure to achieve critical size of the participant base
- Too narrow an assortment of goods and services being offered

- Failure to attract participants from all levels of the supply chain (production/distribution circuit)[144]
- Failure to gain wide acceptance among the mainstream business community

The principles that need to be applied in addressing these problems will be taken up in the next chapter.

14. How Complementary Currencies Succeed or Fail

In our consideration of exchange alternatives, we have been discussing both complementary currencies and credit clearing as viable alternatives and complements to conventional money. The credits that exist within a credit clearing system can be thought of as a complementary currency, even though they may exist only as numbers on a ledger of accounts. Similarly, a currency is simply a manifestation of credits that originate from some issuer who spends them into circulation. Thus we will use the terms *currency* and *credits* interchangeably, since they have the same essence — credit. For the reader's convenience we repeat in Figure 14.1, the depiction of the reciprocal exchange process that was introduced in Chapter 8. It shows the complete circuit of issuance, circulation, and redemption of currency or credits. It is the completion of the circuit that results in reciprocity. This should be kept in mind as we describe the various principles that relate to reciprocal exchange. Note that currency flows in one direction (the outer ring) while goods and services flow in the opposite direction (the inner ring), and that the original issuer eventually redeems the currency they issued by selling their own goods or services.

The level of success of an exchange system is determined by a number of factors, which fall into these four broad categories:

1. the *architecture* of the exchange system or currency itself,
2. the *management* of the exchange system or currency,
3. the *implementation* strategies, and
4. the *context* into which the currency or exchange system is introduced.

Architecture of the Currency Itself

The first requirement of any exchange system is that it accomplish what it is intended to accomplish, i.e., to effectively and efficiently *facilitate the reciprocal exchange of value.* We made the point in Chapter 9 that there are three modes by which economic value changes hands — as gifts, as involuntary transfers, and in reciprocal exchange. It is worth repeating that it is within the realm of reciprocal exchange that money plays its fundamental role as an *exchange medium* or means of payment. Grassroots organizers are often tempted to encumber their fledgling exchange systems with additional baggage that seeks to remedy all sorts of perceived inequities. Well-intended as they may be, these additional requirements cause them to lose sight of the fundamental purpose and to make it more difficult for their systems to "get off the ground."

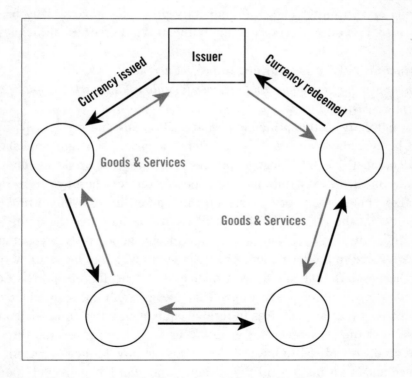

Figure 14.1 The Currency Issuance, Circulation, and Redemption Circuit

So with regard to the currency or credit system itself, *it must be designed in such a way as to assure reciprocity in free-market exchange.* It is necessary to consider both the quality of the currency or credits and their quantity. There are a few critical design questions, the answers to which are all-important in determining the success of a currency, i.e., *its ability to hold its value* and its *ability to circulate widely and rapidly.*

1. Who is qualified to issue currency?
2. On what basis should currency be issued?
3. How much currency may be spent into circulation by each issuer?

What are the factors that determine the limits on the amount of currency that may be issued, and what are the practical limits that should be applied to each issuer? There is an abundance of historical experience from which sound monetary principles have already been derived. It is only necessary to apply them. What are these principles?

Principle 1: Who Is Qualified to Issue Currency?
Anyone who offers goods and services for sale in the market is qualified to issue currency.

A corollary to this principle is that such goods and services should be in everyday demand and be offered at prices that are published and competitive. E.C. Riegel expresses it this way: "A would-be money issuer must, in exchange for the goods or services he buys from the market, place goods or services on the market. In this simple rule of equity lies the essence of money."[145] He further clarifies the point by saying, "He who would create money to buy goods or services must be prepared to produce goods or services with which to buy money."[146]

The point is that money is a device we create for the purpose of facilitating reciprocal exchange. That means enabling a provider of valuable goods and services to receive equivalent value from someone else later on. It is a way of enabling us to indirectly use the things we produce and sell to pay for the things we buy. Money is a kind of placeholder, an instrument that enables one who has delivered goods or services to later on requisition from the marketplace other goods or services that one may desire.

Principle 2: On What Basis Should Currency Be Issued?

Although it is largely ignored in today's banking practice, it is a well-established banking principle that *money should be issued on the basis of goods already in the market or on their way to market.* In its modern manifestation, money is nothing more than credit — but not all credit is suited to serve the exchange function. A distinction must be made between short-term *turnover credit* and long-term *investment credit.* Turnover credit can be thought of as a virtual counterpart of goods that are offered for sale in the market. It is the circulation of turnover credit among potential buyers that provides the means by which those goods can be bought and paid for. The issuance of currency as turnover credit provides the various actors in the economy with the purchasing power needed to buy those goods that they produced, removing them from the market.

Issuance and Reflux

A critical factor in the circulation of any currency is what bankers traditionally refer to as the "reflux rate" — the rate at which a currency returns to the issuer and, having fulfilled its purpose, is extinguished. In the absence of legal tender laws, a currency with too slow a reflux rate will be devalued by traders in the market. It will either be refused as payment or accepted at less than face value. That is why currency should be issued on the basis of goods and services that have a high everyday demand. Such a basis will guarantee that the currency will be quickly returned to the issuer for redemption and not accumulate in the hands of those who have little opportunity to spend it. From historical experience, a minimum daily reflux of 1 percent is necessary for a currency to hold its market value at par.

"Pooling" and stagnation are problems that have afflicted many community currencies. Local currency organizers often complain that their most difficult task is getting people and businesses to accept the currency. My advice is always the same: don't try to push your currency, pull it. Like a string, a currency does not respond well to pushing – but it does respond to pulling, and a properly issued currency will be naturally propelled through the economy. What is this natural force that propels a currency? It is obligation. A currency is a credit obligation of the issuer who must be ready, willing, and able to redeem their currency by accepting it in payment for goods and services. The bottom line is this: most of the issuing power (lines of credit) should be allocated to those businesses in the community that you wish to have accept the currency – the ones at which people wish to spend their currency, the ones who sell what everybody wants to buy. There would be no difficulty in getting a currency to circulate if it were to be issued, say, by the local gas company, or electric utility, or water company, or telephone company, or ... well, you get the idea. I call these entities "trusted issuers." If a company is not already overburdened with debt obligations, and its issuance is not excessive, almost everyone in the community will accept the company vouchers (currency) without hesitation because almost everyone has a gas bill or electric bill or water bill or telephone bill to pay. Even those who do not do business with the issuing company will accept it because of the large number of others in the community who do. So long as such a company agrees to fulfill its obligation by accepting its currency *at face value* in payment for its services, it will have no difficulty in getting its suppliers, contractors, and employees in the community to accept it as a payment medium. From then onward, the currency can pass from hand to hand throughout the community for as long as it remains valid.[147]

It is worth repeating again that in contrast to *turnover credit*, which is short-term, there is also the need for *investment credit*, which is comprised of long-term claims. Investment credit cannot be immediately spent because the activity giving rise to it does not put goods or services into the market until *some later time*. Issuance of currency on the basis of long-term debt, such as mortgages on real estate or long-term government debt, does not compel its timely reflux and redemption by the issuer. Take for example a farmer who decides to plant an orchard. He needs investment credit to acquire land, equipment, and tools, to buy the sapling trees, and to cover his living expenses for a few years until his trees mature and start bearing fruit. The people who provide him with those things deserve to get credit that represents a share of the future produce. How might their investment be recognized? The proper answer is that it should be recognized by giving them a financial instrument (call it a bond) that is redeemable (spendable) only when (and if) the crop is harvested. It would not be appropriate to give them recognition in the form of money – because money is spendable *now*, but the crop will not arrive until *later*. It would not be appropriate for investors to be paid by issuing a currency because the farmer/issuer has no immediate means of redeeming it, i.e., reflux cannot begin until his first harvest. Timing is the salient factor in distinguishing turnover credit from investment credit.

Naturally, there must be some way for turnover credit to be effectively converted into investment credit and vice versa, and in fact such mechanisms are well developed. This is the realm of finance that provides various methods for both saving and investment. At any point in time, there are some who have an amount of turnover credits (the spendable kind of credit) that is in excess of their current needs. They wish to "save." At the same time, there are others who need additional turnover credits to, perhaps, start or expand a business that will *later on* put goods and services into the market. As in the above example, they might spend these turnover credits to acquire the means of producing marketable goods and services. This is the process known as capital formation. So saving and investment are two sides of the same coin. One person saves by reallocating their temporary surplus of turnover credits to someone who wants to invest them in something that will lead to the production of goods and services later on. In this way, turnover credits are transformed into investment credits. The reverse process takes place when the investment is repaid out of income earned at the time that the new products and services go to market. In a currency system, as the product goes to market, currency can be created to redeem the bonds. Consumer credit works in much the same way.

To sum up, money (an exchange medium) should properly be *turnover credit*, created on the basis of the near-term delivery of goods and services to the market. The financing of long-term assets or consumer purchases should not be the basis for money creation, but rather should be financed through the reallocation of money that already exists. In the political money system, this rule is commonly violated. It is one form of inflation that leads to an increasing general price level, which occurs because of the legal tender status of political currencies. In the absence of legal tender status, an inflated currency will begin to pass at a discount relative to an objective value standard. So in sum, the application of this principle requires the following rules regarding the issuing of money (turnover credit):

1. disallow the creation of money on the basis of government debt, which puts no additional product into the market;
2. disallow the creation of money to finance consumer purchases, which take goods *from* the market;
3. disallow the creation of money to finance capital expansion (long-term assets), which does not *immediately* put goods and services into the market.

The relevant argument, then, is not between credit money on the one hand and commodity money on the other, but between credit money that is properly issued and credit money that is improperly issued.

Principle 3: How Much Currency May Be Issued by Each Issuer?
The applicable principle here is best expressed by Riegel: "Each person or corporation is entitled to create as much money, by buying, as he or it is able to redeem by selling."[148] The application of this principle, of course, requires some further definition and measurement. How do we arrive at the amount that each issuer is *able to redeem by selling*? What are the practical limits that should be applied to each issuer?

Here we need to consider the time factor. How long does it take from the beginning of the production process to the end when the product goes to market? Each line of business has its own peculiar production and distribution pattern that determines its annual turnover rate, but we know from experience that average overall turnover is about four times a year. That means that about one quarter of annual production is in the market and ready for sale at any given time. Enough currency or "turnover credit" should be provided to enable that amount of goods and services to be purchased. Based upon the reflux guidelines discussed above, it is reasonable that the issuance limits on each account be based on this practical rule of thumb: each issuer may issue an amount of currency that is no more than their historical average of sales over a period of one hundred days (roughly three months). For example, if a local co-op grocery is a member of a mutual credit clearing association, and it has annual sales of 1 million dollars, its maximum debit balance could be as high as 250,000 dollar credits.

The actual starting point for a complementary currency will be much lower, building up gradually over time, but it should never be allowed to exceed the three months average sales limit. Even this upper limit, however, might need to be adjusted upward or downward in response to actual performance of the currency in the marketplace. The critical indicator is *the value rate at which the currency actually passes in the marketplace.* If it is being accepted only at a discount from face value, that is an indication that it has been overissued or improperly issued, in which case the rate of issuance should be slowed to match the rate of redemption. Remember that we use the word "redemption" to mean the issuer's acceptance, as payment for his goods and services, of the currency that he previously issued. We are not talking about redeeming a currency for official money or any other "currency reserve" like gold or silver.

Implementation Strategies

For alternative exchange media, as for any other innovative product, if one wishes to make inroads in markets where there are entrenched products or patterns of behavior, one must employ means that are capable of making an impression upon the public mind and shifting people's purchasing decisions or lifestyle choices. Having a superior product is not enough. People must be made aware that the superior product exists, they must be persuaded that the advantages of adopting it outweigh the risks and disadvantages, and the product must be made easily available at a price they can afford. There are insights to be gained from the study of natural and social phenomena. In the natural realm, the growth of animal and insect populations and the spread of infectious diseases reveal certain laws that also seem to apply to the market and the spread of ideas. Fashions and fads are phenomena of massive and sudden behavioral change. How do they get started? What gives them their power? How and why do they die out?

Malcolm Gladwell, in his book *The Tipping Point*, highlights three basic elements that can trigger such radical change. He calls them The Law of the Few, The Stickiness Factor, and The Power of Context.[149] The stickiness factor has to do with the nature of the thing being propagated – in our case, the architecture or characteristics of the currency option (which we've already covered above). "The power of the few" means that a few people making small changes can cause a big effect that happens quickly. Gladwell argues that "ideas and products and messages and behaviors spread like viruses do,"[150] and he draws insights on these things from what is known about disease epidemics. So if we wish to foster changes of a cultural, social, economic, or political nature, what lessons from nature can we educe and apply? The salient few, in Gladwell's view, are comprised of three types – the *mavens*, the *connectors*, and the *salesmen*. Mavens "provide the message"; they are teachers or "information brokers." They are the ones who "know everything" about a particular subject – and they not only possess information, they love to share it. Connectors spread it. They are sociable people who tend to "know everyone," and can bridge the gaps between otherwise unrelated social groups. They provide the "weak ties" that help ideas to spread widely and quickly. Salesmen persuade people to adopt, use, or buy it. They have that mysterious knack for getting people to trust them, to agree with them, and to take a particular action.[151] The best salespeople, of course, are those who combine sales talent with belief in what they are selling. They are genuinely trying to be helpful and have a missionary zeal about getting others to use their product.

Gladwell's work has provided a helpful overview, but deeper understanding can be gained by consulting others who have made a thorough study of what are called self-organizing systems or networks. Laszlo Barabasi, in his book *Linked: The New Science of Networks*, shows how networks in diverse and seemingly unrelated fields share similar properties.[152] A detailed elabouration of those points is beyond our scope here, but an example from his book will be helpful in elucidating the point — the impressive success of Hotmail.

At the time that Hotmail was introduced, the use of e-mail communications was already a popular and growing phenomenon, a wave that Hotmail managed to ride in a way that enabled it to capture a major portion of the e-mail accounts then in use. Barabasi asked,

> What is the source of Hotmail's phenomenal success? ... Hotmail enhanced its spreading rate by eliminating the adoption threshold individuals experience. First, it is free; thus you do not have to think about whether you are making a wise investment. Second, the Hotmail interface makes it very easy to sign up. In two minutes you have an account; thus there is no time investment. Third, once you sign up, every time you send an e-mail you offer free advertisement for Hotmail. [At the end of each e-mail sent by a Hotmail user was the Hotmail Web address and an offer to the recipient to set up their own free Hotmail account.] Combine these three features, and you get a service that has a very high infection rate, a built-in mechanism to spread ... Products and ideas spread by being adapted [adopted?] by hubs, the highly connected nodes of the consumer network.[153]

In recent years, similar strategies have been employed by Google, Yahoo!, and other major players in Internet commerce.

The Situational Context

The two most notable cases of complementary currency and exchange, the ones that managed to achieve a high level of success, are the Swiss WIR Bank and the Argentine "credito" currencies that were issued by the so-called *trueque clubs* (trading clubs) from the mid-1990s onward. It is important to observe that each of these was introduced at a time and place in which conventional money was acutely scarce, banking and financial institutions were in disarray, and the national economy was in distress.

WIR

The case of WIR is important for several reasons. As we described in Chapter 10, credit clearing is the highest stage in the evolution of reciprocal exchange, and WIR is the best available example of a credit clearing system that has been able to sustain itself and to thrive over the long term. Over a period of more than seven decades, WIR has struggled with all of the important issues related to the implementation of an independent credit clearing system, and has managed to establish itself as a significant feature of the Swiss national economy.

WIR was founded in October 1934, in the midst of the Great Depression, as a self-help organization to promote solidarity among the "entrepreneurial middle class." At that time, the entire western world was in economic distress. In Switzerland, revenues from exports and tourism had plummeted by 65 percent in the five years between 1929 and 1934 and the domestic economy was wracked with high rates of unemployment and increasing numbers of bankruptcies. The basic objective of WIR was to enable its members to buy from and sell to one another despite the shortage of official money. Initially, members acquired account credit by depositing an equivalent amount in Swiss francs; shortly afterward, WIR deposits were created by making "loans." It was this latter process that created, in effect, a separate monetary system operating in parallel with the national money and banking system. According to Professor Tobias Studer, the function of granting WIR credit loans to members "allows for the creation of an economically significant volume of means of payment, and thus of the needed liquidity for an intense level of barter business, one that can make a significant difference in the economic activity of the individual participant."[154]

The cooperative circle grew quickly, and by the end of 1935 WIR had three thousand participants. In the first year of operation, turnover (sales using WIR credit) surpassed one million francs, which amounted to ten times the volume of WIR account balances. Between 1952 and 1988, the WIR cooperative experienced, as Studer describes it, "tempestuous, near-constant growth and the targeted expansion of the branch network, with no major changes of the WIR credit clearing concept." Then a sequence of peculiar actions commenced that moved the WIR cooperative toward becoming a conventional bank. In the early 1990s, bank ownership was opened up through the sale of stock, and in 1996 the WIR began accepting deposits of Swiss francs and began making loans of Swiss francs. Meanwhile, there was also a significant development on the regulatory front – according to Studer, Swiss law now forbids the organization of banks as cooperatives.[155] What is going on here?

By 1997, the total annual amount of credit cleared by WIR for its members amounted to 2.1 billion Swiss francs (or the rough equivalent at that time of 1.5 billion US dollars). That was still a small fraction of the total Swiss economy, but a significant amount of the members' combined business volume. Available figures for the most recent time period of 2003–6 show that the annual volume of credits cleared has remained about the same as the 1997 level, while the number of WIR accounts has slowly but steadily shrunk from 77,651 in 2003 to 73,134 in 2006. Over the same period the WIR Bank has seen a large and steady increase in its Swiss franc deposits and the volume of its Swiss franc loans, so that the Swiss franc portion of its business is now approximately twice as large as the WIR credit portion.[156]

Considering these developments, and observing that there seems to have been no attempt to propagate the WIR credit clearing model outside of Switzerland, one is led to the conclusion that there must be some effort afoot to suppress it. Though speculative, it is easy to imagine that the success and rapid growth of this upstart exchange alternative must have begun to embarrass and threaten conventional banking interests, who have proceeded to try to quietly neutralize the threat. Attempts by me and others in the alternative exchange movement to meet with WIR Bank management have been unsuccessful. It seems likely that the vested interests in conventional money and banking have managed to influence or control the WIR Bank management and are working to deemphasize the independent credit clearing services which, from its beginning, have distinguished WIR from conventional banks.

Some of the main lessons to be learned from the WIR case are these:

1. WIR took hold during a time of scarcity of national currency and conventional bank credit,
2. WIR continued to thrive even after that time of monetary scarcity had passed,
3. WIR has proven the effectiveness of the direct credit clearing process in improving the vitality of participating businesses and local economies, and
4. when done correctly on a large enough scale, direct credit clearing is fully able to function as a viable complement to conventional money and banking and sustain itself over the long run.

Social Money in Argentina

In 1991 the Argentine government adopted policies favourable to foreign banks and investors. These policies included adherence to IMF rules for "structural readjustment," the sell-off (privatization) of assets owned by the government, and an attempt to maintain parity between the Argentine peso and the US dollar. These policies, supposedly intended to reduce Argentina's international debt, instead caused it eventually to increase further – and in the process, caused large increases in the poverty and unemployment rates as well, even among middle-class professionals.

People at the grassroots responded with their own self-help and mutual aid initiatives. The Argentine "social money" movement began in the mid-1990s when a group of friends and neighbours in a Buenos Aires suburb organized a *trueque club*, or trading club, to barter goods and services among themselves. Very soon, other clubs began to spring up in various places, providing opportunities for people to trade what they had for things they needed without the use of official money. It soon became apparent that some kind of currency was required

Figure 14.2 A Trading Fair in Buenos Aires, February 2001 (Photo by Sergio Lub)

to facilitate trading and to transcend the limitations of direct barter. Various clubs began to issue their own *credito* currency notes and by early 2001 there were several dozen varieties of credito currency in circulation.

The various trueque clubs then formed a loose network known as the *Red Global de Trueque* (Global Trading Network), in which the many different credito currencies issued by the various clubs were being accepted as payment at the various trueque fairs. As might be expected, some unscrupulous people saw this as an opportunity to enrich themselves, either by issuing their own currencies without adequate social or economic backing or by counterfeiting the major credito currencies. Despite these problems the number of participants in the trueque movement continued to grow.

I first visited Argentina in the early part of 2001 as part of a group of economic researchers, social entrepreneurs, and social money advocates who had been invited by Professor Heloisa Primavera to attend a Social Money Conference in Santiago, Chile. Besides a half-dozen South American countries, the participant list included

Figure 14.3 Carlos Sampayo and the Zona Oeste Currency, Buenos Aires, Argentina, March 2003 (Photo by Sergio Lub)

representatives from Europe, Asia, and North America. Following the conference, a group of us traveled to Buenos Aires to observe firsthand the magnitude and vitality of the social money movement as it existed around Buenos Aires at that time. There were numerous trading clubs that operated trading fairs on a daily basis. We visited several venues and saw hundreds of people buying and selling a wide assortment of goods and services, all without the use of pesos. The atmosphere was festive and electric. In each case, the means of payment consisted of the many varieties of *papelitos* (slips of paper) or credito notes issued by the various trading clubs.

By December 2001, the Argentine government could no longer sustain its more than decade long policy of dollar-to-peso parity. There was a rush by foreigners to convert their pesos to dollars and take them out of the country. Very soon dollar and other foreign currency reserves were exhausted and the Argentine economy collapsed. The peso was devalued by about two-thirds and chaos reigned. Banks were closed for long periods of time and even people who had money

Figure 14.4 A Collage of Some Credito Currency Notes (Collage by Sergio Lub)

on deposit were not allowed to withdraw more than a small amount each week, making the shortage of official money even more acute. Without sufficient access to cash to buy necessities, huge numbers of people clambered into the trueque "lifeboats." Between December 2001 and July 2002, the amount of trading in the trueque clubs and the amount of credito currency in circulation exploded. For millions, it was the trueque clubs that literally made the difference between survival and starvation.

By August 2002, however, the Argentine trueque network had disintegrated and the social money movement had all but collapsed.

What happened? On my second visit in early 2003 with colleagues Sergio Lub and Chuck Feil, we interviewed a number of key leaders of the movement to try to discover reasons for the rapid decline. Amid conflicting stories and sketchy documentation, hard facts were difficult to come by, but we concluded that the longer term viability of the network and the credito currencies had been undermined by a combination of mismanagement, fraud, misplaced trust, and counterfeiting. From that time to the present, the movement has been rebuilding, one local system at a time. Hopefully, these will be built upon more solid foundations, and adequate standards, procedures, and protocols will be developed before renewed attempts are made to network the local clubs together.

It is apparent from these two case studies, WIR and the Argentine social money movement, that complementary currencies will take hold most easily when introduced into markets that are starved for exchange media. That is not to say that they cannot be successful otherwise, but that some situational contexts make it easier than others. Conventional money is always scarce in the aggregate, but there are times when the mismanagement of conventional money brings about shortages that are even more extreme and widespread. It has been at such times that complementary currencies have been widely conceived and rapidly adopted. Further, there are sectors of the economy that are chronically underserved by conventional banks in the allocation of credit (money). These include small producers who lack assets that might be used as collateral, and those who have for various reasons been economically marginalized as well as producers who are located in particular geographic regions. These might seem ideal ground for the introduction of alternatives, but initiating complementary exchange programmes within these sectors can be problematic because they are usually highly dependent upon imports from outside and are able to exchange only a very limited range of goods and services among themselves. For that reason, it is better to organize exchange alternatives over a wider geographical region, and as part of a more comprehensive economic development programme like the one we will describe in Chapter 16.

15. Commercial Trade Exchanges – Their Present Limitations and Potential Future

The commercial trade exchange industry has been growing and developing over a period of almost four decades and has achieved enough market success to suggest that it could become a significant economic force. However, most commercial trade exchanges – while they have had greater levels of successes and profitability than their grassroots, not-for-profit counterparts – remain small and barely visible within their local economies. In this chapter, we will address the question of why commercial trade exchanges have not yet been able to tap more than a tiny fraction of their potential markets.

Commercial trade exchanges, often improperly called "barter exchanges," provide services that enable business-to-business trading (1) outside of conventional marketing channels and (2) to a large extent, without the use of conventional money. These two elements together constitute the value proposition that is offered to trade exchange members (clients), and for which they pay sizeable cash fees. According to the International Reciprocal Trade Association (IRTA, the leading trade association for what is now being called the "modern trade and barter industry") the hundreds of commercial trade exchanges operating in various parts of the world now collectively enable billions of dollars of sales annually among their members. Although hard, up-to-date figures are not readily available, IRTA estimates that in 2007 the industry enabled trades worth more than 10 billion US dollars – a figure that is growing at an estimated annual rate of 8 percent. IRTA further estimates that more than 400,000 business firms – most of them small- and medium-sized businesses, but including a significant

---

This chapter is an elabouration of the keynote presentation I gave to the 2006 Annual Convention of the International Reciprocal Trade Association (IRTA) in St. Petersburg, Florida.

and growing number of well-known larger firms – use the services of commercial "barter" companies.

In the early days, many so-called "barter exchanges" sprung up, thrived for a season, and then passed from the scene. Most of those that failed were ill conceived or mismanaged, many being operated by entrepreneurs and marketers who had little understanding of the business and even fewer scruples. The industry has matured a great deal since then and those exchanges that remain are, for the most part, reasonably well run and profitable. In moving from the "entrepreneurial stage" to the "consolidation stage" the industry seems to have reached a plateau, and there is a rising discontent among exchange operators that it is not thriving as it should.

I believe that most operators of commercial "barter" exchanges have not fully comprehended either their *main* value proposition or the enormity of the potential market. In conversations I had with a number of leading exchange executives in 2006, I was told by many that there is a great deal of complacency among their peers. Most of those who have managed to achieve some moderate size and profitability are reluctant to risk making any change in the way they do things. Of those, more than a few are approaching retirement age and are hoping to be bought out. This has helped to spur the wave of consolidation that is now underway. Firms like IMS, ITEX, and BarterCard have been buying up a number of small local exchanges and thereby creating larger, more geographically dispersed transaction networks that provide more trading opportunities to their clients. Industry veteran and IRTA President David Wallach expects this pattern to continue for some time into the future. Despite continued improvement in standards, there are still some widespread practices within the industry that have been limiting and counterproductive. I will offer below an assessment of these limiting perceptions and practices and provide some recommendations that I consider necessary for the industry to move into the mature stage of its development. These recommendations, if followed, can enable the modern trade and barter industry to achieve unprecedented levels of service and prosperity.

Limiting Factors

These are the limiting factors that pertain to current commercial trade exchange operations, which will be addressed in order.

1. Limited scope and scale of membership
   a. Inadequate number and diversity of member businesses
   b. Limited geographic coverage
   c. Failure to penetrate all levels of the supply chain (almost exclusive focus on recruiting members who operate at the retail level)
2. Failure to perceive and promote credit clearing as their most valuable service
3. Certain clauses that are commonly included in their membership agreements that result in conflicts of interest with their members and debasement of the value of their internal trade credits (currencies)

Limited Scope and Scale

The vast majority of commercial trade exchanges are small local operations that average between a few hundred to a little over one thousand members. In most cases, the bulk of the member businesses offer services or "soft goods" rather than "hard goods" like manufacturers and commodities that are in everyday demand. Media, advertising, hospitality, tourism, and entertainment comprise a large portion of the offerings in many trade exchanges. These and other business lines that have prices that are "fuzzy" and negotiable, rather than fixed and advertised, are usually well represented — making the value of the internal trade credits harder to pin down.

Further, trade exchanges have been limited by their almost exclusive focus on the *retail level* of business-to-business trading. While retailers and service providers are the most readily available client prospects, the greatest potential lies in connecting suppliers and customers throughout all levels of the supply chain, including wholesalers and manufacturers (more about this later).

The Value Proposition
Trade exchange operators generally recognize that the main value propositions that they offer to their members consist of

1. the competitive advantage of having privileged access to an existing membership base, providing a group of potential new customers;
2. the active brokering of trades, by which exchanges help their members to find customers for their offerings and suppliers of their needs and wants; and
3. the ability to pay for purchases using internal trade credits instead of cash.

However, their emphasis has been too much upon the marketing advantages of membership inherent in the first two of these items and not enough on the financial advantages of the third. It is the credit clearing service that is the most distinctive feature of trade exchange operations. The dysfunctions and flaws in the political money system result in most businesses having excess capacity (i.e., the ability to provide more value than they actually sell). Excess capacity is not so much a matter of overexpansion as it is a lack of money on the part of potential buyers. The greatest value proposition is the credit clearing service that provides additional exchange media — a cashless payment alternative and an interest-free line of credit — that enables businesses to sell more of what they are able to produce.

Many exchanges intentionally limit the number of members in a particular line of business that they will accept in order to assure them a competitive advantage. If one sees the marketing advantages as the main value proposition provided to exchange members, then it makes sense to accept only a few restaurants, for example, in a particular neighbourhood. But if the main value proposition of exchange membership is the cashless "clearing" or offset of purchases against sales, then the more the merrier. The value and usefulness of a credit clearing network, just as with any other network, grows geometrically as the size of the network increases. Grounds for exclusion and offers of exclusivity to prospective members need to be seriously reconsidered.

The fact is that credit clearing can work for everyone who provides desired goods or services to the market, and the larger the number of participants in the trade exchange, the more useful membership will be.

Operations and Agreements

Certain clauses that are commonly included in membership agreements have jeopardized the viability of trade exchanges and retarded their growth. Specifically, these are clauses related to the trade exchange's own trading account and its ability to participate as a member as well as a service provider. But such a dual role can easily, and often does, lead to serious conflicts of interest. As third-party record keepers and managers of their members' collective credit, trade exchanges have a professional responsibility to put their members' interests first. They must earn the trust of their clients, and must assure the continued value of their internal trade credits.

There are two major conflict-of-interest issues that have arisen in the management of trade exchanges. The first is called "cherry-picking," which is the ability of a trade exchange operator, based on its insider information and prior knowledge, to acquire the best offerings of its members before the other members even get to know about them. This has become less prevalent among established exchanges, but may still be an issue in some newer and smaller exchanges.

The second and more serious issue derives from the "borrow and spend" clause that is typically contained in trade exchange membership agreements. This clause grants to the exchange account a virtually unlimited credit line that allows the exchange management (1) to spend beyond its means and (2) to out-compete other potential buyers (members) in the system. The resultant ballooning of debt in the system account results in the debasement of the value of the internal trade credits and the loss of confidence in the trade exchange management. Members are usually denied access to definitive information about the extent of these practices, but their effects are "felt" in the internal marketplace as trade credits become harder to spend and therefore less valued. As a result, members may seek ways to differentiate their cash prices from their trade credit prices, or may require a blend of cash with trade credits when they sell something within the trade exchange. Both of these practices diminish the usefulness and credibility of the trade exchange system.

Proposed Remedies

How might these problems be remedied? I suggest that the problem of cherry-picking can be handled by limiting both *what* the system account can buy and *when* it can buy. The system should *not* be allowed to buy anything from its members for the purpose of resale, but should be restricted to buying only those goods and services that it commonly needs to conduct its business operations, i.e., to provide services to its members. Further, it should not make any purchase until the offering has been made generally available to the entire membership for some reasonable period of time.

With regard to the line of credit allocated to the system trading account, it should be determined on the basis of the same qualifying criteria as for any other account — it should have no special privileged access to trade credit. Ideally, the credit allocation process should involve broader participation by the members and be based on objective criteria, primarily the internal trade credit earning history of each account averaged over some reasonable period of time.

In regard to these practices, some trade exchanges are better managed than others, but the remedies and restrictions proposed above need to become industry standards and formally specified in membership agreements. (A generalized draft of such a proposed membership agreement, which could be applied either to for-profit or mutual exchanges, is provided in Appendix A.) If exchange operators do not voluntarily discipline themselves, they will eventually see discipline imposed on them from outside, either by government regulation or by the requirements for participation in an eventual wide-area network of exchanges. But more importantly, by adopting these measures and making prospective members aware of them, a trade exchange will gain a big competitive advantage over other trade exchange operators that are more closed and inclined to exploit their members. Exchange owners that subject themselves to such restrictions can still be active traders — and by the quality and volume of trading they do, become living examples to their members of the advantages of cashless trading without risking debasement of their internal currency (trade credits). Industry trade associations like the IRTA have done much to foster the adoption of such standards of practice through their own certification and branding programmes.

The Real Deal — Credit Clearing Services

I firmly believe that *the most important value proposition that trade exchanges can offer to their members is the cashless clearing of their transactions* — i.e., the operation of mechanisms that enable the members to use their sales to pay for their purchases. The market for such clearing services is virtually unlimited and worldwide, but to tap that market it will be necessary for exchange operators to think outside of the conventional box. What are the necessary actions required to realize that potential?

Tapping the Vast Potential Market

The short answer to that is that credit clearing exchanges need to attract a much larger, more diverse membership base. As pointed out above, the value and usefulness of a credit clearing network grows geometrically as the size of the network increases. The obvious way to achieve that is to make it easy and inexpensive to join an exchange. Existing pricing schedules for trade exchange services needs to be completely reviewed and revised. Trade exchange operators need to find ways of reducing the costs of participation in order to make membership more attractive. It costs nothing to open a bank account. Any alternative payment system must justify its membership fees in comparison to that.

It is said that "nothing succeeds like success," and the challenge is to find the right combination of services and implementation strategies to get the success spiral started. During the early stages, it has been appropriate for trade exchanges to emphasize the "competitive advantage" and brokering services that they provide for their members

– but as the size and diversity of the network is increased, the financial advantages of membership become much more significant and obvious.

Another aspect of member diversity has to do with the supply chain. If geometric growth in both membership and trading volume is to be realized, a trade exchange must include members, products, and services from *all levels of the supply chain* – not only retailers, but also wholesalers, manufacturers, basic commodity producers, independent professional service providers, and ultimately employees. Trade exchange operators must actively solicit membership on these other levels. If a trade exchange has a retail member, it should try to recruit the wholesale companies that supply that retail member, then try to recruit the manufacturing companies that supply those wholesalers, then try to recruit the basic commodity producers that supply those manufacturers, and so on – until the loop is eventually closed by recruiting the employees/customers who are supplied by the retailers. In this way, each participant will be able to pay their suppliers by means of credit clearing, as depicted in Figure 15.1 on page 167.

Achieving this may take a trade exchange far afield from its local base of operations, since many suppliers will not be located within the local area in which the trade exchange operates. That implies the need for exchanges to either operate over a wider geographical area, or (perhaps more importantly) to have effective reciprocity agreements with other trade exchanges in other regions. The vision of a global network of independent trade exchanges that could result from such agreements is an attractive one that the industry should work toward establishing. At the present time, this broader reach is being achieved by a process of acquisition of small local exchanges by a few larger companies leading to consolidation within the industry.

Finally, each member of a trade exchange should be allocated an internal line of credit – which, I strongly recommend, should be interest-free. If it is not, the credit clearing alternative could end up replicating the dysfunctional political money system. It is these lines of credit that constitute the "money supply" within a credit clearing circle. As described in previous chapters, it is necessary, at any given time, for some members' balances to be negative in order for other

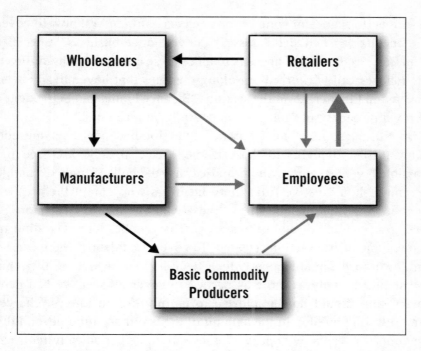

Figure 15.1 The Circulation of Credit through All Levels of the Supply Chain

members' balances to be positive. The total of all account debits should always equal the total of all account credits, making the overall system balance equal to zero. The interest-free feature follows the usual and long-standing business practice of trading on "open account," by which a supplier ships goods to a customer and allows that customer a certain period of time in which to pay the invoice. A commercial trade exchange is a credit clearing association in which that practice of selling on credit is organized on a multilateral basis. If the industry is to tap the huge potential market for cashless credit clearing services, the provision of no-interest credit will be crucial. Unlike banks, then, trade exchange system revenues will be obtained on a fee-for-service basis – deriving mainly from transaction fees, brokerage fees, advertising revenues, and risk premiums.

The issues that are raised in regard to lines of credit are (1) how to determine an appropriate debit limit for each account, (2) how to assure performance of contract on each account, and (3) how to cover the inevitable "bad debt" losses. Conventional business, especially banking, has developed answers to all of these questions, but improved approaches can be worked out along the lines that have already been covered in Chapter 12, in the sections "Balance Limits and Settlement", "Providing Surety of Contract", and "An Insurance Fund".

On the question of an insurance fund for bad debts, let me add some further thoughts to those above. We've already discussed the possible revenue sources and proposed that the bulk of trade exchange revenues should derive from those members who obtain the greatest benefit from their membership — those who are able to clear more of their transactions through the system. That implies fees according to the volume of transactions cleared. To cover "bad debts," there can be an "insurance fund" against which defaults can be written off. This fee should be only as large as needed to cover prospective bad debt losses, and should not be allowed to morph into an interest charge. Any resulting buildup in the amount of the insurance fund beyond the amount of reasonably expected losses should be periodically returned to the members.

A further important feature is transparency in the operation of the exchange. Full and timely disclosure is necessary to enable the participants to evaluate the soundness of the operation and the value of their trade credits at any point in time.

What About Taxes?

People often ask me about the tax implications of trading that is mediated using private currencies and direct credit clearing. The short answer is that they are the same as conventional money transactions. The purpose of alternative exchange is not the avoidance of taxes, but to provide traders with greater control over their own credit, to circumvent the dysfunctions inherent in the money and banking system, and to save the costs associated with conventional banking — including the interest on borrowed money. In the early days of the commercial "barter" industry, exchange operators and their members were subjected to harassment by the IRS because the IRS acted on the presumption that their intention was to avoid paying taxes. In the US that was brought to an end years ago by an agreement that trade exchanges would provide the IRS with annual reports about the members' barter income using a form 1099B, which is similar to the form used to report money income of independent contractors.

An Eventual Cashless Trading Network

Trade exchanges must eventually associate into a network that will enable members of one exchange to trade with members of others. This capacity for cross-system trading will add tremendous value to exchange membership. But networking exchanges together will require that they adopt and adhere to standard procedures and protocols. The electricity grid is one good example. Any individual or company is at liberty to produce electricity in any form it wishes for its own use or for distribution within its local isolated domain. But if it wishes to connect to the power grid, it must conform to the established grid standards. In North America, for example, the electricity one produces must be 110-volt, 60-cycle alternating current. Nothing else is acceptable. Standards need not be imposed by any political authority, but can be worked out by voluntary agreement among those players who have the greatest interest in the development and use of the network.

So such a network of credit clearing exchanges must be founded upon standard procedures, protocols, and ethical standards that each member exchange agrees to adhere to as a condition of participation in the network. Primary among these would be the procedures for allocating credit lines to members and the way in which the system account is managed. By way of comparison, one might consider the conditions that apply in order for any particular bank to issue transaction cards under the Visa or MasterCard brands. If a bank wishes to issue cards under one of those brands, it must do it in a way specified by the entity that manages that brand. So, too, the emerging trade exchange network brand must be founded upon a set of agreed standards that can assure that the various trade exchange credits have comparable value, and that the risks to the viability of the network will not be excessive.

Cashless payment based upon direct credit clearing among buyers and sellers is a revolutionary innovation in reciprocal exchange that might be compared in importance to the invention of the printing press, which empowered masses of people by making literature widely and cheaply available and freeing them from dependence upon scribes and scholars. Cashless trading has, over the past thirty years, gone through a stage of experimentation, trial and error, and small-scale application analogous to early letterpress technology. The principles of credit and exchange are now better understood; as they are more effectively applied, the tremendous possibilities will become generally apparent, sufficient amounts of resources will be allocated to their further development and implementation, and the world will be forever changed.

16. A Regional Economic Development Plan Based on Credit Clearing

Throughout the world today, local communities are struggling to maintain their economic vitality and quality of life. The reasons for this are both economic and political, and are largely the result of external forces that are driven by outside agencies like central governments, central banks, and large transnational corporations. In brief, decisions made by others outside of the community are having enormous impacts on life within the community. Be that as it may, it is possible for communities to regain a large measure of control over their own welfare and to ameliorate the effects of those external forces by employing peaceful approaches that encourage human solidarity and are based on private, voluntary initiative and creativity.

I often use the analogy of the small boat harbour to convey the general idea of how local communities can protect their small enterprises while remaining open to the global economy. The process of globalization, while having many positive aspects, has thus far been carried out in such a way as to be destructive to small businesses, local economies, and democratic governance. It is as if there were a policy to remove the breakwaters from every small boat harbour in the world, the effect of which is to expose small boats to the turbulence of the open sea. As I put it in one of my lecture presentations – *a rising tide may lift all boats, but the tidal wave of globalization smashes all but the biggest.*

But a healthy global economy and a peaceful world require healthy communities. Is there still a place for small businesses? Must every advantage be given to the corporate megaliths at the expense of small enterprises? The ancient economic debate that poses "free trade" against "protection" is too limiting and outmoded. Healthy economies require *both* free trade *and* protection, each confined within its appropriate

Figure 16.1 A Typical Small Boat Harbour (Drawing by Dennis Pacheco)

bounds. Communities must create the equivalent of breakwaters to protect their small enterprises and workers, while at the same time remaining open to the national and world economies.

It is encouraging to note that there has been a recent major awakening about the mega-crisis that is developing worldwide, and a plethora of creative responses to it. *Sustainability, relocalization, human scale,* and the *devolution of power* are the current buzz. The big question, of course, is how are they to be achieved in the face of the tremendous forces that are driving us toward the precipice?

Approaches to Community Economic Development

Sadly, the orthodox approach to community economic development over the past several decades has centreed upon efforts to recruit some large corporation to come and set up operations in the local region — with the expectation that they will provide additional jobs for local people, stimulate business for peripheral industries and the service sector, and ultimately add to local tax revenues. The consequent competition among cities and states in pursuing that strategy has resulted in corporations wresting enormous concessions from host communities in such forms as tax abatements and infrastructure provided at taxpayer expense. But capital is notoriously fickle and recent developments have given it unprecedented mobility. Quite often the experience has been for companies to leave town as soon as the "free lunch" has expired, only to play the same game again somewhere else.

It is widely acknowledged that, in comparison to large corporations, small and medium enterprises (SMEs) contribute proportionately more to the economy in jobs, productivity, and innovation. According to the Organization for Economic Cooperation and Development (OECD), "SMEs play a major role in economic growth in the OECD area, providing the source for most new jobs. Over 95% of OECD enterprises are SMEs, which account for 60%–70% of employment in most countries. As larger firms downsize and outsource more functions, the weight of SMEs in the economy is increasing. In addition, productivity growth – and consequently economic growth – is strongly influenced by the competition inherent in the birth and death, entry and exit of smaller firms."[157] The same pattern would seem to hold in other parts of the world, including America.

Doesn't it therefore make more sense to nurture the businesses that are already part of the local economy? Doesn't it make sense to support those companies that are locally owned or managed and have a stake in the prosperity and quality of life in their home communities? Communities that have a high quality of life, an able workforce, and a clean and pleasant environment do not need to offer bribes to outsiders. Relocalization efforts cannot get very far without the creation of metasystems that support buying locally, selling locally, investing locally, and saving locally. Conventional political forms of money, and huge banking companies that are owned and managed by remote entities, by their very nature militate against relocalization. There is no need for antagonistic opposition to those entities; they can be made less relevant and less destructive by implementing creative methods that localize control over both exchange and finance.

I propose that groups and organizations that seek to promote healthy, sustainable local economies should make it a priority to organize *regional mutual credit clearing associations* as the centrepiece of a comprehensive programme. As these associations develop and grow, they will provide their regions with an increasing measure of independence from the outside forces that control conventional money and banking, enabling communities to rise above "the race to the bottom" that has resulted from the kind of globalization that has been architected and forced upon the world by the World Trade Organization, the International Monetary Fund, and the World Bank. *The credit clearing exchange is the key element that enables a community to develop a sustainable economy under local control and to maintain a high standard of living and quality of life.*

The possibilities inherent in such a plan should not be judged by past experience with local currencies and other exchange alternatives. Just as a modern jet aircraft bears little resemblance to the Wright brothers' first airplane, so too are the more optimized exchange structures proposed in this book unlike any community currency, LETS, or commercial "barter" exchange with which people might be familiar. Based on the principles we have outlined, it is now possible to engineer and build exchange systems to carry heavy economic loads within local bioregions and to operate them according to sound business principles. This is a multistage project that will proceed in the following sequence:

1. Institute measures that promote import substitution
2. Provide an alternative payment medium, independent of any political currency and banking establishment
3. Issue a supplemental regional currency
4. Develop basic support structures that strengthen the local economy and enhance the community's quality of life
5. Develop an independent value standard and unit of account

Stage 1: Mapping the Territory and Import Substitution

Jane Jacobs has argued that cities, not nation states, are the salient economic entities, and that city and regional economies develop through a process of import substitution.[158] That being the case, it would seem reasonable that a regional economic development programme should begin with actions that support that process.

The first stage of the development programme might look rather conventional and similar to some "buy-local" programmes of the past, but it will be more comprehensive in its social, economic, and political aspects. It begins by organizing solidarity groups that include *all* sectors of the constituent communities – particularly the locally owned and controlled businesses, municipal governments, the nonprofit sector, social entrepreneurs, and activists. By building bridges between these groups and identifying common objectives, it should be possible to achieve the commitment to do the hard work necessary to move together toward greater regional economic self-sufficiency.

The first major task is to launch a "buy-local" campaign in which the economic resources and business relationships within the region are clearly mapped. That database can then be used to assist businesses in finding local sources for the things they buy and local customers for the things they sell. The services of brokers can be employed to help match up supplies with wants and needs. Critical gaps are identified and local entrepreneurs can be encouraged to find ways to fill them, perhaps with support from a local microlending agency. As this process proceeds, the community becomes less dependent upon outside entities and more resilient and self-determining.

These measures alone, however, are far from sufficient. Given the fact that conventional money and banking are themselves externally controlled and act in ways that are parasitic upon the local economy, some way must be found to reclaim at least a portion of the "credit commons" and bring it under local control. So unlike conventional buy-local initiatives, this project moves quickly to implement the second stage.

Stage 2: Mutual Credit Clearing Provides
an Alternative Means of Payment

The second stage is the most important and unique stage of the project. It provides an alternative means of payment based on the community's own credit through the process of *direct credit clearing.*

Working capital in the form of conventional money is always scarce and expensive for most businesses. Mutual credit clearing is an extension of the common business practice of selling on "open account," but it is done on a more organized multilateral basis, which has the effect of sharing the risks and enabling a participant's sales to pay for purchases without the use of any third-party credit instrument such as conventional money. As a member of a mutual credit clearing exchange, a business can have an interest-free line of credit, it will be able to acquire the things it needs without the use of cash, and (because it accepts payment in the form of exchange credit) will be a preferred source of supply for others who are members of the exchange.

The allocation of credit in a clearing exchange involves the granting of an "overdraft privilege," which means that a member's account may have a negative balance up to some specified limit. In allocating lines of credit, it is important (especially in the beginning) to allocate the greatest share of credit to "trusted issuers" – i.e., those that are well established, financially sound, and whose products and services are in greatest demand within the local region. This is the key to maintaining a rapid circulation of credits through the system, avoiding defaults, and preventing the excessive accumulation of credits in the hands of businesses that cannot easily spend them. In brief, the businesses that you wish to have accept community credits in payment are the ones that should be issuing them in the first place. By beginning with "trusted issuers" the value and usefulness of the community credits is quickly demonstrated beyond any doubt. As the process gains credibility and general acceptance in the community, more businesses and individuals will want to join the credit clearing exchange and as each member develops a trading history they too can earn an overdraft privilege commensurate with their volume of sales within the system.

Like any network, a credit clearing system becomes more valuable and useful as it continues to expand and a greater variety of goods and services become available within the network. By way of example one may note that the first fax machine was very expensive – but useless. As more fax machines were deployed and connected in an expanding network, the fax became more valuable to *all* users – even as prices plummeted and quality improved. The same will happen with clearing networks, but it is essential that the network and each node in it be properly designed and operated from the very start.

Stage 3: The Credit of "Trusted Issuers" Provides an Alternative Currency for Regional Circulation

The third stage of the programme will be the joint issuance of credits into the general community by the members of the clearing association. This is accomplished by the association members buying goods and services from nonmembers who are outside the credit clearing circle. They make these purchases by using some form of uniform credit instrument, like a voucher or certificate, which all association members are obliged to redeem – not for cash, but for the goods and services that are their normal stock in trade. That provides a sound regional currency based on the productive capacity of the region's leading enterprises, a currency that can circulate among any and all as a supplemental medium of exchange. The availability of such a currency to supplement the flow of official money *insulates* but does not *isolate* the local economy. Just as a breakwater protects a small boat harbour from the turbulence of the open sea, a sound regional currency provides a measure of protection from the turbulence of the global economy and centralized banking and finance.

This externalization of credits from the clearing association into the general community can be achieved using any of several available forms and devices. Credits may take the form of paper notes, coupons, vouchers, or certificates; they might be placed on stored value cards like the gift cards that are commonly issued by major retailers and are so popular these days with consumers; or they could manifest as credits in accounts that reside on a central server that can be accessed by use of a debit card and point-of-sale card reader. (For more on the issuance of an alternative currency, refer back to Chapter 14, particularly the section "Principle 2: On What Basis Should Currency Be Issued?").

Stage 4: Support Structures for Localization — Saving, Investment, Finance, and Education

While the most fundamental need is for mechanisms that enable local control over the exchange function, the health and independence of local economies also requires the localization of savings and investments. In today's world, locally owned and managed banks have become increasingly rare, most having been acquired or replaced by branches of huge bank holding companies that are owned and controlled by entities outside the region. Local savings deposited in those banks can and do get invested anywhere in the world, often in ways that are detrimental to the interests of the saver and the health of their local economy. They often leave homegrown enterprises starved for capital while funding megacorporations, weapons, war, and projects that are socially or environmentally destructive. Structures can be created that channel temporary surpluses of both conventional money and exchange credits into enterprises that enhance local production and quality of life. This has already been outlined in Chapter 11 and will be considered further in Chapter 20.

Additional support structures are suggested by the experience of the Mondragon cooperatives in the Basque region of northern Spain. Over a period of more than fifty years, the Mondragon network has grown and thrived on the basis of cooperation and social solidarity. In addition to more than 250 industrial and service cooperatives and associated companies, it has developed structures to provide finance, education, and research in support of its regional cooperative economy. The Caja Laboral Popular (CLP, or Working People's Bank), for example, is itself a cooperative that invests the savings of the local community and provides financing for the other cooperative enterprises. This, along with the educational and social service aspects of the "Mondragon experience," will be described more fully in Chapter 18.

Stage 5 and Beyond: Transition to an Objective Measure of Value and Accounting Unit

Eventually, it will become necessary to denominate local credits in some independent, objective, nonpolitical unit of account based on a concrete standard of value. This will become especially important as political currencies continue to be inflated and their monetary units are debased, and as local clearing networks become interlinked regionally and across national boundaries. Trade credit units originally defined as being equivalent to the dominant political currency unit (like dollars, pounds, euros, and yen) will shift over to a value unit that is objectively defined in terms of valuable, commonly traded commodities. Such a unit will facilitate trading across national borders by obviating the need for foreign exchange and eliminating the exchange rate risk, and will be immune to the inflationary and deflationary effects that beset national political currencies.

The remaining design details and implementation strategies can be settled upon as the programme unfolds. For now, it is sufficient to say that all of the necessary monetary science is well established and all of the major system components are readily available. With a modest amount of funding or investment, programmes designed along these lines can be quickly launched and a credit clearing system can quickly reach critical mass. It is expected that the success of this model in one or two local regions will inspire others to implement it, leading to a rapid proliferation of healthy and sustainable communities that might associate to form a worldwide economic democracy.

17. The Next Big Thing in Business: A Complete Web-Based Trading Platform

"Visa, it's everywhere you want to be." That's the familiar slogan for the Visa card. Almost everyone I know has one, and it's the way I pay for many of the things I buy. But what is a Visa card, anyway, and how did it come to be such an important part of our lives and the global financial landscape? There was a time not so long ago when most purchases were paid for using paper currency, or by cheque — and not so long before that they were paid for using gold or silver coins. It is in the nature of things to evolve, to change form, and to adapt to new conditions. So it is with money — or to be more precise, "payment media" and exchange systems. It hardly makes sense to use the word "money" anymore given its muddled meaning and careless usage, which derive from the successive transformations that have taken place in the realm of exchange, banking, and finance. As we've shown, money today is not what it used to be, and tomorrow ... well, tomorrow we won't use money at all.

The Convenience of Cards

A Visa card may be either a *credit card* or a *debit card*. I have one of each. If the former, the card-issuing bank allows the card holder to make purchases and cash withdrawals against a line of credit, i.e., the bank will "lend" the cardholder enough money (up to some limit) to pay for their purchases or cash advances. Most card issuers provide a grace period within which no interest is charged on purchase balances, but if a balance is carried beyond the current billing period, the cardholder must pay interest on that balance at rates which are usually somewhere around 18–20 percent, but some card-issuing banks may charge rates approaching 30 percent − and if one is late in making a payment, the bank may impose a penalty as well as raise the interest rates on remaining balances.

A debit card, on the other hand, works like a cheque. The cardholder must already have money in his or her account. Purchases and cash withdrawals are charged immediately against the balance in the cardholder's account. In either case, a Visa card allows the holder to pay for purchases made at millions of businesses scattered all around the world. In short, Visa is a self-described "global payment system." Visa (along with its sister, MasterCard, and a few lesser card systems) has been enormously successful, and provides great convenience to the cardholder. I do quite a bit of international travel and it is remarkable that I can walk up to a hole in the wall in almost any country of the world, insert a piece of plastic, and get some slips of paper that allow me to acquire whatever I might need for my sustenance and comfort.

Visa cards and MasterCards are issued by banks that, while they may compete with one another to some extent for your business, also cooperate together as members of a financial services cartel to make their common business extremely profitable. While the card payment system provides a great deal in the way of convenience, it has (as presently structured) a major downside for the user and for the economy as a whole. We've already described the dysfunctional nature of the political money system; the fact that it is inequitable, unstable, unsustainable, and overly expensive. As part of that system, credit cards and debit cards simply provide new ways of using the political debt-money that banks create by making loans.

Further, while they are more efficient than cheques, the use of cards is much more expensive to the users (both consumers and merchants) than they need to be. While service providers deserve to earn a fair profit, the privileged status that the banks enjoy limits competition and makes the emergence of other payment systems difficult. We've already mentioned the high rates of interest that cardholders must pay on outstanding balances, but there is also a charge to the merchants − who typically pay 3 percent or more on the amount of each transaction involving a card. That is a business cost that must ultimately be passed on to the consumer. People with low incomes, or those who lack a solid credit history, may have difficulty gaining access to credit cards or be required to pay higher rates of interest.

Improving the Exchange Process — Challenge and Opportunity

We can do better. While there has been recurrent debate about reforming the system of money and banking by new legislation and political initiatives, improvement is much more likely to come through private, voluntary, free-market approaches that apply technological and business innovation. The implementation of such systems provides both a transformational advance for civilization and a huge market opportunity for entrepreneurs. Imagine a democratically structured global payment system operated in the interests of the general welfare with membership open to all, in which the exchange medium is abundant and readily available to mediate as much trading as people need to do, and which provides each member with an interest-free line of credit. This is more than a pipe dream. Such a system is entirely feasible using well-established principles and procedures of sound money and banking. Like so many other reasonable things, the main obstacles to implementation have been political, not technical. However, recent social and technological developments provide the means by which those obstacles may be overcome.

As we proceed to consider emerging technologies and their expected impact upon money and the exchange process, it is useful to recapitulate some essential points that were made earlier.

- The primary role of money is to serve as a medium of exchange.
- Money is nothing more than credit.
- Current methods of allocating and managing credit are neither optimal nor sustainable.
- New methods that are more effective, efficient, and equitable are already available and are being profitably applied.

- Complementary currencies and credit clearing exchanges can be established by community groups, NGOs, entrepreneurs, business associations, and municipal and regional governments.

Significant Trends and "Disruptive Technologies"

In his book *The Innovator's Dilemma*, Clayton Christensen contrasts two types of technologies – "sustaining technologies" and "disruptive technologies." He uses a broad definition of technology, saying that "Technology ... means the processes by which an organization transforms labour, capital, materials, and information into products and services of greater value." By this definition, technology includes marketing, distribution, investment, and managerial processes, as well as design and production. This makes his concepts quite applicable to our present subject.

Christensen's technological dichotomy is reminiscent of Thomas Kuhn's distinction between "ordinary science" and "revolutionary science," which also seems relevant. Ordinary science is "tradition-preserving," while revolutionary science is "tradition-shattering." Mark Buchanan's account makes this distinction: "In normal scientific work, theories are extended, observations are made more accurate, and understanding grows by a process of accumulation. A scientific revolution, on the other hand, involves throwing out cherished ideas and replacing them with new ones; scientists come to see the world in a different light."[159]

Likewise, sustaining technologies are comprised of improvements to established ways of doing things that enhance the position of dominant companies, while disruptive technologies consist of new approaches that, in Christensen's words, "Bring to market a very different value proposition than had been available previously." They typically "underperform established products in mainstream markets. But they have other features that a few fringe (and generally new) customers value."[160] While disruptive technologies may underperform in the short run, they often have the potential to eventually dislodge established

technologies and dominant companies. Among the numerous examples is that of digital photography. Initially, digital photography was
greatly inferior to the established technology of chemicals and film, but
there were a few applications where it was "good enough" and found a
sufficient market to support its further development. Eventually, digital
photography became the norm and companies that had been dominant
in the field of imaging were dislodged from that position.

Strengths and Vulnerabilities of Political Money and Conventional Banking

In order to comprehend the points of vulnerability of political monies,
we must be aware of the main features that have made them so dominant in the market.

- They are universally accepted within wide national,
  continental, or even global domains.
- Inertia – the public is habituated to their use.
- Political monies are easily exchanged for one another
  through well-organized foreign exchange currency
  markets and widespread money change offices and kiosks.
- General lack of viable alternatives for mediating exchange.
- The intensive support and protection they obtain from
  national governments.
- Their true costs and "side effects" are obscured and not
  widely recognized.

But despite these enormous advantages, they also have inherent
weaknesses and vulnerabilities that we have already described. As
Christensen points out, dominant companies often "overshoot their
markets." This makes them vulnerable to displacement for a number
of reasons.

- Their focus is mainly on continuing improvement of
  established products or services.

- They eventually give established customers more than they
  need or are willing to pay for.
- They often overplay their dominant position and
  overexploit their customers.

Others simply become complacent, ossified, or unresponsive to developments and the demands of both established and emerging markets.

Remember that the credit card companies are actually consortia of banks. It is the banks that issue the cards, and the banks that reap the profits. The credit card industry is dominated by two major brands, Visa and MasterCard. The banks that participate as members of this duopoly, while engaging in some limited competition with one another to attract cardholders, have cooperated to raise interest rates, add fees upon fees, and gradually add more stringent clauses to the cardholder agreements. All of this has made them ever more exploitative of users, especially those who are caught in the "debt trap" and who carry a balance from month to month and are sometimes late in making a payment.

Christensen observes that dominant companies often ignore or try to suppress disruptive technologies. This has been particularly true in the case of money and alternative credit institutions. Whenever competing currencies have appeared, the power of government has been used to quash them. The successful Great Depression–era currencies in Wörgl and Schwanenkirchen are but two among numerous such examples.[161] The Swiss WIR, described earlier, is one notable exception that seemed (for a while at least) to have somehow slipped through and been allowed to subsist.

Finally, if dominant companies ever do adopt the new technology, they are usually too late to be competitive with nimble start-ups. Banks especially should be expected to be very late in adopting technologies that will create a wholly different, more competitive economic and financial playing field.

From Disruptive to Sustaining — Moving Upmarket

If exchange alternatives are to gain a foothold within such a protected (for the banks) milieu, they will need to first find small niche markets where their special qualities are recognized and valued. As performance improvements are achieved, they will be able to attract more of a mainstream market. This has already been happening for some time in both the grassroots and commercial sectors. In the former, the attraction has been mainly ideological. Complementary currency and exchange has been seen as a means for achieving social justice, economic equity, local self-determination, and environmental restoration. Most grassroots initiatives have tried to incorporate features that promote such ideals. In a few cases, like Argentina, the impetus has been more practical, as we've already described. Within the commercial sector, the features that have been most highlighted are the ability of trade exchange membership to mobilize the excess capacity of members in the face of scarce official money by providing a supplemental medium of exchange (credit), and the marketing advantage that comes from preferred access to the membership base. In both cases, a strategic approach will need to be taken to avoid the legal and regulatory minefields that have been laid to inhibit market advances from newcomers to the field of exchange services. Since the usefulness and marketability of credit clearing services is determined by both the scale and scope of the network, it would seem essential that critical mass must be quickly achieved. That goal necessitates that all levels of the supply chain must be included from as early on in the process as possible. But how does one recruit participants into an emerging network?

The Emergence of a Complete Web-Based Trading Platform

Over the past decade, commerce has been increasingly migrating onto the World Wide Web. Barring some major catastrophe that would disrupt our information and communications infrastructure, that trend is sure to continue accompanied by ever-greater functionality and additional services. If there is such as thing as a "monetary science," it is presently undergoing a revolution – and the technologies that are arising from it are sure to bring about enormous changes. Compared to conventional money and banking, the complete Web-based trading platform we will describe here will achieve the innovative potential that Christensen writes about.

Within my own lifetime, I have seen a number of companies that were so entrenched in their industries and so much in control of their markets that it was unthinkable that they might ever be dislodged from their position of dominance. This was especially true in the fields of computers, telecommunications, and photography. Yet many of those companies have either ceased to exist or have been eclipsed by others that developed and marketed what seemed initially to be inferior technologies.

In the early 1980s I was working as a consultant with a company on projects that required a considerable amount of statistical analysis. We had been buying time (at some considerable expense) on a university mainframe computer, and had to put up with long turnaround times. It began to seem sensible to consider acquiring a computer system that would enable us to do that work in-house. Among the proposals that were submitted to us was one from DEC (Digital Equipment Company) for a multistation minicomputer. This was at the time when desktop microcomputers were just beginning to provide some significant computing power, and local area networks (LANs) were becoming a real possibility. Fortunately, we realized that the DEC system and other minicomputers would soon become obsolete. We decided instead to acquire one of the new AT-type microcomputers, thinking that it could serve our immediate needs and be networked with other similar computers, if needed, later on. That solution did prove to be quite satisfactory for our purposes, and at a small fraction of the price we would have paid for the obsolescent minicomputer. DEC was not nimble enough to adapt to the fast-changing computer technologies and market conditions. It made an early foray into the microcomputer market with the DEC Rainbow desktop machine, but it was overly expensive and not "IBM-compatible." Where is DEC today? An interesting analysis of DEC's failure to succeed in the personal computer market is provided by Christensen.[162] He notes that DEC had all the necessary resources to succeed but their processes and values did not permit them to effectively compete in that market. IBM, Eastman Kodak, and Xerox are still viable companies, but they are nowhere near as dominant in their industries as they once were.

The entrenched position of the money and banking establishment far exceeds that of any single company or other kind of cartel. Its position, as we have described, has been established and sustained through political privilege and the suppression of competition rather than by the quality and value of the services it provides. Given that situation, is there any chance that new technologies might enable the emergence of significant exchange alternatives? I think there is. The US Postal Service enjoys a monopoly in the delivery of mail, but that did not stop the massive shift to newer, faster, electronic communications channels like fax, text messaging, e-mail, instant chat, and Internet file transfers. Now voice-over-Internet is mounting a similar challenge to telephone and cable companies.

What are the "disruptive technologies" that are emerging within the realm of money and banking?

- Direct credit-clearing among buyers and sellers
- The use of the Internet to create Web-based marketplaces
- Transparency in Web-based accounting, information, and exchange systems
- Strong identity verification
- Secure encryption of information over the Internet
- Social networking
- Reputation ratings of vendors and buyers that are continually updated and available on-demand
- The reemergence of mutual companies, coresponsibility, and localized Web-based markets

It is not any of these individually but *all of them in combination* that will, I believe, result in structures that will provide superior performance in mediating the exchange process. Worsening economic and financial conditions, such as those experienced in 2007 and 2008, will create enhanced market opportunities for this sort of nonpolitical trading platform, and will assure their eventual implementation and wide acceptance.

Essential Components of the Web-Based Trading Platform

Management guru Peter Drucker has expounded the following "law" — *profits migrate to the supplier of the missing component necessary to complete the system*. What system are we talking about, and what is needed to complete it? It is what I call a *complete Web-based trading platform*, and it requires these four basic components.

1. A marketplace
2. A social network
3. A means of payment
4. A measure of value or pricing unit

There are already numerous Web-based marketplaces — eBay, Amazon, and Craigslist, to name just a few — and there are numerous social networks — Facebook, Friendster, Linkedin, MySpace, the Living Directory, and so on. But what about payment systems? And what about measures of value? This is where gaps remain. Yes, PayPal is a payment system of sorts — but it only allows the transfer of the same old bank-created debt-money. The only real advantage it provides is in enabling you to pay an online vendor without the risk of revealing to them your credit card or debit card information. PayPal plays the role of a trusted intermediary. That is a useful service but it does not provide a true alternative payment system. PayPal could conceivably become a full-blown credit clearing service if it were to allocate interest-free lines of credit to some or all of its account holders.

With regard to value measures, we have numerous ones (like dollars, euros, pounds, and yen) but each is a political unit, the value of which is dependent upon the policies of their respective government or central bank issuer. These are the very measures that are unstable and problematic. But before proceeding with that line, let us consider each of the four components a bit more fully.

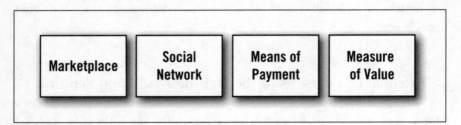

Figure 17.1 The Four Essential Components of a Complete Web-Based Trading Platform

A *marketplace* is a "space" where buyers and sellers come together to display their offerings, express their needs and wants, and negotiate the terms of trade. It need not be a physical space, as we see with the emergence of marketplaces on the Web. It is important to recognize that there are marketplaces that bring businesses together with consumers (B2C), marketplaces that specialize in business to business transactions (B2B), and some that enable all types – B2C, B2B, and even C2C.

A *social network* enables participants to make themselves known to one another and to communicate more effectively. It allows one to establish their identity online, to post their credentials, and to provide other information for others to see. It also can track correspondence and behaviour within the network, establishing one's reputation and enabling an impersonal medium to serve as a tool for building a matrix of trusting relationships that can lead to collaboration and coordinated action on many levels.[163] Social networks are enabling an inherently impersonal medium to become an effective tool for forging very personal relationships across all sorts of boundaries.

A *means of payment* facilitates the exchange process and transcends the barter limitation of coincidental wants and needs. Possible payment media include

- official money,
- private currencies, and
- direct clearing of traders' credits and debits.

Everyone understands the use of official money as a means of payment. Thus far, Web-based payment systems have been mainly limited to the transfer of conventional bank-created money from one party to another. It does not usually occur to people that there might be any other payment possibility. But private currencies have a long history and have often served the payment function, especially during times of financial malfunction and economic distress like the Great Depression of the 1930s. We have already discussed a number of such payment possibilities.

A *measure of value* enables comparison in the marketplace of the values of distinctly different kinds of goods, services, and contracts – including financial claims. In times past, values and prices were expressed in terms of some standard commodities, most notably a specified amount of gold or silver. As described earlier, those value measures were obliterated by legal tender laws that made the various national currencies both the means of payment and the measure of value. At some point, legal tender laws will be abolished. In the meantime, buyers and sellers can adopt some nonpolitical measures of value to use in pricing their goods and services for sale.

Completing the Web-Based Trading Platform

Recalling Drucker's Law, we propose that the missing components that are needed to complete the edifice of a complete Web-based trading platform are (1) a means of payment that utilizes no political currency as a payment medium and (2) a concrete, objective, universal measure of value that provides a unit of account that is independent of all national currency units. Of these, the first is more critical; the second can be temporarily deferred, as we discussed in Chapter 9.

What we propose as the innovative means of payment is direct credit clearing, which has already been described. And what we propose as the objective measure of value is a composite commodity standard such as that described in my earlier book, *Money and Debt: A Solution to the Global Crisis*,[164] and summarized in Appendix B. These missing components need to be properly integrated with an online marketplace and adequate social networking tools. When these things are accomplished, the trading platform becomes an integrated milieu that subsumes the functions of both a marketplace *and a bank.*

Who are the dominant players in Web-based commerce today? Will eBay or Amazon be able to exploit this opportunity, or will it be some nimble start-up that is still fluid enough to develop the necessary internal processes, lean enough to accept the small initial returns, and venturesome enough to develop new markets? The past three decades have seen great progress in the development of private commercial "barter" or trade exchanges that provide direct credit clearing among their business members. These and other historical examples provide adequate proof of concept. Optimizing their design, putting all the pieces together, and taking these networks to scale are the remaining tasks that will revolutionize money and banking and enable the evolution of civilization toward greater peace, prosperity, and sustainability.

18. Organizational Forms and Structures for Local Self-Determination and Complementary Exchange

It is a hopeful sign that there are increasing grassroots and entrepreneurial efforts springing up to address the various problems that are now becoming acute. These efforts include broad-based community coalitions that are focused on addressing all aspects of sustainability along with social justice, economic equity, and personal freedom. "Community building" and "relocalization" have become rallying cries — but in western societies at least, the social fabric has become a flimsy mesh and we remain isolated from one another, often not knowing even our closest neighbours.

Humans have demonstrated a great capacity for brutal and violent conflict based on competing values, attitudes, and beliefs that constitute our diverse cultures, ideologies, and religions — but we have also exhibited tremendous capacity for organization, cooperation, compassion, and mutual support. The survival and advancement of civilization will depend upon our ability to transcend religious, ideological, and cultural differences; to recognize that we all have fundamental interests in common; and to organize and coordinate our actions to achieve common goals. While competition has a role to play in urging each of us to higher levels of realization, science shows us that *life thrives more on cooperation than on competition*.[165] It is from nature that we must take our cue.

There are some things that can be accomplished individually, but within the context of the complex global economy the effectiveness of isolated individual action is greatly limited. It will require organized, coordinated, collective action to save civilization. It may seem paradoxical to some, but that kind of action is more likely to come from the collective intelligence and wisdom of ordinary people dealing with their own problems in small groups in their own local communities, than from the knowledge and impulses of a few self-appointed "leaders" who have somehow managed to climb to the top of the heap in the global game of Monopoly.[166]

Toward Economic Independence

The key to personal and community survival is to gain a substantial degree of economic independence and to provide for our material needs in ways that are community controlled and sustainable over the long run.

What is required is organized action that

- enhances community solidarity – socially, economically, and politically;
- restores every aspect of "the commons," including the "credit commons";
- supports the localization of economic activity, including local production for local distribution and consumption, local sourcing of inputs, and local investment of local savings and resources; and
- provides a significant measure of independence from the structures and mechanisms of conventional money, banking, and finance.

The first three cannot be effectively achieved without accomplishing the fourth, and all of this implies local organization at a relatively small "human scale." This must be mainly a transcendent, bottom-up process driven by self-empowerment and personal responsibility. This chapter outlines organizational strategies and structures that might be employed, and briefly describes a few cases from which necessary lessons might be learned.

The "Banjar" and the Balinese Governance Structure[167]

The upland community of Ubud is the self-proclaimed cultural centre of Bali. That's where my longtime friend and colleague Stephen DeMeulenaere was living when I went to visit toward the end of 2007. Stephen, a specialist in local economic development and community currencies, has been working and living in Bali and other parts of Indonesia for more than ten years. He speaks the language and is well acquainted with the local culture and customs.

Bali has become one of the most popular destinations for western tourists — and like other such destinations, has been somewhat spoiled by it. For me, Bali was a bit disappointing. After just a couple days in the heart of Ubud, I felt harassed and a bit sad. Despite their efforts to maintain their culture and way of life, it seems to me that the people of Ubud have become far too dependent upon foreign visitors. The competition for the tourist dollar, euro, and yen is intense. A leisurely, peaceful walk down the street is all but impossible. I was continually pressured to engage taxis I did not need and to buy stuff I did not want. When out and about, it feels as if one is the object of some predatory presence that keeps manifesting in slightly different form, often like some big overly friendly dog craving attention. That situation is not unique to Bali, of course — it's one that is common to virtually all popular destinations. Tourists attract ever more hawkers and eventually the place becomes overrun. I've had similar experiences in other places, including Goa (India), which was even worse.

Still, the Balinese culture has proven to be more resilient than most. Its social structure remains very tightly knit, its elaborate religious ceremonies still meaningful, and its governance structure highly decentralized and democratic. I was impressed with the apparent power of the local communities, especially since Hindu Bali is a part of Indonesia, which is predominantly Muslim. Not only have the Balinese managed to retain a large measure of independence from the central government in Jakarta, but also the local communities seem to be able to control their own affairs.

In 2002, Stephen teamed up with Bernard Lietaer on a research project to try to explain the relative resilience of Balinese society in the

wake of the tourist onslaught, and to understand its governing structures. Besides researching the literature, they conducted interviews
with Balinese leaders in and around Ubud. They reported that there
are "three overlapping but separate local organization structures" that
combine to provide "a strong social and cultural fabric." These are:

- The *Banjar* that orders the civil aspects of the community;
- The *Subak* that regulates the irrigation facilities (for
  farmers who are still active in rice production); and
- The *Pemaksan* that organizes the religious rituals.[168]

Of these, the banjar is the most significant structure in Balinese
governance. DeMeulenaere and Lietaer, citing various scholarly references, report that

> The Banjar is the fundamental civil unit in Bali, operating in
> a decentralized, democratic, cooperative manner at the local
> level. It is an ancient organization structure, as the first written
> reference to it goes back to 914 AD ... In a small village, there
> is often only one Banjar; in larger towns, there may be several.
> In Ubud for instance, there are four Banjars in the town itself,
> and 9 additional ones in the immediately surrounding villages.

Virtually everyone belongs to a banjar, which provides each person
with a large measure of his or her identity.

Each banjar has an unpaid elected head who can be removed at
any time by vote of the membership. Scale seems to be an important
feature of the banjar in that none of them is very large. According to
DeMeulenaere and Lietaer, "In the Ubud area each Banjar has between
750 and 1200 members, who are represented at the council by the 150
to 260 male heads of each household. The largest Banjars in Bali are
the urban ones (Denpasar [the island's main city] has councils with
more than 500 family heads); in villages they can be as small as 50."

Every member of a banjar is required to provide both money and
services to the various projects that are discussed and decided upon at
the monthly meetings. Those decisions include the necessary "contri-

butions of time and money [needed] for each project... In short, the Banjar functions as a community-based planning and implementation unit which budgets always its activities using two currencies, both Time as well as Rupiah."[169] DeMeulenaere agrees with me in thinking that it is too much of a stretch to call the time commitment a "currency" as Lietaer does, but the work/service requirement of each Balinese adult has, no doubt, been a major factor in maintaining power at the local level and preserving the social and cultural fabric. I surmise that it does this in three ways: (1) it mobilizes local resources independently of the monetary system, (2) it provides opportunities for families and neigh-bours to work together, continually renewing their bonds of kinship and solidarity, and (3) by its egalitarian nature, it tends to inhibit class differences that might otherwise arise. Add to this the small scale of the banjar units, and we may have the beginning of a model for local democratic governance and self-determination.

What you won't find in Ubud is discotheques or western fast-food chains. With the object of maintaining the cultural authenticity of the place, all of the banjars that comprise Ubud have agreed that such disruptive influences and manifestations of foreign cultures will not be allowed. Their avowed intention is to avoid "becoming like Kuta," which is one of the main tourist destinations in Bali, best known for its excesses and debauchery. One can imagine that the pressures to allow the KFCs and McDonalds must be intense, but it seems the banjars have enough power to call the shots, at least for now. Still, one wonders how long they will be able to resist the pressures that large corporations typically assert through central governments.

The Mondragon Cooperatives

The town of Mondragon is nestled among the mountains in the Basque region of northern Spain. Called Arrasate in the Basque language, Mondragon is the hub of what is probably the most progressive and successful cooperative economy in modern history. It is an economy that has been built up over more than half a century on the basis of humane ideals and cooperative principles – an economy that puts people above profits. I first became aware of it in the late 1970s but did not have occasion to visit until 2005. During my visit I enjoyed the privilege of a full day briefing by Mikel Lezamiz, one of the executives of the Mondragon Cooperative Corporation.

The story begins in 1941 when Father José María Arizmendiarrieta was sent by his bishop to Mondragon. This twenty-six-year-old priest was "dynamic, enterprising and bursting with ideas."[171] Just two years earlier, Generalísimo Francisco Franco had emerged the victor in the Spanish civil war, and had established his fascist regime. Franco was resentful of the support the Basques had given to the Republican opposition, and instituted repressive measures against them – including

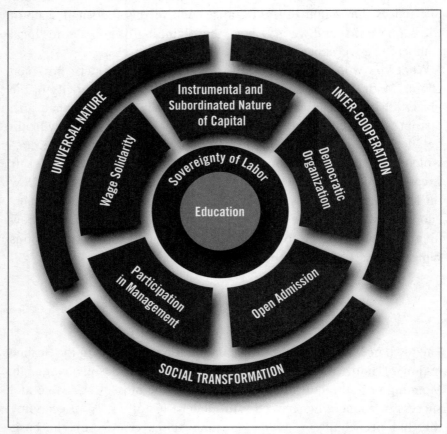

Figure 18.1 Basic Cooperative Principles of the Mondragon Management Model[170] (Courtesy of the Mondragon Cooperative Corporation)

outlawing use of the Basque language. In the face of high unemployment and economic hardship, Arizmendiarrieta made economic development and education his main concerns, so in 1943 he set up a democratically managed Polytechnic School devoted to providing a good technical education based on principles of social solidarity and dedication to the common good of the community.

Under Arizmendiarrieta's guidance, the first worker-owned-cooperative enterprise (named Ulgor) was established in 1956 by a few of his former students to manufacture oil stoves and heaters. A few years later they organized a credit union, called the Caja Laboral Popular (CLP, or Working People's Bank), to provide financial services to co-op members and start-up funds for new co-operative enterprises. "This stroke of genius resulted in the constitution of an entity which became the backbone of the co-operative project, enabling a growth rate that would have otherwise been impossible."[172] But more than financing, this entity provided critical business advice to new cooperative ventures.

Over the next decade, the number of cooperatives proliferated rapidly. Their emphasis was on regional self-reliance and production was mainly for sale within the region. "Before long the co-operatives began to set up their own R&D departments with the aim of developing their own products, thereby avoiding both the need to pay royalties and the limitations imposed by the obligation to export to specific countries."[173] As time went on the cooperative network spread throughout Spain and eventually to other countries, so that now there are 250 companies with plants in a dozen different countries on four continents under the Mondragon Cooperative Corporation. While only about half of these are cooperatives, the corporation has made a commitment to "the gradual application in our main subsidiaries of a 'participative enterprise' model that will channel worker participation in company ownership and management."

Network activities cover three distinct areas – financial, industrial, and distribution – which are coordinated under the corporate centre involving an elabourate governing structure. The Mondragon Cooperative Corporation tries to achieve balance in these dimensions:

- Efficiency and democracy
- Economic and social concerns
- Equality and hierarchical organization
- Private interests (of staff and the companies) and the general interest
- Identification with the cooperative model and cooperation with other business models

As of 2006, the most recent year for which figures are available, total employment numbered 83,600, total assets amounted to more than 27 billion euros (roughly 42 billion dollars), and sales exceeded 13 billion euros (more than 20 billion dollars).

What factors account for the phenomenal success of the "Mondragon experience"? Official company documents highlight the following[174]:

- The vision and influence of José María Arizmendiarrieta
- The corporate culture in which people are given priority over capital
- "A decidedly business-like approach" that emphasizes "company profitability and planned, rigorous and demanding management efficiency"
- "Re-investment of practically all resources generated"
- Adaptability to changing conditions
- The creation of "efficient inter-cooperation instruments – financial, social welfare, innovation, and R&D, and coordinated methods of dealing with management issues and crisis situations"
- Emphasis upon training and education, including retraining to meet changes in market demands

When a cooperative in the network experiences a drop in demand for its products, it does not respond in the normal fashion of cutting jobs — rather it may cut prices to make its products more competitive or it will work aggressively to develop new products, it may reduce wages to keep everyone employed, or it will shift personnel to jobs in other cooperatives within the network. None of this is done in isolation, but is guided and supported by the entire network infrastructure. Additional capital may be provided by the CLP, and workers retrained at one of the many vocational training centres. Other elements of the support infrastructure include a centre for research and development, the Mondragon University, a management training centre, and social services like health care.

The strong ethnic identity and social solidarity of the Basques was no doubt a major factor in the early success of the Mondragon Cooperative model. This raises a number of questions: Can it be replicated elsewhere? Under what conditions might similar efforts have a chance of succeeding? What prior steps might be necessary to "prepare the soil" for cooperative enterprises to thrive?

I tend to believe that the Mondragon experience is replicable, but only in conjunction with the simultaneous weaving of a strong social fabric. That effort need not necessarily be centred around ethnic identity and culture, but could be based on other commonalities – such as religious affiliation, geographical proximity, shared values, or other factors that create common interests (but with concern for the greater common good always foremost). Social entrepreneur and Mondragon scholar Terry Mollner makes a distinction between the declining "material age" and the emerging "relationship age," and concludes that the success of the Mondragon cooperative economy derived from the fact that Arizmendiarrieta "set about building a Relationship Age society by extending into more sophisticated realms the Relationship Age values which were already present in Basque society."[175] He explains that this was done amid the repressive fascist occupation by avoiding confrontation, not by being passively servile but by doing what was for the good of all. As Mollner describes it,

> Arizmendi simply extended this relationship of oneness known by all in friendships and between lovers into the relationship with all things, even with those who see themselves as our enemies – like Franco and his Guardia Civil soldiers which were nearly always in view. *Arizmendi pointed out that they were powerless to decide what people were thinking in their minds.* Thus, rather than confront them, which would be acting

as if they could, Arizmendi separated what people were doing from the language and belief system within which they were doing it. "Let's do what we want to do and then simply talk about it in their language and ideas," is the kind of thing Don Jose Maria might have said. "Since in their worldview they do not think what we are doing is possible, they will think we are doing what they want us to be doing because we are talking their language. We will be left alone to do exactly what we want to do right under their noses. They will be happy and we will be happy without there being any need for confrontation. Soon they will discover that we are growing and they are not because they are stuck standing there watching us." Of course, they also wanted the occupation to end and they would work for that as well, but in the meantime they would be happy and prosperous and be building a society of their own. Thus, as you can see, Father Arizmendi's non-violent or loving methods of dealing with an oppressor in this setting did not even necessitate confrontation. (This makes me think that perhaps Father Arizmendi took non-violent political action to another stage of maturity beyond where Mahatma Gandhi had taken [it] ...to post-confrontation.)[176] [emphasis added]

Ways of Organizing Credit Clearing Exchanges

There are many possible ways of organizing to provide complementary exchange services. Up to now, most grassroots initiatives have either had no formal organization at all, or they have had the sponsorship of some existing nonprofit corporation acting as a legal umbrella and fiscal agent. The commercial trade exchanges have mostly been organized as for-profit corporations or limited liability companies. In considering forms of organization, it would be well to think beyond the immediate needs of the exchange, to forms that will support the general objectives of relocalization and the emergence of economic democracy within communities. Forms of organization will play a major role in answering the key question – *how to build networks that are globally useful while maintaining power and control at the local level.*

Corporations

As corporations have become larger, more powerful, and international, there is increasing doubt about whether they are capable of serving the common good. Small closely held corporations reflect the values and ethics of their owners and managers, and they can often be good community citizens – but it seems that once a corporation exceeds some threshold in size, and the ownership of its shares becomes widely dispersed, it becomes increasingly sociopathic in its behavior, seeking as much as possible to internalize profits while externalizing costs. This is not only a matter of "greedy management" but also is driven by the existing laws pertaining to corporate management, taxation, and the definition of "fiduciary responsibility" (which requires managers to maximize profits and to put other social objectives aside). David Korten, in his book *When Corporations Rule the World*, has described the abuse of corporate privilege and the increasing power that corporations wield in the modern world. The question remains, "Is it possible to tame the corporate 'beast'?"

One possible way is suggested by the work of Peter Barnes, journalist and cofounder and former president of Working Assets Long Distance. In his book, *Capitalism 3.0: A Guide to Reclaiming the Commons*, Barnes proposes that, rather than trusting government to protect the commons and restrain the corporations (an approach that has failed badly), the management and allocation of access to the various aspects of the commons could be done by "trusts." These entities would collect rents for access and distribute to the citizenry what has been called by Jeff Smith and others a "citizen's dividend." Private corporations would continue to maximize profits, but because the commons would be protected by numerous trusts, the corporations would have to internalize many of the costs they now externalize.

I have suggested a corporate structure as a possibility for the regional economic development project in India that I have been collabourating on since 2006. That project, which is centreed on the international community of Auroville and the nearby city of Puducherry, will follow the multistage regional economic development plan that I described in Chapter 16 — and could be undertaken by a "regional development trust," which would hold the majority interest in the corporation. As I envision it, that trust would have a diverse membership representing various interests and sectors of the communities within the bioregion. Unlike typical political offices, trustees might be appointed by each constituent group to serve a limited term and be subject to immediate recall, in a way similar to the Balinese practice.

Limited Liability Companies and Limited Liability Partnerships

The US Limited Liability Company (LLC) and the UK Limited Liability Partnership (LLP) are relatively new organizational forms. Like the corporation, these legal forms provide limited liability to the owners, but without the disadvantage of "double taxation."[177] In the latter respect, they resemble partnerships. More importantly, LLCs and LLPs have a greater potential for harmonizing the interests of the various stakeholders — clients, managers, investors, and the general community — because all of these groups can be members of the "partnership." Chris Cook is a former petroleum exchange director and current enterprise architect and consultant who has been specializing of late in partnership enterprise models. He has articulated how these legal forms might be applied to complementary exchange systems as well as to capital projects involving renewable energy and other green technologies. He is promoting the ideas of risk guarantee, revenue sharing, and temporary equity under the rubric of "Open Capital."

> Open Capital is the concept of partnership finance through the sharing of risk and reward. *Risk* is shared through a guarantee society or clearing union, where trade credit between buyers and sellers is subject to a mutual guarantee.
> *Revenues* are shared through co-ownership of a productive asset by the investors and investees.[178] [emphasis in orginal]

Cook describes one mainstream example of the use of the LLP form to align the interests of the "provider of capital" with those of the "user of capital."

The optimal nature of the UK LLP is already becoming apparent, and a number of technology start-ups have utilised the form. Moreover, a transaction entered into in late 2002 by the Hilton Hotel Group serves as an example of how "Temporary Equity" may operate in practice (although it is extremely doubtful that the parties realised quite how ground-breaking their transaction was to be). The Hilton Hotel Group sold a portfolio of 10 hotels for some £350m to an LLP in which Hilton (the Occupier) holds 40% and the balance of 60% is owned by another LLP linking the 3 Investor Members — one of whom is Bank of Scotland. The Investors receive for 27 years 28.8% of the gross revenues from these hotels plus a further £3m pa [per year] all subject to a floor of £17.5m pa or 5%.

There were two conventional routes Hilton Group could have taken to raise Capital from these assets.

1. a loan secured by a mortgage over the hotels;
2. a "sale and leaseback" transaction.

which give rise to an interest and rental overhead respectively and to a divergence of interest between the provider of Capital and the User, i.e., between the Lender and Borrower or the Freeholder and Leaseholder, respectively. In this transaction, however, the interests of the provider of Capital and the User are aligned, as both have an interest in maximising the overall Value creation of the LLP in terms of revenues.[179]

We can note from the above example that there are two characteristics of such arrangements that distinguish them from conventional equity arrangements:

1. the shares pertain, not to profits, but to revenues; and
2. the sharing arrangement is not permanent but temporary.

Space does not permit a thorough discussion here, but these emergent forms and innovative approaches seem to merit further investigation and development.[180]

Mutual Companies

Although the concept is mainly unknown among younger generations, mutuals have a long history. There have been, and still are, structures known variously as mutual savings banks, mutual insurance companies, credit unions, savings and loan associations, and guarantee societies (in the United Kingdom). Unlike ordinary corporations or *stock companies*, mutual companies have no stockholders. They are owned by, and operated for the benefit of, their depositors, clients, members, or policyholders.

There has been in recent years an unfortunate trend toward demutualization, a process of converting mutual companies to stock companies. This is a matter with which I have some personal experience. When I was around seven years of age, I received as gifts a small amount of money. It totaled perhaps thirty dollars. My parents, knowing that I would quickly spend it if it were kept at home, decided that I should deposit the money in a bank – and thereby learn a lesson in thrift and deferred gratification. One day, they took me downtown to open an account. I can still remember the feeling of awe as we entered that impressive structure that sat across the street from my dad's office. The building, both outside and in, seemed more extravagant than any church I had been in up to that time. It had a bright, spacious interior, with a high vaulted ceiling covered in mosaic tiles depicting various bucolic scenes. A long line of teller windows ran the entire length on one side, while the other side was furnished with massive wooden desks at which were stationed well-dressed men and a handful of women ready to do business. That bank happened to be a mutual savings bank. Many years later, while in graduate school for my MBA, I was a sad to learn that one of my professors was instrumental in the demutualization of that bank.

Those were the days when a family could live pretty well on one income. During my undergraduate days at Villanova, the ten dollar allowance that my dad sent faithfully every week was enough to take care of my incidental expenses and pay for an occasional lark, like a weekend in New York or Atlantic City. My dad, with his seventh grade education, had made a successful career of selling life insurance. He managed to put both me and my sister through college, with my mother at home for all but a few years of their marriage (during which she went to work to help make a down payment for a house). The company my dad worked for was another mutual company, Metropolitan Life Insurance Company, now known as MetLife. Many years later, after he had long been retired, that company was demutualized too. Most policyholders, not knowing the original philosophy behind mutualization, voted in favour of the change. They gained a few shares of stock, but I think they lost a great deal more — another case like Esau selling his birthright for a "mess of pottage."

Many mutual savings banks were forced to demutualize during the crisis of the 1980s. A fairly clear picture of the situation is provided by a report of the Federal Deposit Insurance Corporation. It states that,

> In the early 1980s, many mutual savings banks failed because both macroeconomic forces and changes in the financial services marketplace were inhospitable to the industry's traditional mode of operating. By law and regulation, MSB assets were permitted to be invested primarily in fixed-rate mortgages and long-term bonds, but as short-term interest rates rose to historically high levels between 1979 and 1982, the market value of these assets plunged. At the same time, MSB liabilities were composed almost exclusively of short-term deposits paying rates of interest subject to deposit interest-rate ceilings — and as market rates rose, even small savers began to think like investors. MSB deposits were withdrawn and placed in higher-yielding investments. Regulators fought this disintermediation by permitting the introduction of a variety of time deposits paying market rates of interest. These certificates of deposit helped MSBs retain funds, but they also raised the industry's cost of funds. Yields on assets rose much more slowly, and net interest margins shrank and became negative. Operating losses

were so great that capital levels built up over a century or more
of profitable operations quickly eroded.[181]

The report further concludes that "MSB failures were predictable and,
arguably, preventable."[182] All of this sounds too familiar. Has the more
recent subprime mortgage crisis any relationship to these earlier financial crises? Why, one must ask, has the "remedy" of demutualization
been pushed forward so strongly?[183]

Scale of Organization

If we seek to ultimately create a global exchange network that is *globally useful while locally controlled*, we need to pay attention to the
element of scale. The size of each unit or node in a network may well
be even more important than its legal form. The interpersonal dynamics within a group change drastically as its size increases. This is something that Malcolm Gladwell highlights in his book *The Tipping Point*.
Referring to "The Rule of 150" he says, "Above that point, there begin
to be structural impediments to the ability of the group to agree and
act with one voice."[184] He cites the unusual organizational structure of
the highly successful company Gore Associates. This is the company
that is best known for its Gore-Tex fabric and high performance
outdoor sportswear and gear. It is a company with a very flat hierarchy and no titles; everyone is simply an "associate." Gore also has a
policy of not allowing any plant to get bigger than 150 people. They
will, instead, start a new plant when market demand requires greater
output. Gladwell observes that, "Gore doesn't need formal management structures in its small plants – it doesn't need the usual layers of
middle and upper management – because in groups that small, infor-
mal personal relationships are more effective."

The Rule of 150 is something that has been discovered time and
again. It applies in a variety of contexts from the military to high-
tech business to religious organizations. British anthropologist Robin
Dunbar, based on his primate research, has explained it on the basis
of a physical characteristic of the brain. He says it is the size of the

neocortex that limits the capacity to maintain stable interpersonal relationships. In humans, that capacity seems to be around 150.

Achieving a system of reciprocal exchange that is locally controlled yet globally useful is totally dependent upon keeping the scale of the basic organizational unit small. The structure that I envision consists of local mutual credit clearing exchanges comprised of small affinity groups that are networked regionally and, eventually, globally. Affinity groups that are small and coresponsible enable high levels of trust and democratic self-regulation, but they interact with other affinity groups in ways that enable intergroup trading and the development of social solidarity. As Gladwell concludes, "That is the paradox of the epidemic: that in order to create one contagious movement, you often have to create many small movements first."[185]

19. The Role of Governments in Establishing Economic and Financial Stability

The early chapters of this book traced the events and actions that have led to the politicization of money and banking. They described how national governments in collusion with global financial interests have arrogated power to themselves by their abusive issuance of money, abandoning all semblance of monetary and fiscal responsibility. I recommended the separation of money and state, now let us consider what central governments *could* and *should* do if they were truly interested in serving the common good and promoting a just and harmonious world. In this chapter, I will also examine the more likely possibilities for action at lower levels of state, provincial, and local government.

What National Governments Should Do

The emphasis throughout this book has been on guiding private, voluntary initiatives toward mobilizing resources, empowering communities, and restoring the "credit commons," and while I am not at all sanguine about the near-term prospects for the success of political approaches to monetary reform, it is necessary to recognize the power of national governments and the role they might *eventually* play in producing positive outcomes. Furthermore, it is at least conceivable that some enlightened government in some small country somewhere might be willing to lead the way by renouncing its abuse of the money issuance power and by supporting the kinds of community-based and private exchange mechanisms I have described. So let us explain the specific kinds of legislative and executive actions that are needed.

Objectives

In light of the dysfunctions inherent in the present global monetary regime that have already been described, I would advocate for legislation that would achieve the following objectives:

- protect against both inflation and deflation;
- eliminate involuntary unemployment;
- protect against the effects of international economic and financial instabilities;
- provide a greater measure of independence from foreign economic and political manipulations; and
- enable the emergence of effective and efficient means for mediating the exchange of goods, services, and financial instruments.

It is well within the realm of possibility to achieve all of these objectives, and there exists a solid base of knowledge and experience that makes evident the structural changes that are necessary to do so. The main obstacles to implementing these changes are governments' addiction to deficit spending and their subservience to the vested interests of international finance.

Rationale

As described in Chapter 7, inflation is possible only under the circumstance where there is a monopoly on the issuance of money and that money is compelled by means of legal tender laws to circulate at par. By putting an end to the issue monopoly and repealing all general legal tender laws, the inflation problem will be solved. These actions, of course, imply the existence of an objective, concrete standard of value, as well as competing exchange mechanisms (competition in currency). Government must allow private alternative exchange media that are subject to free-market valuation and the right of anyone except the issuer to refuse to accept such currencies.

The central banks of all countries are closely interlinked — enabling a few individuals to control the national and global economies, to subvert democratic government, and to exploit the people through their monopolization of credit. By their alternating policies of credit liberalization followed by credit restriction they cause recurrent inflations and recessions with their attendant miseries of diminished purchasing power, bankruptcies, foreclosures, and unemployment.

The global interlinking of banking and finance, and the institutions and procedures that promote chronic indebtedness, have enabled the banks of the developed countries to dominate the economies and governments of lesser developed countries (LDCs). Countries like Ecuador, which have accepted the US dollar as their own domestic medium of exchange, have made themselves completely dependent upon the dollar and the US banking system. In no case should the exchange of goods *within* a country be rendered impossible because there are disturbances in finance *outside* the country. The ill effects of such disturbances can be avoided if private exchange alternatives exist. Thus, governments should permit private entities to establish clearing associations as a self-help measure – *without any government restrictions, discriminatory taxes, or subsidies.* Only mechanisms that ensure openness and transparency should be required. The task of these clearing associations should be to bring into contact the available raw materials with the existing labour power, and the available products with buyers' needs, without requiring payment in conventional money. They will thus contribute significantly to the general facilitation of the exchange of goods and services and the abolition of involuntary unemployment. *These clearing associations are able to guarantee domestic liquidity regardless of conditions elsewhere.* The disadvantages suffered by the provinces and certain deprived sectors, such as agriculture, will be diminished, and the exchange of goods within the country will become independent of the currencies of foreign countries.

Legislative Proposals in Brief[186]

Proposal I: Stable Value Reckoning and Protection against Inflation and Deflation
Stable value reckoning in all transactions is essential to an orderly, equitable, and efficient economy. It is therefore necessary that a unit of account be defined in unambiguous terms. The avoidance of infla-

tion (and deflation) requires that there be a measure of value that is independent of, and separate from, any national or other currency — and that no currency, either public or private, be invested with general legal tender status. A truly stable value reckoning is quite impossible as long as legal tender exists. It is therefore proposed that:

1. all laws granting general legal tender status be repealed, and
2. that the official unit of account be declared on the basis of a specific value standard that is defined in concrete physical terms. It should be comprised of a specified amount of some commodity or group of commodities — e.g., 371.25 grains of fine silver (the original definition of the US dollar) — or, much preferably, a composite standard comprised of specified weights or volumes of selected standard commodities (see Appendix B).

Proposal II: Exchange Utilities
The substance of modern money is credit and every currency is a credit instrument. The proper functioning of an economy requires that the exchange process be unencumbered by monopoly control over credit by any government, private entity, or cartel. To restore the disturbed private economy, eliminate unemployment, and enable a more complete matching of economic needs with actual and potential supplies, institutions must be established that make free reciprocal exchange in the economy possible. It is therefore proposed that:

1. The government should not interfere with, and indeed should encourage (but not subsidize), the establishment and operation of private credit clearing utilities that are voluntarily subscribed to, and operated according to agreed standards of honesty, openness, and transparency.
2. That there should be no interference with the issuance and circulation of private currencies that are issued upon proper foundation and in accordance with agreed standards of honesty and transparency.

Proposal III: Public Finance

There should be a strict separation between money and the state. Any financial instruments issued by the government must be made to stand upon their own merits in the financial markets. It is therefore proposed that:

1. No government-issued security – including bonds, warrants, notes, vouchers, or other instruments intended to circulate as currency – should be forced to circulate at face value by means of legal tender laws or otherwise. Likewise, long-term government debts in such forms as bonds or notes should enjoy no special privilege regarding their acceptance or value in the market.

2. Government may, if it wishes, finance its short-term needs through the direct issuance from the treasury of noninterest-bearing tax anticipation warrants – but the rate, relative to the value standard, at which such warrants are accepted as payment by private parties shall be determined by the parties themselves in the free market, and *not* be compelled by legis-lation. *Only the government itself shall be compelled to accept its own financial instruments at par.*

3. There should be no further monetization of long-term government debts by "open market operations" or otherwise.

4. Outstanding government debt should be gradually reduced.

5. Since there is no longer any role for it, the central bank shall be abolished, and government finances should be managed directly by a department of the government.

Such actions would force central governments to balance their budgets, but would not totally preclude them from issuing their own currencies. But if a government currency is made to circulate on its own merits in competition with other exchange media, the amount of currency issued would need to be kept within reasonable limits (in proportion to its anticipated revenues from taxes and fees) to prevent its being discounted or refused. A government could spend its own small denomination no-interest bonds into circulation as a way of paying for its immedi-ate needs – guaranteeing to redeem these bonds, not in gold or other currency, but by accepting them *at face value* in payment for taxes and fees. Additional longer-term financial needs would have to be financed in the conventional way of selling interest-bearing bonds to the public at the market rate.

Given the financial turmoil as I write this and the likely deep recession into which the global economy seems to be headed, many readers may object to the imposition of such severe restrictions on the central government's fiscal policy options, specifically the option for deficit spending to counteract deflationary pressures in the downside of the business cycle. That "cure" is part of the Keynesian orthodoxy that has been sold to both academics and lay people over the past two or three generations. I hope that I have succeeded here in showing that it is the system itself that creates such pressures and that when these restructuring prescriptions are adopted in their entirety, they will greatly ameliorate and even, I believe, eliminate the problem of the business cycle. This is because productive resources of capital and labour never have reason to stand idle, since artificial restrictions on the credit needed by the productive sector to enter the market and to have their products exchanged will have been removed, in which case the "need" for Keynesian deficit spending ceases to be relevant.

The Rentenmark, described in Chapter 7, provides a good model for a government-issued currency. At this point it is useful to refer back to Beckerath's description:

> The Rentenmark had neither a forced market rate nor was its acceptance in general circulation enforced [it was not "legal tender"]. It was not redeemable in gold, although it was made out in gold. It was guaranteed by tax foundation (par. 14, no. 3 of the Act), that is, all taxation offices accepted the Rentenmark at its face value irrespective of any market discount. Inasmuch as the aggregate amount issued (2,000 million marks) corresponded to the revenues of those offices for only two months, Lorenz von Stein's "safety coefficient" (namely total of State paper money not more than a third to a half of the annual requirements of the public revenue offices) was far from reached. In order to make a concession to popular opinion, the

Act referred to a cover by landed property, but at the same time the Act provided that no one was obliged to surrender real estate property for Rentenmarks. Also, a small annual contribution was imposed on landowners and manufacturers; but this was not collected because it naturally proved superfluous for safeguarding the currency. An "intercepting organization" was established by allowing everyone to exchange Rentenmarks for a long term loan, (i.e., an annuity) made out in gold and bearing 5% interest. When the certificates stood at a discount say 3% or more, this naturally led to the loan being subscribed with the certificates, with the result that the certificates together with their discount disappeared from the market. This safeguard ultimately proved to be unnecessary as almost no use was made of the option of exchanging certificates.[187]

Recapping what we said earlier, the features that enabled the Rentenmark to maintain its value were that

1. the Rentenmark was acceptable by all tax offices *at face value* in payment of taxes;
2. there was no legal compulsion for anyone else to accept it, thus it was made to stand on its own merits in the marketplace and might legally pass at a discount from face value in private transactions; and
3. the amount issued was modest in relation to the tax revenues that supported it.

The Role of State, Provincial, and Local Governments

It is often assumed that only national governments have the power to issue money and that lower levels of government have no leeway by which to issue or support alternative exchange media. While it may be true that in many cases the power of local, regional, and provincial governments to act within the realm of money, banking, and finance is legally restricted by higher level constitutions or statutes, one should not presume that they are completely powerless to do so. As any lawyer knows, much depends upon the interpretation of such laws and the words one uses to describe the instruments and actions one wishes to implement.

There are numerous possible ways in which these lower levels of government might act to enable or assist alternative exchange media and systems. First, within their legal authority to do so, they can take direct action by issuing their own complementary currency after the Rentenmark model — for example, spending it into circulation by using it to pay suppliers and employees, and redeeming it by accepting it back in payment of taxes and fees. Tax anticipation warrants or bonds are not uncommon and might be spent into circulation instead of being sold for national money. Issued in small convenient denominations, they can circulate as currency within the region and later be redeemed as payment for taxes.

There are numerous examples of provincial government currencies that were issued by Argentine provinces during the 1990s. These "provincial bonds" were issued in small denominations by provincial governments by using them to pay part of the salaries of their employees. The currency note shown in Figure 19.1 overleaf, called a "Petrom," was issued by the province of Mendoza on the basis of its petroleum royalty income.

If it should be the case that this door is completely closed to them (but not only in that case), local and regional governments should, as much as possible, support the development of complementary local currencies and local community development banks by the private sector, especially as mutuals and cooperative associations. They can, at the very least, encourage inquiry, dialogue, and discussion of these topics

Figure 19.1 A Petrom Note from Mendoza Province (Photo by Sergio Lub)

throughout the community. They can also engage consultants with expertise in these areas to provide input to the new or ongoing development departments and agencies that often undertake "public-private partnerships" to promote local economic development. In pursuing such public-private cooperation in providing exchange media, lower-level governments have the potential to keep factories producing and workers working despite economic setbacks or shortages of official money.

An Early Example of a Local Currency

Henry George, Jr., describes a successful private currency issue that his father had suggested as a way of ameliorating the effects of the financial panic of the 1890s that was exacerbated locally by the famous Johnstown flood disaster of 1893. It is not clear what role was played by the local government in this episode, but it suggests how a local government, private companies, or a public-private partnership might effectively monetize their credit outside of the banking system – thus putting into circulation a generally accepted payment medium that enables production and trade to continue despite the machinations and dysfunctions of banks, central governments, and the conventional political money system.

> An instance of the highly practical cast of Mr George's mind
> when responsibility concentrated his faculties was given in 1893,
> when a general financial stringency was squeezing the banks

of the country, and crippling and destroying strong and weak industrial enterprises. The large steel rail manufacturing company named after Tom L. Johnson, and located at Johnstown, Pa., was soon brought face to face with this problem. The president of the company, Arthur J. Moxham, had come into the single tax faith soon after Mr Johnson's conversion in the middle eighties. His strength of character and high executive ability were attested by the people of Johnstown when the never-to-be-forgotten flood lay the centre of the city in ruins, killed thirty-six hundred persons, and sweeping away all established authority and order, gave place to horror, terror and frantic confusion. In that time of disaster Mr Moxham was made dictator, with life and death powers; and for three days he held that extraordinary office.

Mr George happened to visit Johnstown and Mr Moxham in 1893, at the moment when the financial stringency had brought the affairs of the Johnson Company to a crisis. He was told by Mr Moxham that no course seemed to be left but to shut down, for while he could get plenty of orders for rails, he could get no money in payment. Whereupon Mr George suggested that the bonds of the street railroad companies ordering rails should be taken in payment of their orders; and that certificates to be used as money be issued against them. Mr Moxham took the idea and developed a plan, calling a meeting of his employees, explained to them the proposal to take steel railroad bonds, place them in the hands of a trustee mutually acceptable to the company and its men, and against these bonds to issue certificates in small denominations with which to pay salaries and wages by the Johnson Company. The employees gladly accepted the proposal and appointed a committee to act for them, and the plan was put into execution, one-third of all salaries and wages being paid in currency and the other two-thirds in these bond certificates. The store-keepers and other townspeople accepted the certificates as readily as money; and the company, with its several thousand employees, passed through the "tight" period without further trouble. Indeed, the earnings of the employees were greater at this time than at any other period in the history of the company.

Subsequently every one of the certificates was drawn in and redeemed. Mr George regarded this as an illustration of what the United States Government could do to clear up the currency difficulties — issue from its own treasury, a paper currency based upon its credit and interchangeable with its bonds.[188]

This account provides a good example of the simplicity with which value in the form of marketable goods and services can be monetized independently of the central government and the banking system. Once the concepts and processes are understood, the keys to economic liberation are at hand.

20. Exchange, Finance, and the Store of Value

In Chapter 6, I described the distinction between the *exchange* function and the *finance* function. I explained that the exchange function requires *short-term* credit that bridges the gap between the delivery of goods to market and the sale of those goods, while the finance function requires *long-term* credit to enable the renewal or expansion of the economy's production capacity. We concluded that capital *investments* should therefore be financed out of *savings* rather than by the creation of new money. We also saw that borrowing to purchase consumer durables (consumer finance) should, as well, be provided from savings. Let us now turn to a more complete consideration of saving and the store of value function.

The Store of Value

Think for a moment about how you save, i.e., how you store value. Do you have much of your wealth in the form of cash (paper notes) or checking account deposits? I would guess that, like most of us, you have very little of your wealth in those forms. They function as exchange media that are kept for the convenience of making transactions. More likely, if you have any savings at all (aside from ownership of your home), they are in the form of "investments" in various financial assets – like corporate stocks, bonds, or mutual fund shares; insurance policies; annuities; and credit default swaps (CDs). These are all *long-term financial claims* but they are not money. We tend to not distinguish them from money because markets are so highly developed that such financial claims can be readily liquidated, i.e., converted into money by selling them. Your savings do not remain idle, they provide the investment financing needed for capital formation – business expansion and development that brings new value into the market later on.

Saving and Investment

It is a necessary feature of any organized economy to have a set of mechanisms that provide for financial security. This is a particular concern in countries where the traditional social fabric, with its built-in family and tribal supports, has been eroded. The increasing concentration of power and the appropriation of resources by the centralized government/banking/corporate nexus has rendered traditional social units economically impotent. In this atomized social context, and with the increasing attacks on government-managed programmes like Social Security and Medicare, individuals must now provide as best they can for their own future needs. Let's examine how financial security is typically achieved.

We all begin, and most of us end, our lives as dependent and unproductive creatures. In between, there are often times of illness and misfortune. Without the assurance of support from a prosperous extended family, clan, or tribe, each of us is thrown into the sea of mass society within which we must provide for our own financial security. Whether we do it individually or collectively, privately or through government, people must be able to save some of what they earn during the productive periods of their lives in order to provide for their needs during unproductive periods – and to cover unusual expenses and emergencies. The latter can be handled to some extent by insurance, but an investment "nest egg" is necessary to financing large consumer goods purchases and to provide a source of income that does not depend upon the sale of one's labour.

In addition, as already mentioned, an economy must have some means of financing new productive enterprises, the renewal of the material infrastructure of economic activity, and business expansion. All of those things that enhance the production and delivery of goods and services – factory buildings, hotels, machinery, railroads, ships, planes, etc. – require large up-front expenditures for their creation, but produce benefits, not immediately, but gradually over a long period of time. In order to be able to make such investments, an economy must produce a surplus over its current consumption needs. These two functions, *saving* and *capital formation*, are complementary processes. It is our collective savings that provide the financing for the creation of new productive capacity. Those of us who have a surplus that we are able to save provide the resources needed by others to become more productive.

In a developed economy in which there is specialization of labour, saving is essentially a social phenomenon. It is possible for an individual to save directly by purchasing tangible goods and commodities that can easily be sold later, but this method of saving has distinct disadvantages and costs. One might purchase such things as extra food stocks, precious metals, gemstones, useful tools, other types of merchandise, or various collectibles (like works of art) for which there is a persistent market demand. But the expenses of storage, safekeeping, and physical depreciation make the holding of most physical assets less desirable than holding sound financial assets.

Savings more commonly take the form of financial claims such as bank deposits, bonds, corporate stocks, mutual fund shares, and some forms of insurance. Your "money in the bank" is not really money in the bank. Unless you have a stash of bills in a safe deposit box, your money is not just sitting there in the bank waiting for you to come and get it. Balances in savings accounts, checking accounts, and CDs are simply claims to so much wealth. When you make a deposit, the bank uses that money. It lends it out – or more accurately, uses it as "reserves," which allow it to create new money of an even greater amount to lend out. Your monetary income, if it is not spent, can be used in only two other ways – it can be hoarded or it can be saved/invested. Money is hoarded when it is held out of circulation, e.g., when you stuff it in a mattress or bury it in a hole in the ground. That money is not available for mediating exchanges of goods or services. Only concrete forms of money, like coins and notes, can be hoarded. Money in the form of bank deposits remains in circulation, since the bank has the option of using it.

For our purposes, we will consider money used to accumulate

tangible goods and commodities to be spent money, since that money takes goods off the market and does not finance capital formation. We will define savings as financial claims. In this sense, then, saving and investment are two sides of the same coin. For example, when you allocate your surplus income to me and in return obtain a financial claim from me, that surplus income is then spent by me – perhaps to start a business of some kind. You have agreed to forego spending the money yourself, making it possible for me to spend it instead. In that case, money that was part of the common credit pool is transformed into a private credit obligation to you by me. The expectation is that you will recover that saved income from me later on when you need it. You can either allocate your savings directly (as when you make a loan to me or purchase corporate stocks and bonds) or you can accomplish it through some financial intermediary (like a bank or insurance company) that will do it for you.

As an example, when you deposit money in a savings account at a bank, the bank may lend it to a business or use it to buy government or corporate securities. When you deposit money in a credit union, that money is loaned out to another member, perhaps to buy a house or car. The latter, however, enable *consumer spending* – not capital formation. As the other member repays their loan, money becomes available for you to withdraw part of your savings. In practice, there are many such loans being made and repaid at any given time. Financial institutions keep a portion of their total deposits in liquid form, e.g., cash and short-term government securities, just in case many depositors wish to withdraw their savings at the same time. Liquidity is also achieved by cooperation among banks in which they agree to provide one another with cash to cover unusual withdrawal demands.

Liberating Saving and Investment

Concurrent with the liberation of the exchange process, we are also seeing developments that attempt to liberate savings and investment by bypassing the banks in their role of *depositories*. This is a form of *disintermediation* in which people with surplus cash can lend it directly to those who need it by making private arrangements. This approach has been widely practiced historically by particular ethnic groups and immigrant communities and has recently become a more general phenomenon with the emergence of Web-based peer-to-peer lending intermediaries that are supposed to help borrowers and lenders come together online. How far this will get remains to be seen. Two notable examples of such attempts are Zopa.com, which started in the United Kingdom, and a US effort called Prosper.com. This process, now being referred to as the "social lending" movement, should ideally work like this.

- When someone applies for a loan, the system authenticates their identity and a credit history report is obtained.
- The loan is then given a risk level rating.
- The request is posted on the Website as an offer to prospective lenders.
- Lenders can then offer some amount of their choosing to that particular request.

Thus the risk of default is spread among many lenders, with each lender deciding how much of their money they wish to risk on any particular loan. Lenders can diversify their investments among many different borrowers. Further, borrowers are able to specify the maximum interest rate they are willing to pay for money they borrow, while lenders can specify the minimum rate of return they will accept on money lent. The online system then, in an automated auction-type process, matches them up in a way that is most advantageous to the parties involved. Compared to banks, these peer-to-peer arrangements typically provide savers with a higher rate of return on their savings, while enabling borrowers to obtain capital at lower rates of interest. To paraphrase a familiar commercial message, "When savers and borrowers compete, everybody wins."

The Zopa Principles that constitute part of the lender's application are rather lengthy and contain a number of restrictions based on UK laws. A clause that makes the role of Zopa clear is this: "Zopa Limited is not a party to any Loan Contracts between Lenders and Borrowers. Our function is to operate the Lending Platform." As such, it's a process that (at least initially) approached the ideal. I've not kept close tabs on developments, but I have the sense that increasing regulatory restrictions may over time erode its effectiveness.

Zopa USA operates in a completely different way. Instead of connecting borrowers and lenders directly, it offers lenders an account in a credit union through which loans are made. The particular credit union partner is USA Fed, which describes itself as follows:

> Born and bred in San Diego, California, USA Fed is a non-profit, international credit union with over 61,000 members worldwide and over $700 million in assets — a member-owned financial cooperative with branches in California, Nevada, Japan and Korea.[189]

Zopa USA's partnership with the credit union enables it to offer insured CDs, but at a low fixed rate of interest. On the borrowing side, the loans are not made by individual investors, but by the credit union at their usual rates and only for consumer finance — not entrepreneurial purposes.

All that pretty much takes the bloom off the rose, reverting to the same-old, same-old. If Zopa USA is but a marketing device for a credit union, one must wonder — why bother?

Prosper.com describes itself as "America's largest people-to-people lending marketplace. Connecting people to people eliminates the need for borrowers to go through a bank for a loan — and fewer middlemen means Prosper lenders also benefit."[190] But Prosper seems to be in a continual state of flux. When I explored their Website in mid-2008, they were saying that "lenders' deposits are covered up to $100,000 by FDIC pass-through insurance provided by our banking partner, Wells Fargo Bank."[191] More recently, I find no mention of that and it appears that Prosper.com has run up against some legal barriers. Their Website (as of November 28, 2008) announces that they are "not accepting new lender registrations or new commitments from existing lenders at this time." A linked page explains that they are in a legally imposed "quiet period," which is part of the registration process they are embarked upon.

Until we complete the registration process, we will not accept new lender registrations or allow new commitments from existing lenders ... As the appropriate securities authorities may consider a new loan listing to constitute the offer of a security, *we are unable to post new loan listings on our site until our registration statement becomes effective* ... A successful registration can take several months, but we assure you we will do our best to move forward as quickly as possible. Until this process is complete, we're required to be in a quiet period and will be unable to respond to press, blogger or other inquiries about Prosper or the registration filing until it becomes effective.[192] [emphasis in original]

It appears that Web-based peer-to-peer finance, in the United States at least, is in the process of being hogtied. Whether it will be able to maintain any empowering features at all remains in question.

Debt Claims Versus Equity Claims

There are two basic types of financial claims, *debt* and *equity*. Quite simply, when you lend money to someone, that becomes a debt they owe you. You are their creditor and they are your debtor; you have a *debt claim* against them. The loan agreement will usually specify some repayment schedule and a rate of interest. As the creditor you may also ask for the pledge of some collateral, a house, a car, or some other asset that can be legally confiscated if the debtor fails to live up to the agreement.

An equity claim, however, is a partial ownership. It is an arrangement in which the various parties to the agreement hold a more equal position. There are various kinds of equity agreements — but the basic character of an equity claim is such that there are no fixed obligatory returns, repayment schedules, or collateral demanded of one equity holder by another. Consideration of some common financial securities will serve to distinguish more precisely between debt and equity claims.

In the securities markets, debts take the form of bonds, notes, and bills; equities are represented by such things as preferred and common stocks of corporations, or shares of limited partnerships. Mutual fund shares represent claims against an assortment of securities, often a combination of corporate shares and corporate or government bonds. There are very important distinctions between debt claims and equity claims. Debt claims are contracts that take legal priority over equity claims in the payment of money. A corporate business, for example, might be financed through the use of both debt and equity. It might issue several types of bonds, and both preferred and common stocks. The agreed interest on debt must be paid regardless of the level of profits, and even if the company makes losses. Also, if the company goes bankrupt and is forced to liquidate its assets, the bondholders (along with the other creditors) must be paid before the stockholders can receive anything. Consider the following example.

The ABC corporation sells a million shares of common stock for $10 per share, yielding $10,000,000. It also sells 1,000 shares of preferred stock for $1,000 per share yielding $1,000,000. The preferred shares have a specified yearly dividend of $100 per share. The company also sells $5,000,000 of first mortgage bonds, secured by its factory building, and $5,000,000 of subordinated debentures (a debenture is a bond that is not secured by any specific assets, but by the general assets of the company). The first mortgage bonds carry an interest rate of 7 percent per year, and the interest rate on the debentures is 9 percent.

Profits will be distributed in this way. The bond and debenture holders must receive their interest payments before the stockholders can receive any dividends at all. Even if there are no profits, the interest must be paid. The first mortgage bond holders usually have priority over the debenture holders. They must receive their interest before the debenture holders can receive any interest payments. Once the bond and debenture interest has been paid, the preferred stockholders can receive their dividends, but only if there is enough profit available to pay them. The common stockholders are last in line for the distribution of profits. They may or may not receive dividend payments, and the amount will be at the discretion of the board of directors of the corporation.

What happens if the interest on the bonds or debentures is not paid?

In that case, either group can force the company into bankruptcy, and secure payment of the debts through liquidation of the company's assets. In the event of liquidation, the first mortgage bond holders get paid out of the proceeds from the sale of the collateral (in this case, the factory building). Any remaining amount due on the principal and accrued interest will be paid from the proceeds obtained from sale of the remaining assets. This part of the bondholders' claim may or may not take precedence over the debenture holders' claim, depending on how the contracts are written. Next in line for payment come the debenture holders. Once they are paid in full, the preferred stock holders can receive the par value of their stock. Common stockholders come last and divide up whatever may be left, which is why they are called "residual owners."

As pointed out earlier, one of the problems with a debt contract is that it forces the entrepreneur to assume all of the business risk. Another problem is that interest must usually be paid according to a specified time schedule, along with a portion of the principal. This requirement holds regardless of the level of profits earned and the ability of the business to pay. Any failure to comply with the terms of the loan contract constitutes default, which allows the creditors to foreclose and force liquidation of the business assets as a way of recovering their investment. The relationship between the lender and borrower is, therefore, an antagonistic one. Creditors will sometimes renegotiate the terms of repayment, but only if it is more to their advantage than seizing the collateral assets. On the other hand, an equity investment, since it represents a part ownership in the business, makes the entrepreneur and the investor partners who share both the risks and the rewards of the enterprise. In my opinion, shared ownership (equity) financing is preferable to borrowing and lending at interest, because it does a better job of harmonizing the interests of the parties involved by sharing both the rewards and the risks associated with a venture, thus being more favourable toward social justice and cooperation. Shared equity also satisfies the requirements of various religious traditions mentioned earlier.

A Shared Equity Mortgage*

Suppose you wish to buy a house for yourself and your family to live in. The usual procedure in contemporary western society is to go to a bank and apply for a mortgage to finance the purchase. Suppose the purchase price is $100,000. The bank may require that you make a down payment equal to 10 percent of the appraised value, which may or may not be the same as the purchase price. Let's suppose that the appraised value and the purchase price are the same, in which case the bank will require $10,000 down and will lend you the remaining $90,000. You will sign a mortgage contract, which will require you to make monthly payments over a period of years. Typically, home mortgages run for a period of twenty, thirty, or sometimes as much as forty years. The bank, of course, charges interest based on the amount of the unpaid principal. The rate of interest you are asked to pay depends on the prevailing market conditions and the term (time period) of the loan.

Let's assume the bank agrees to give you a thirty-year mortgage for $90,000, at an interest rate of 8 percent per year. People usually prefer to make equal payments to amortize (repay) such a loan. In this case, the monthly payments would be $660.39. Each payment will consist partly of interest due and partly the repayment of principal. Since the interest is figured on the basis of the remaining unpaid principal balance, the interest portion will decline over time while the principal portion increases.

A loan amortization table shows that, over the thirty-year term of the mortgage, you will pay the bank $237,740.40, or more than two and a half times the $90,000 you borrowed. The bank will have collected interest totaling $147,740.40. Now what happens if you miss a few payments? If you fail to make the payments as scheduled, the bank can foreclose and sell the house to recover the amount of principal and interest you still owe. You may or may not recover any of your own investment. Since the bank's claim has priority over yours, it will probably not try very hard to get the best price. The bank is mainly

---

* I first completed this study and analysis in the late 1990s and an abridged version was published in *Islamic Horizons* magazine.

concerned about recovering its own investment, not yours, so it may set the selling price low in order to liquidate the property quickly – leaving little or nothing for you to recover.

There is another way to finance a large purchase based on equity sharing. This is nothing new. During the thirteenth century, a time when laws against usury were strictly enforced, it was common practice among the Dutch banks to provide this sort of financing for business ventures. Some present day Islamic banks have been using a similar approach to provide a so-called "halal mortgage." (Something that is in accordance with Islamic law is *halal*, analogous to the term *kosher* in Jewish custom.) It avoids usury by avoiding debt. Let's imagine a different kind of bank – a cooperative bank, perhaps. Instead of making a loan and asking you to sign a mortgage contract, the cooperative bank takes a *temporary* equity share in your house. How does this work? How do you achieve full ownership, and how does the bank earn a return on its investment?

Just as in the conventional arrangement, the co-op bank will require some down payment. That will be your initial equity share. Let's assume you make the same down payment as before, 10 percent, or $10,000. The co-op bank puts up the remaining $90,000. Now you and the bank are co-owners. You own 10 percent of the house and the coop bank owns 90 percent of the house. There is no interest to be paid on the co-op bank's capital – but if you occupy the house, you will be required to pay rent to the owners. Of course, since you are a part owner, part of that rent comes back to you. At the outset, the bank will get 90 percent of the rental payments and you will get 10 percent. But you are also allowed to increase your ownership share at any time by making additional payments to the co-op bank – in effect, buying out the bank's interest in the house. As you do so, your proportionate share increases while the coop bank's share decreases and the distribution of the subsequent rental payments will change accordingly.

Let's compare this arrangement with the conventional mortgage in the example given above. The big question, of course, is what is a fair amount for the monthly rent? It might be reasonable to assume that it is equal to the monthly payments you would have made under the conventional mortgage arrangement – in this case, $660.39. At the outset, you will receive 10 percent of that rent as your ownership share and the co-op bank will receive 90 percent. Let us also assume that you apply your share of the rental payments to increasing your share of the ownership. My calculations show that, under this arrangement, you will own 100 percent of the house after making the 350th payment, or in twenty-nine years and two months. You will have paid total rent of $231,018.30. The bank's total share will have been $141,018.30. This is a saving of more than six thousand dollars over the amount of interest paid on the conventional mortgage. In percentage terms, this is a saving of a little over 4.5 percent. This may not seem like much, but as we shall see when we compare this approach with conventional mortgages carrying higher interest rates, the savings can be quite substantial. Additionally, if the "fair rent" had been set at a lower level, but you had made the same monthly payments of $660.39, you would achieve full ownership of the house more quickly and would have saved yet more relative to the total interest payments on the conventional mortgage.

However, the more important advantage derives from the risk sharing inherent in the shared equity approach. Under this arrangement, if you are unable to make the additional principal payments, you will not be foreclosed – you simply do not add to your ownership share. If you are unable to pay the rent, however, your equity share will diminish accordingly; and at some point, perhaps when your equity share falls below a certain percentage, you could be required to vacate the house, just as if you were renting from anybody else – but you would not lose your ownership equity. When the house is rented to someone else, you would still receive your share of the rent – or if the house were to be sold, you would get your share of the proceeds based on the percentage of the equity that you own. Of course, since the co-op bank's claim does not take priority over yours, it is in the best interests of both you and the bank to try to get the highest price possible from the sale.

Compared to the conventional mortgage debt, the relationship between you and the co-op bank is amicable rather than antagonistic and your interests are congruent rather than opposed. The conventional mortgage tends to be exploitative. It creates conflict, stress, and insecurity while contributing to greater disparities of income and wealth – the rich get richer and the poor get poorer. The shared equity financing (or halal mortgage), however, reduces conflict, stress, and insecurity, and makes for a more harmonious and equitable society.

To fully appreciate the advantages of the shared equity approach, we need to examine the numbers pertaining to higher conventional mortgage interest rates. Table 20.1 is a summary table that shows the figures for conventional mortgages at various interest rates (6 percent, 8 percent, 10 percent, and 12 percent) along with figures for comparable halal mortgages. It can be seen how seemingly small

Table 20.1 Summary Comparison Between Conventional Mortgage and "Equity Mortgage"

Conventional Mortgage

Comparative figures for different interest rates

30 year conventional mortgage: $90,000 principal; $10,000 down

Interest rate	Monthly payment	Total payback	Total interest paid	Number of payments	Time to complete payback	
6%	$539.60	$194,256.00	$104,256.00	360	30 yr	
8%	$660.39	$237,740.40	$147,740.40	360	30 yr	
10%	$789.81	$284,331.60	$194,331.60	360	30 yr	
12%	$925.75	$333,270.00	$243,270.00	360	30 yr	

Shared Equity ("halal mortgage" or "equity mortgage")

$90,000 initial bank equity (90%); $10,000 initial buyer's equity (10%)

Buyer's share of monthly rent applied to repurchase of bank's share

	Monthly rent	Total payout	Bank's share of rents	Number of payments	Time to complete buyout	Savings relative to conventional mortgage
	$539.60	$230,879.35	$140,879.35	428	35 yr 8 mo	($36,623.35)
	$660.39	$231,018.30	$141,018.30	350	29 yr 2 mo	$6,722.10
	$789.81	$231,167.29	$141,167.29	293	24 yr 5 mo	$53,164.31
	$925.75	$231,323.14	$141,323.14	250	20 yr 10 mo	$101,946.86

changes in the interest rate cause huge increases in the amount of money you must pay back. At 12 percent interest, for example, you will repay $333,270.00 on your $90,000 loan over thirty years, giving the bank interest income of $243,270.00. However, a shared equity or halal mortgage with the same monthly payment of $925.75 would give you full ownership in twenty years and ten months. The total rent shares to the co-op bank would be only $141,323.14, saving you over $100,000.

The reader may note from the chart that at an assumed mortgage rate of 6 percent you would end up paying more for equity mortgage financing than for the conventional mortgage. This is partly the result of the assumptions we are making about the amount of a fair market rent. Setting it to be the same as the monthly payment on the conventional mortgage may not be realistic in all of these cases. However, the greater total payment to the co-op bank is mainly due to the fact that with the lower monthly payment assumed in this case you would have taken considerably longer to repay the co-op bank's share — thirty-five years and eight months, as opposed to an even thirty years for the conventional mortgage. For those who might care to pursue this possibility further, it would be instructive to run the numbers for a conventional mortgage of that same duration — and further, to make some similar comparisons based on actual rental market data.

Savings and Investment within Complementary Exchange Systems

When I tell people about alternative exchange systems, the question invariably arises as to how one would save up for retirement or to make some major purchase later on. The answer is that it would occur in much the same way as with conventional money. As credit clearing and complementary currencies develop, those who accumulate surpluses in the alternative currencies or credit systems will want to save or invest them. This will give rise to opportunities for entrepreneurs to use the alternative currencies as another means of financing new enterprises or expanding existing ones. Some process to match complementary currency *savings* with complementary currency *invest-ments* will be set up either as part of the credit clearing exchange or by independent entities. Your temporary surplus of credits or comple-mentary currencies can also be allocated to be used by someone else in consumer finance, just as your savings at a credit union might be loaned to another member to enable them to buy a new car.

Consider this example. Suppose you have a successful business and as a member of a local credit clearing association you have been accu-mulating credits faster than you care to spend them. You might wish to save your surplus credits to enable you to make a large purchase (say, for replacement office equipment) two years from now, a purchase that would exceed your allowed line of credit. What might be your avail-able options?

The simplest case would be to make a direct loan to someone who has a present need for purchasing power. Let's suppose that Geoffrey is also a member of the credit clearing exchange. He owns a success-ful coffee shop that is now too small to adequately serve his growing customer base. He would like to rent an adjacent space, knock out the wall in between, and renovate and re-equip the entire shop. He needs to hire a carpenter, an electrician, and a plumber, and needs to buy some new restaurant equipment. All of these are available within the credit clearing association but his credit line is not high enough for him to acquire these things on his current account. He makes it known that he will borrow the necessary credits on favourable terms from any members who have extra credits to spare for, say, one year.

Being a faithful customer of Geoffrey's shop and knowing him to be a competent businessperson, you agree to make the loan. Geoffrey gives you a promissory note describing the terms and the duration of the loan, and you transfer your surplus credits to Geoffrey's account at the credit clearing exchange. Now you've accomplished your savings goal and Geoffrey has the credits he needs to spend to expand his business.

Note that the credits are still in the system, but now they belong to Geoffrey instead of you. They will circulate to other members of the exchange as Geoffrey spends them to acquire the services and equip-ment he needs. Note too that these credits, which had been a collective obligation of the associated members to you, have now become a private obligation of Geoffrey to you. You have taken on some additional risk because if Geoffrey defaults the loss will be borne by you personally and not by the collective membership. So it is with *any* investment, though many ways have been devised to mitigate such risks. This is the business of finance. Assuming that all goes well, Geoffrey's business will thrive, his credit earnings will increase during the coming year, and he will have the credits needed to repay his loan to you.

This is but one possibility. As in the conventional money realm, there is an endless array of possible private debt, equity, and hybrid arrangements that might serve as vehicles for savings and investment.

As these long-term savings and investment possibilities develop, the protection of the purchasing power of alternative currency credits over time will require that they be denominated in concrete units such as were described previously and in Appendix B, making them independent of political currency units like the dollar, which will surely continue to be debased and lose purchasing power.

Epilogue

Just as it is vain to judge history, it is equally vain to try to predict its future course. While one can try to discern patterns and causal relationship from the past and extrapolate trends out into the future, it is very likely that even relatively short-term predictions will prove to be erroneous. We simply cannot account for what Nassim Taleb calls the "black swans"[193] — those highly improbable events that virtually no one sees coming, that take us by surprise, and often change the course of history. Yet we can see that particular conditions bring about particular kinds of outcomes, and we are not entirely powerless to change those conditions.

I have described in this book a particular worldview and traced the development of significant human institutions that have enabled the ever-increasing concentration of power and wealth. By projecting this long-standing trend we can arrive at some very disturbing possibilities. It appears that the fate of the world, and everyone in it, is now to be determined by a very small group of individuals who have the power to decide for all of us without consulting any of us. They have their own worldview, their own values, and their own agenda that is mostly hidden. We have seen the development of a mode of governance in which, as C. Wright Mills described it, "Public relations displace reasoned argument; manipulations and undebated decisions of power replace democratic authority."[194] At the same time, the world is being confronted with geophysical changes, human-made or otherwise, that are bound to have major impacts on how we live.

Fortunately, we still have a little bit of wiggle room in which we are free to act, but time is running out. Most of our political, economic, and religious leaders seem to be taking us in the wrong direction. That makes expressions of dissent more important than ever. There is always some risk in expressing contrary views, but it is the dissidents who are the most valuable in society and politics — for it is their dissent that focuses attention on the matters that, if left unattended, will rend the social fabric and cause greater pain to the body politic later on. It is the dissidents who force those in positions of power to justify themselves and their actions to their constituencies. The British notion of the "loyal opposition" probably had much to do with the success of British civilization, but such opposition is barely noticeable these days, either in Britain or America or elsewhere. The increasing suppression of dissent is making it necessary to devise ever more creative forms for peacefully expressing it. There is a facetious aphorism that says that, "No good deed goes unpunished." While as a general statement that may be overly cynical, it seems to bear a lot of truth when the good deed threatens the agendas and narrow self-interests of the power élite.

The Prospects for Civilization

In assessing the current prospects for civilization, I think we need to take very seriously Carroll Quigley's observations and conclusion that, "sooner or later, an authoritarian political system that reflects the inequality in control of weapons will be established," just as Supreme Court Justice Louis Brandeis warned that "We can have a democracy in this country or we can have great wealth concentrated in the hands of the few. We cannot have both." It appears that western civilization has already arrived at that point. Neither man lived to see the virtual shredding of the Bill of Rights and negation of the Constitution that has transpired over the past few decades, largely under the guise of the war on drugs and then drastically worsening in the "war on terror" following September 11, but even from his vantage point of the mid-1960s Quigley had concluded that "there is little reason to doubt that authoritarian rather than democratic political regimes will dominate the world into the ... foreseeable future."[195]

Civilization is at a critical juncture where circumstances require that each of us take greater responsibility – not only for ourselves and our close communities, but also for the common good. We are, after all, one human family sharing one planetary home. Giving our leaders the benefit of the doubt and assuming the best of intentions on their part, I share the opinion of Mahatma Gandhi that, "Good government is no substitute for self-government." My own preference follows that of President Woodrow Wilson who said "I do not want to see the special interests of the United States take care of the workingmen, women, and children. I want to see justice, righteousness, fairness and humanity displayed in all the laws of the United States, and I do not want any power to intervene between the people and their government. Justice is what we want, not patronage and condescension and pitiful helpfulness. The trusts are our masters now, but I for one do not care to live in a country called free even under kind masters. I prefer to live under no masters at all."[196]

What needs to happen to reverse the destructive and despotic trends, and prevent our sliding into a modern form of materialistic feudalism? In my opinion, we need (at a minimum) to find ways of achieving a number of goals.

- Power and control need to be decentralized
- Wealth must be more fairly distributed
- Local economies must be nurtured
- The commons, especially the credit commons, must be restored
- Monopolies must be eliminated or circumvented
- The basic necessities of life – especially water, air, food, and energy – must be brought under popular control
- Ecological restoration must be a high priority

As I have argued throughout, none of this can be achieved to any significant degree under the present politicized global debt-money regime. It is therefore essential that the processes of exchange and finance be recreated. None of this needs to involve coercive measures or violent confrontation, but simply the assumption of personal responsibility, voluntary cooperation, and organization. The greatest results will derive from a willingness to share and to work together. Still, these are a few things that we can do as individuals to reduce our dependence upon the dominant institutions and to prepare the way.

- You've certainly heard this numerous times before, but it bears repeating: every dollar spent is a vote. Think before you spend your money – consider more than price.
- Promote the establishment of private complementary exchange systems – and *use them.*
- Buy from your friends and neighbours whenever possible.
- Contribute your time, energy, and money to whatever moves things in the right direction.

We will either learn to put aside sectarian differences, to recognize all life as one life, to cooperate in sharing earth's bounty, and yield control to a higher power – or we will find ourselves embroiled in ever-more-destructive conflicts that will leave the planet in ruins and avail only the meanest form of existence for the few, if any, who survive. The only rational course now is for the people of the earth to embrace one another in familial love and without judgment, sharing what we have and supporting one another to each realize our fullest potential while at the same time dedicating ourselves to nurture our Mother Earth so that she may continue to nurture us. For it is, as always, the same fundamental choice that creation puts before us, so plainly expressed in the Mosaic scriptures: "I call heaven and earth to record this day against you, that I have set before you life and death, blessing and cursing: therefore choose life, that both you and thy seed may live" (Deuteronomy 30:19).

As for the élite rulers, grudges will do us no good and only create new hurdles. Let us thank them for their service and bid them welcome as members of our human family.

Acknowledgments

Writing is thought to be a solitary pursuit but there is so much more to producing a book or an article than typing out the words. It is impossible to credit all of those whose support and influence have played a role in the emergence of this work, but there are some whose immediate assistance with this book must be recognized. I hope no one will feel slighted if I neglect to mention them by name.

I am especially indebted to my dear friends, Sergio and Gaye Lub, who have supported me and my work in so many ways over a long period of time. I am especially appreciative of their having provided me with an ideal setting in which to live and work during the completion of the first draft of this book, and of permission to use some of Sergio's photo images as illustrations.

I am also greatly indebted to Dr Laurence Victor for lending his extraordinary intellectual talents and wide-ranging knowledge to the review of chapter drafts and for providing deeper insights into many of the book's topics. Thanks as well to Theo Megalli for his enormous assistance with research items, review of draft chapters, consultation on technical points, valuable suggestions, and translation of German texts; to Dr Philip Beard for additional translation assistance; to Stephen DeMeulenaere, David Wallach, Mike Aldana, Dr Ahamed Kameel Meera, Dr Aziuddin Ahmad, Curtis Priest, and Frank Nuessle, for their comments on particular sections and chapters; to Peter Etherden for his topical dialogues and diligent and expert preparation of related texts for online presentation, particularly those relating to the subject of usury; and to my editor at Chelsea Green, Jonathan Teller-Elsberg, for his excellent advice on edits and revisions.

Finally, to all of my many friends, colleagues, and correspondents who have over many years provided encouragement and various kinds of support, thank you, and may our work become a blessing to all.

Appendix A

A Model Membership Agreement for a Credit Clearing Service[197]

The following draft agreement is applicable to either a for-profit credit clearing service or to a nonprofit mutual credit clearing association. While this draft is worded in terms of the latter, the same provisions should apply to for-profit clearing services such as the commercial "barter" exchanges that have been proliferating for the past three decades. The terms highlighted in bold type are of particular relevance in providing safeguards and remedies for certain suboptimal, inappropriate, or exploitative practices that have, in the past, been prevalent in credit clearing services.

The Mutual Credit Clearing Union (MCCU)

Membership Terms, Conditions, and Agreement

This agreement is made and entered into on the date shown herein by and between The Mutual Credit Clearing Union — hereinafter referred to as either MCCU, "the Union," or "the Exchange" — and the individual, corporation, partnership, or other entity (hereinafter referred to as the Member) who do mutually agree as follows.

1. About These Terms

1.1 Nature of Terms: The terms set out in this agreement specify:

    (a) the basis upon which each Member is entitled to participate in the MCCU;

    (b) the rights and obligations of each party to the agreement, including the roles of, and limitations upon, the MCCU administration.

1.2 Alteration of Terms: MCCU may alter any of these terms (including the fees and charges payable) by giving notice to each Member. Any alteration will be effective from the date specified by MCCU, which date must not be earlier than 30 days from the date on which notice of the alteration is given.

1.3 No partnership: Nothing in these Terms creates any partnership, agency, or joint venture relationship between MCCU and any Member or between any two or more Members.

1.4 Definitions: Some words that are used in these Terms are defined in section 24.

2. MCCU's Role

2.1 The essential purpose of the MCCU is to facilitate trade among its members on a noncash basis. **Except as stated in section 2.3, MCCU's role is that of a third-party record keeper and clearing agent.** The parties to any Transaction made through the Exchange are entirely responsible for its fulfilment and the quality or acceptability of the goods or services involved. The MCCU has no liability to either party in relation to the quality of the goods or services, timely delivery, prices, warranties, or commitments made by either party to the Transaction. Members are expected to exercise the same discretion that they would in undertaking a cash transaction.

2.2 Any disputes in relation to a Transaction are to be resolved between the parties to that Transaction. MCCU has no responsibility in relation to any such dispute, but it will provide for appropriate adjustments to be made to Members' MCCU accounts where a request is made in accordance with the Operating Procedures.

2.3 **The MCCU may also transact business through the Exchange as a principal for its own account; however, to avoid any conflict of interest between the Exchange and its members, such transactions will be strictly limited as follows:**

1. Transactions through the system account shall be limited to receiving service fee revenues from exchange Members for services rendered, and the disbursement of payments to Members for the purchase of services and goods necessary for system operations.

2. Any credit line allocated to the system account must be determined using the same criteria that are applied to other member accounts, as outlined in section 5 below. The MCCU shall have no special privileged access to credit within the Exchange.

3. MCCU Clearing Accounts

3.1 The MCCU will maintain a clearing account for each Member. The internal currency used in the Exchange is denominated in units called *VALs*. Credits and debits to clearing accounts are made in terms of VALs, which are not legal tender and have no value other than to enable Members to make purchases from other Members on a noncash basis in accordance with these Terms. Each VAL shall be valued at par with the official currency unit in the legal jurisdiction in which the MCCU is established, or in some other unit mutually agreed to by the members.

3.2 In no circumstances is MCCU, or any other person, obliged under these terms to redeem VALs for cash. However, **anyone wishing to buy or sell VALs for cash may do so at any rate of exchange that may be negotiated between the parties to the transaction.**

3.3 MCCU will credit to a Member's VAL account:

(a) the number of VALs received from each sale or supply made by that Member through the Exchange in accordance with these Terms; and

(b) any other amounts as may be provided for in these Terms or agreed between the Member and MCCU.

3.4 MCCU will debit from a Member's VAL account:

(a) the number of VALs paid for each purchase made by that Member through the Exchange in accordance with these Terms;

(b) the VAL component of the fees payable to MCCU by the Member in accordance with section 7;

(c) any other amounts as may be provided for in these Terms or agreed between the Member and MCCU.

4. Authorization Of Transactions

4.1 MCCU will credit a selling or supplying Member's VAL account only where the Transaction is authorized by MCCU. Any request by a Member for authorization of a Transaction must be made in accordance with the Operating Procedures.

4.2 MCCU will not authorize a Transaction if:

(a) at the time of the Transaction either party's right to engage in Transactions has been suspended, in accordance with section 14;

(b) the Transaction would result in the purchasing Member's credit limit being exceeded.

4.3 While MCCU will use all reasonable endeavours to ensure that its approval system is functioning properly at all times, it is unable to guarantee uninterrupted operation. MCCU excludes all liability to Members arising out of:

(a) any Transaction being improperly declined or improperly approved by MCCU; or

(b) any failure of MCCU to provide a prompt response to any request for authorization of a Transaction.

5. Credit Limits

5.1 Each Member agrees that MCCU is allowed to establish for each Member a line of credit on their VAL account (i.e., a maximum debit balance or "overdraft"), the amount of such credit lines being as MCCU, in its discretion, considers appropriate.

5.2 MCCU may at any time increase or reduce a Member's credit limit, although it will not increase a Member's credit limit beyond the level requested by the Member or beyond the maximum level determined according to section 5.3 below.

5.3 The line of credit (debit balance) on any account may not exceed a maximum determined as follows:

1. Maximum credit lines (debit balances) will be determined according to each Member's recent record of sales into the network, or the value of goods currently offered and available for sale within the Exchange, not upon the value of any nonliquid collateral that may be pledged as surety of contract.

2. For each account, credit lines may not exceed one quarter of annual sales into the Network, based on the most recent twelve-month period (six-month period for those who have been members for less than one year).

3. New members may be granted a minimum line of credit based on their sales history prior to membership but such credit lines may not exceed two months' sales averaged over the past twelve months.

5.4 MCCU may at its discretion require a Member to provide a guarantee, cash deposit, or other security acceptable to MCCU as surety for the performance by the Member of its obligations under these Terms. Such security shall be used only to provide surety of contract, not to determine the amount of credit lines.

5.5 The maximum line of credit (debit balance) on the MCCU credit clearing account shall be determined according to the same criteria as applied to any other Member account, as outlined in section 5.3 above.

6. Commitments By MCCU

6.1 MCCU agrees to use its best efforts to:

(a) Encourage a wide range of businesses to become Members of the Exchange;

(b) **Recruit the companies or individuals that typically supply goods or services to existing Members;**

(c) Operate the Exchange in accordance with sound and ethical industry practice;

(d) Respond to queries from Members in a timely manner;

(e) Authorize (or decline, where appropriate) transactions between Members on a real-time basis;

(f) Maintain an accurate and up-to-date database of Members that can be accessed by Members during normal business hours. Every attempt will be made to provide continuous online access to this database via the Internet.

6.2 MCCU agrees to act in good faith toward each Member, **and avoid, as much as possible, any actions that would conflict with the interests of its members.**

7. Payment Of Fees

7.1 In consideration of MCCU performing services as specified in these Terms, each Member agrees to pay MCCU, **in a timely manner, all fees due as defined by its current fee schedule.** Such fees may include, but are not necessarily limited to:

(a) transaction fees on the Transactions (either sale or purchase) made by that Member through the Exchange (as a set percentage of the total transaction value);

(b) **initiation fees on new memberships;**

(c) **annual membership fees;**

(d) **fees associated with credit checks and assurance of lines of credit requested by the Member, at the rates applicable at the time of request.**

7.2 MCCU will send each member a monthly statement and invoice **showing all the transactions done in the previous month including the fees charged by MCCU.** Any cash amount owing to MCCU by the Member must be paid within fourteen days of receipt of that statement. Any fees that are payable in VALs will be deducted from the Member's VAL account by MCCU seven days after the date of the statement.

7.3 Direct debit: Each Member must provide MCCU with a direct debit authority for the cash payments referred to in the fee schedule, if required by MCCU.

7.4 Interest: If any sum owing to MCCU by a Member is not paid on the due date the Member shall pay MCCU interest at twice the prevailing prime rate on the outstanding sum from the due date for payment, until the date when payment is made in full.

8. Obligations Of Members

8.1 Terms of Sale. Members of the Exchange shall offer their goods and services for sale to other Members at their prevailing and customary cash prices and accept VALs same as cash without any price discrimination.

8.2 Blended Trades. Blended trades shall be allowed only on transactions that exceed 1,000 VALs according to the following schedule:

If the amount of a single transaction is less than 1,000 VALs, seller must accept 100 percent of payment in VALs.

If the amount of a single transaction is between 1,000 VALs and 2,000 VALs, the buyer may be required to make partial payment in cash, but in no case shall the cash portion exceed 30 percent.

If the amount of a single transaction is between 2,000 VALs and 5,000 VALs, the buyer may be required to make partial payment in cash, but in no case shall the cash portion exceed 50 percent.

If the amount of a single transaction is greater than 5,000 VALs, the buyer may be required to make partial payment in cash, but in no case shall the cash portion exceed 70 percent.

8.3 Code of Conduct. Each Member agrees

(a) to act in good faith towards MCCU and other Members;

(b) to do nothing that is likely to diminish the good name or goodwill of MCCU or the Exchange;

(c) to comply with all relevant laws when engaging in Transactions;

(d) to comply with all relevant tax obligations;

(e) to not use the name or any trademark of MCCU, except in a manner approved by MCCU.

8.4 Taxable Transactions. It is the obligation of each Member to pay any sales or value added taxes that may be due on sales made to other Members. MCCU is not responsible for any tax liability incurred by any of its Members.

9. Liability

9.1 All liability of any kind of MCCU to any Member with respect to the services provided by it (whether arising under the Consumer protection laws, or any other enactment, or otherwise) is excluded to the fullest extent permitted by law.

10. Entire Agreement

10.1 These Terms contain all of the terms relating to each Member's participation in the Exchange.

11. Waiver

11.1 No exercise or failure to exercise or delay in exercising any right or remedy by MCCU will constitute a waiver by MCCU of that or any other right or remedy available to it.

12 .Confidentiality And Publicity

12.1 Terms and agreements: In the interests of transparency and the public interest, these Terms are to be considered public record and may be disclosed to any individual for any purpose.

12.2 Member's transaction and account information: MCCU will, to the best of its ability, maintain the confidentiality of Member's transactions and account information, except as follows:

(a) If required by law, MCCU will disclose such information to government investigators and/or tax authorities.

(b) MCCU may publish its membership directory online or otherwise, including Members' contact details.

(c) MCCU, in the course of recruiting Members' suppliers, may divulge to said suppliers the identities of its Member customers.

13. Privacy

13.1 MCCU will treat information regarding Members in accordance with MCCU's Privacy Policy and, where applicable, in accordance with the State and Federal privacy regulations.

14. Suspension

14.1 MCCU may suspend a Member's ability to engage in Transactions if MCCU reasonably believes that the Member has breached any of its obligations under these Terms.

14.2 Any suspension under section 14.1 will be lifted when MCCU is reasonably satisfied that no breach has occurred, or that any breach that did occur has been remedied.

15. Termination Of Membership

15.1 Termination on notice: A Member may cease to be a Member by giving five working days written notice to MCCU. MCCU may terminate a Member's membership by giving five working days written notice to the Member.

15.2 Termination by MCCU on default: MCCU may terminate a Member's membership with immediate effect by giving written notice to the Member:

(a) if the Member has committed any material breach of these Terms; or

(b) if the Member becomes insolvent, or a receiver or manager of any asset of the Member is appointed, or an order made or resolution passed for the liquidation of the Member's business.

16. Consequences Of Termination

16.1 Upon termination of a Member's membership for any reason the Member must immediately pay to MCCU:

(a) the cash equivalent of any debit balance remaining in the Member's VAL account; and

(b) all charges that have accrued in accordance with section 7.

16.2 If MCCU reasonably believes that the Member is unable to pay their cash fees and/or that the Member may be insolvent, MCCU reserves the right to seize stock, goods, fittings, and fixtures to the value of all cash and VAL fees *plus* the Member's VAL account balance. MCCU can seize these goods immediately upon termination of the Member's account. For the purpose of seizing goods these shall be:

(a) Valued at wholesale price.

(b) MCCU shall return said goods only on the condition that the member meets their obligations as defined in 16.1 (a) and 16.1 (b).

16.3 MCCU may add the reasonable cost of recovery of any debts that require the assistance of a third-party debt collection agency to collect, to the total amount payable to MCCU.

17. Termination Of The Exchange

17.1 If for any reason the MCCU ceases to operate each Member that has a debit balance in its VAL account must immediately pay to MCCU the cash equivalent of that debit balance. Any payments made pursuant to this section will be held in trust by MCCU and will be distributed pro-rata among the Members having credit balances in their VAL accounts.

17.2 Cessation of the Exchange's operations does not release any Member from liability to make any payment due to MCCU at the time the Exchange's operations cease.

18. Receipt Of Cash By MCCU

18.1 Where a Member pays cash to MCCU in respect of any debit balance in that Member's VAL account MCCU will debit an equivalent number of VALs from its own MCCU VAL account, so that the payment has a neutral effect on the Exchange.

19. Taxes On Services

19.1 Payments to be made **by Members** under this Agreement are exclusive of any taxes that may be levied, which must be paid by the person to whom the goods or services are provided.

20. Assignment

20.1 No Member may assign its rights under these Terms. MCCU may by notice to the Members assign its rights under these Terms.

21. Partial Invalidity

21.1 If any provision of these Terms or its application to any party or circumstance is or becomes invalid or unenforceable to any extent, the remainder of these Terms and their application will not be affected and will remain enforceable to the greatest extent permitted by law.

22. Third Parties

22.1 Nothing in these Terms is intended to confer a benefit upon anyone other than MCCU and the Members.

23. Notices

23.1 Service of notices: Any notice given pursuant to these Terms will be deemed to be validly given if personally delivered, posted, faxed, or e-mailed to:

(a) in the case of a notice to MCCU, to the address set out below the signatures of this agreement or to such other address as MCCU may advise.

(b) in the case of a notice to a Member, the address or facsimile number that is listed in MCCU's records as the address or facsimile number of that Member.

23.2 Time of service: Any notice given pursuant to this Agreement will be deemed to be validly given:

(a) in the case of delivery, when received;

(b) in the case of facsimile transmission, when sent provided that the sender has a facsimile confirmation receipt recording successful transmission;

(c) in the case of mailing, on the second working day following the date of mailing; provided that any notice personally delivered or sent by facsimile either after 5:00 pm on a working day or on any day that is not a working day will be deemed to have been received on the next working day.

24. Interpretation

24.1 Definitions: In these Terms unless the context otherwise requires:

1. "Exchange" means the credit clearing union known as MCCU, which was established by and is operated by MCCU;

2. "Member" means a person, company, or organization that has applied to become a member of the exchange and whose application has been accepted by MCCU;

3. "Operating Procedures" means the procedures applicable from time to time relating to the operation of the Exchange, which are set out on the MCCU Website;

4. "MCCU" means MCCU the Mutual Credit Clearing Union;

5. "Terms" means these Terms and Conditions of Membership of the MCCU;

6. "Transaction" means the supply of goods and/or services from one Member to another made through the Exchange in accordance with these Terms;

7. "working day" means a day (other than a Saturday, Sunday, or legal Holiday) on which chartered banks are normally open for business in the jurisdiction in which MCCU has its headquarters;

8. "Blended Trade" means a transaction in which payment is rendered partly in VALs and partly in cash;

9. "Fee schedule" means the schedule of fees established by MCCU and charged to Members and others who receive its services.

24.2 General construction: In interpreting these Terms the following rules must be applied unless the context otherwise requires:

(a) Headings to sections are for reference only and are not an aid in interpretation.

(b) References to statutory provisions will be construed as references to those provisions as they may be amended or reenacted or as their application is modified by other provisions from time to time.

(c) References to sections are to sections of these Terms.

(d) References to cash are to the official currency in the place in which MCCU has its headquarters.

(e) Any date that is not a working day, upon or by which anything is due to be done by any party, will be deemed to be a reference to the next working day.

(f) Words importing the plural include the singular and vice versa and words importing gender import all genders.

(g) Any obligation not to do something will be deemed to include an obligation not to suffer, permit, or cause that thing to be done.

Date: _____

Member name: _____

Member mailing address: _____

Member phones: _____

Member fax: _____

Member e-mail: _____

Member Website: _____

Member signature _____

Member agent: _____ , Title: _____

For MCCU

MCCU agent: _____ , Title: _____

MCCU agent signature: _____

Appendix B

An Objective Composite Standard Measure of Value

It seems indisputable that a composite commodity standard of value would provide a much more stable measure than a fixed weight of gold, silver, or any other *single* commodity. It is true that the market prices of all commodities fluctuate according to the levels of supply and demand, which are influenced by many factors including changing tastes and fashions; new technologies; and weather, civil, and political disturbances. Therefore, the averaging process inherent in a composite standard should provide a closer approach to constancy in value measurement over time than any other conceivable measure.

There is an important distinction to be made between using commodities as a standard for defining an accounting unit on the one hand, and using them as backing for the issuance of a currency on the other. It is not necessary that a currency be redeemable for the specific commodities in which it is denominated. So long as the standard commodities are actively traded, they can provide a benchmark for measuring value. If a currency is properly issued on the basis of goods and services changing hands, it should be able to hold its value at or close to par with the standard unit without redeemability. A properly issued currency will always be redeemable in the marketplace for whatever the holder wishes to buy with it. Under monetary freedom, traders will choose to use those currencies that show themselves to be most stable in terms of their purchasing power.

Selection of the Standard Commodities

In 1972, Dr Ralph Borsodi and a few associates set out to create and circulate a private currency called the *Constant* to prove that a private currency could (1) gain public acceptance and (2) be denominated in such a way as to hold its value in the marketplace.[198] While the experiment was not carried to completion, the currency did gain a wide measure of public acceptance. Borsodi, in defining his

Constant currency, selected thirty basic commodities. In preliminary studies of commodity prices, I have concluded that twelve to fifteen commodities might be sufficient for defining the standard unit. More importantly, I have decided upon some appropriate selection criteria for the commodities that should comprise the "market basket." The chosen commodities should be

1. traded in one or more relatively free markets (freely exchanged),
2. important in world trade (high volume),
3. important in satisfying basic human needs (necessity),
4. relatively stable in price (in real terms) over time (stability), and
5. uniform in quality, or standardized quality (uniformity).

Definition of the Unit of Account

Once the commodities have been selected, the definition of the unit of account can be achieved by completing the following steps:

1. Determine the "economic importance" (I) of each commodity by multiplying its average price (P) during the base year in one specified market (e.g., New York) by world production (V) of that commodity in the base year. Thus

$$I_x = P_x \bullet V_x$$

2. Determine the fractional weight (W) for each commodity in the market basket by dividing its economic importance by the sum of all the economic importance figures. Thus

$$W_x = \frac{I_x}{(I_1 + I_2 + I_3 + ... + I_n)}$$

3. Selecting the initial value of the market basket arbitrarily to be equal to, for example, $1,000,000, determine the initial value amount (D) of each commodity to be included by multiplying its weight (W) by $1,000,000. Thus

$$D_x = W_x \bullet \$1,000,000$$

4. Determine the physical quantity (Q) of each commodity to be contained in the market basket by dividing its value amount by its average price (P). Thus

$$Q_x = \frac{D_x}{P_x}$$

5. Adjust the quantities (Q), discarding fractional units in such a way as to not disturb too greatly the relative makeup of the market basket while maintaining its initial value close to $1,000,000.
6. Consider the value of the final market basket to be (arbitrarily) equal to 500,000 (five hundred thousand) standard accounting units (call it a *Val*). Thus, the Val will be initially equivalent to about $2 US, or $1 will equal one half a standard unit, or 50 Val cents.

Determining the Value of Currencies in Terms of the Standard Unit (Val)

Once the standard value unit has been defined as being one five hundred thousandth of the specified "market basket," the value of any currency (e.g., the US dollar) can be easily determined at any time by computing the current cost of the market basket in dollars using prices reported in actual trading. Dividing by 500,000 will give the dollar equivalent of one standard accounting unit. The reciprocal, of course, would be the value of the dollar expressed in standard accounting units.

References

Adams, Frank T., and Gary B. Hansen. *Putting Democracy to Work: A Practical Guide for Starting and Managing Worker-Owned Businesses.* San Francisco: Berrett-Koehler Publishers, 1992.

Ammer, Christine, and Dean Ammer. *Dictionary of Business and Economics.* New York: Free Press, 1977.

Barabasi, Laszlo. *Linked: The New Science of Networks.* Cambridge, MA: Perseus, 2002.

Barnes, Peter. *Capitalism 3.0: A Guide to Reclaiming the Commons.* San Francisco: Berrett-Koehler Publishers, 2006.

Beckerath, Ulrich von. *Does the Provision of Employment Necessitate Money Expenditure.* London: Williams & Norgate, 1935.

Benyus, Janine M. *Biomimicry: Innovation Inspired by Nature.* New York: Harper Collins, 1997.

Bilgram, Hugo, and L. E. Levy. *The Cause of Business Depressions.* Philadelphia: J. B. Lippincott Company, 1914.

Borsodi, Ralph. *Inflation and the Coming Keynesian Catastrophe: The Story of the Exeter Experiment with Constants.* Published jointly by the E. F. Schumacher Society (Great Barrington, Mass.) and the School of Living (Cochranville, Penn.), 1989.

Bridgwater, William, and Seymour Kurtz, eds. *The Illustrated Columbia Encyclopedia.* New York: Columbia University Press, 1972.

Buchanan, Mark. *Nexus: Small Worlds and the Groundbreaking Science of Networks.* New York: Norton, 2002.

Christensen, Clayton M. *The Innovator's Dilemma.* New York: Collins, 2003.

Clark, Kenneth. *Civilization.* New York: Harper and Row, 1969.

Corporate Management Model. Mondragon, Spain: Mondragon Cooperative Corporation, 2007.

Cunningham, Noble E. *Thomas Jefferson Versus Alexander Hamilton: Confrontations that Shaped a Nation.* Boston: Bedford/St. Martins, 2000.

Davies, Glyn. *A History of Money from Ancient Times to the Present Day.* Cardiff, UK: University of Wales Press, 1994.

DeMeulenaere, Stephen, and Bernard Lietaer. "Sustaining Cultural Vitality in a Globalizing World: The Balinese Example." *International Journal of Social Economics* 30, no. 9 (2003). pp. 967-84.

Diamond, Jared. *Collapse: How Societies Choose to Fail or Succeed.* New York: Viking, 2005.

Dunbar, Robin. *Grooming, Gossip, and the Evolution of Language.* Cambridge, MA: Harvard University Press, 1996.

Fisher, Irving. *The Money Illusion.* New York: Adelphi, 1928.

Fuller, R. Buckminster. *Critical Path.* New York: St. Martins Press, 1981.

Galbraith, John K. *American Capitalism: The Concept of Countervailing Power.* Boston: Houghton Mifflin Company, 1952.

— — — . *Money: Whence It Came, Where It Went.* Boston: Houghton Mifflin, 1995.

George, Henry Jr. *The Life of Henry George.* Garden City, New York: Doubleday, Doran & Company, 1930.

Gladwell, Malcolm. *The Tipping Point.* Boston: Little, Brown, 2000.

Gordon, John Steele. *Hamilton's Blessing: The Extraordinary Life and Times of Our National Debt.* New York: Walker and Company, 1997.

Greco, Thomas H. Jr. *Money and Debt: A Solution to the Global Crisis, 2nd Edition.* Tucson, Ariz.: Thomas H. Greco, Jr., 1990.

— — — . *New Money for Healthy Communities.* Tucson, Ariz.: Thomas H. Greco, Jr., 1994.

— — — . *Money: Understanding and Creating Alternatives to Legal Tender.* White River Junction, Vermont: Chelsea Green Publishing, 2001.

Greider, William. *Secrets of the Temple.* New York: Simon & Schuster, 1987.

Griffin, G. Edward. *The Creature from Jekyll Island: A Second Look at the Federal Reserve.* Westlake Village, Calif.: American Media, 1994.

Hamaker, John D., and Donald A. Weaver. *The Survival of Civilization.* Woodside, Calif.: Hamaker-Weaver Publishers, 1982.

Hayek, Friedrich von. *The Road to Serfdom.* London: Routledge, 1944.

— — —. *Choice in Currency: A Way to Stop Inflation.* London: Institute of Economic Affairs, 1976.

— — —. *Denationalization of Money: The Argument Refined.* London: Institute of Economic Affairs, 1990.

The History of an Experience. Mondragon, Spain: Mondragon Cooperative Corporation, 2006. Available at www.mcc.es/ing/index.asp.

Hixson, William F. *Triumph of the Bankers: Money and Banking in the Eighteenth and Nineteenth Centuries.* London: Praeger, 1993.

Hock, Dee. *Birth of the Chaordic Age.* San Francisco: Berrett-Koehler Publishers, 1999.

— — —. *One from Many: VISA and the Rise of the Chaordic Organization.* San Francisco: Berrett-Koehler Publishers, 2005.

Homer, Sidney. *A History of Interest Rates.* New Brunswick, New Jersey: Rutgers University Press, 1963.

Jacobs, Jane. *Cities and the Wealth of Nations.* New York: Vintage, 1984.

— — —. *The Nature of Economies.* New York: Vintage, 2000.

Johnson, Chalmers A. *Blowback: The Costs and Consequences of American Empire.* New York: Metropolitan Books, 2000.

— — —. *The Sorrows of Empire: Militarism, Secrecy, and the End of the Republic.* New York: Metropolitan Books, 2004.

— — —. *Nemesis: The Last Days of the American Republic.* New York: Metropolitan Books, 2006.

Klein, Naomi. *Shock Doctrine: The Rise of Disaster Capitalism.* New York: Henry Holt, 2007.

Knox, John J. *A History of Banking in the United States.* New York: Bradford Rhodes, 1900.

Korten, David. *When Corporations Rule the World.* 2nd ed. San Francisco: Berrett-Koehler Publishers, 2001.

Linton, Michael, and Thomas Greco, "The Local Employment and Trading System,"

Whole Earth Review, no. 55 (Summer 1987).

Lipscomb, Andrew A., ed. *The Writings of Thomas Jefferson.* vol. 1. Washington, D.C.: Thomas Jefferson Memorial Association of the United States, 1904.

Meadows, Donella H., Dennis L. Meadows, Jørgen Randers, and William W. Behrens III. *The Limits to Growth.* New York: University Books, 1972.

Meadows, Donella H., Jørgen Randers, and Dennis L. Meadows. *Limits to Growth: The 30-Year Update.* White River Junction, Vermont: Chelsea Green Publishing, 2004.

Mencken, H. L. "Women as Outlaws" in *A Mencken Chrestomathy.* New York: Knopf, 1949. This essay was first published in *The Smart Set,* December 1921.

Meulen, Henry. *Free Banking.* London: Macmillan, 1934.

Mills, C. Wright. *The Power Élite.* New York: Oxford University Press, 1956.

Mollner, Terry. *Mondragon: The Loving Society That Is Our Inevitable Future.* Northampton, Mass.: Trusteeship Institute, www.trusteeship.org/Articles/Trusteeship_Mondragon_theLovingSociety.html. Accessed Dec. 31, 2008.

Moore, Richard. *Escaping the Matrix — How We the People Can Change the World.* Redwood City, Calif.: Cyberjournal Project, 2005.

Perkins, John. *Confessions of an Economic Hit Man.* San Francisco: Berrett-Koehler Publishers, 2004.

Phillips, Kevin. *Bad Money.* New York: Viking, 2008.

Quigley, Carroll. *Tragedy and Hope: A History of the World in Our Time.* New York: Macmillan, 1966.

Remini, Robert V. *Andrew Jackson and the Bank War: A Study in the Growth of Presidential Power.* New York: Norton, 1967.

Riegel, E. C. *Private Enterprise Money.* New York: Harbinger House, 1944.

— — —. *The New Approach to Freedom.* San Pedro, Calif.: Heather Foundation, 1976.

— — —. *Flight from Inflation: The Monetary Alternative.* San Pedro, Calif.: Heather Foundation, 1978. Available at www.

newapproachtofreedom.info.

Rittershausen, Heinrich. *Die Zentralnotenbank (The Central Bank)*. Frankfurt a.M.: Knapp, 1962.

— — —. *Unemployment as a Problem of Turnover Credits and the Supply of Means of Payment*. Translated by John Zube. Available at www.reinventingmoney.com/documents/RittershausenUnemployment.pdf.

Rolnick, Arthur J., and Warren E. Weber. *The Free Banking Era: New Evidence on Laissez-Faire Banking*. Federal Reserve Bank of Minneapolis, 1982.

Rothbard, Murray Newton. *A History of Money and Banking in the United States: The Colonial Era to World War II*. Auburn, Alabama: Ludwig von Mises Institute, 2002.

Rothkopf, David. *Superclass: The Global Power Élite and the World They Are Making*. New York: Farrar, Straus, Giroux, 2008.

Sachs, Jeffrey. *The End of Poverty*. New York: Penguin Books, 2005.

Schlesinger, Arthur. *The Age of Jackson*. Boston: Little, Brown, 1988.

Sechrest, Larry J. *Free Banking: Theory, History, and a Laissez-Faire Model*. London: Quorum Books, 1993.

Selgin, George A. *The Theory of Free Banking: Money Supply under Competitive Note Issue*. Totowa, New Jersey: Rowman and Littlefield, 1988.

Smith, Adam. *An Inquiry into the Nature and Causes of the Wealth of Nations*. New York: Modern Library, 1937.

Somers, Robert. *The Scotch Banks and System of Issue*. Edinburgh: Adam and Charles Black, 1873.

Staloff, Darren. *Hamilton, Adams, Jefferson: The Politics of Enlightenment and the American Founding*. New York: Hill and Wang, 2005.

Steil, Benn. "The End of National Currency." *Foreign Affairs*, May/June 2007.

Studer, Tobias. *WIR and the Swiss National Economy*. English translation by Philip H. Beard, Sonoma State University, Rohnert Park, Calif. Originally published in German as *WIR in unserer Volkswirtschaft*. Basel, Switzerland: WIR Bank, 1998. Available online at www.lulu.com/content/301348 (for an electronic version) and www.lulu.com/content/268895 (for a print version).

Taleb, Nassim Nicholas. *The Black Swan: The Impact of the Highly Improbable*. New York: Random House, 2007.

US Congress. House. Committee on Banking and Currency, Subcommittee on Domestic Finance. *A Primer on Money*. 88th Cong., 2nd sess., September 21, 1964.

US Congress. House. Committee On Banking And Currency, Subcommittee on Domestic Finance. *Money Facts — 169 Questions and Answers on Money*. 88th Cong., 2nd sess., September 21, 1964.

Vieira, Edwin Jr. *What Is a "Dollar"?: An Historical Analysis of the Fundamental Question in Monetary Policy*. Monograph No. 6. Manassas, Virginia: National Alliance for Constitutional Money, 1996.

Weatherford, Jack. *Indian Givers*. New York: Fawcett Columbine, 1988.

— — —. *The History of Money*. New York: Three Rivers Press, 1997.

Wilson, Woodrow. *The New Freedom: A Call for the Emancipation of the Generous Energies of a People*. Project Gutenberg, 2005. www.gutenberg.org/etext/14811. (Originally published in 1913).

Withers, Hartley. *The Meaning of Money*. 7th ed. London: John Murray, 1947.

Wolf, Naomi. *The End of America: Letter of Warning to a Young Patriot*. White River Junction, Vermont: Chelsea Green Publishing, 2007.

Zander, Dr Walter, "Railway Money and Unemployment," *Annals of Public and Cooperative Economics*, vol. IX, (1933). Available at www.reinventingmoney.com/zanderRailway.php.

— — —. "A Way Out of the Monetary Chaos," *Annals of Public and Cooperative Economics* Vol. 12, No. 1 (1936): 285–305. Available at www.reinventingmoney.com/documents/wayout1.html.

Zimbardo, Philip. *The Lucifer Effect: Understanding How Good People Turn Evil*. New York: Random House, 2007.

Notes

1. Dee Hock, *One From Many: VISA and the Rise of the Chaordic Organization*, p. 291.
2. I held positions of Instructor and Assistant Professor at Rochester Institute of Technology (RIT) in Rochester, New York, from 1965 to 1979.
3. C. Wright Mills, *The Power Élite* pp. 3–4.
4. Ibid., p. 343.
5. Philip Zimbardo, *The Lucifer Effect: Understanding How Good People Turn Evil*.
6. *Money Facts — 169 Questions and Answers on Money*.
7. *A Primer on Money*.
8. Edwin Clarence Riegel, born 1879 and died 1954.
9. Several of Riegel's books, essays, and monographs can be accessed in their entirety at the Websites http://reinventingmoney.com and www.newapproachtofreedom.info. The latter contains his three major books — *Flight from Inflation*, *Private Enterprise Money*, and *The New Approach to Freedom* — in both html and pdf formats.
10. Dee Hock, *Birth of the Chaordic Age*, p. 117.
11. Irving Fisher, *The Money Illusion*, p. 182.
12. From his newsletter titled *The Bailout and What's Next*, dated October 1, 2008.
13. The number of grains accumulated by day sixty-four would be 9,223,372,036,854,775,808. These figures come from a Wikipedia entry at http://en.wikipedia.org/wiki/Second_Half_of_the_Chessboard#Second_Half_of_the_Chessboard. Accessed December 3, 2008.
14. Donella H. Meadows, Dennis L. Meadows, Jørgen Randers, and William W. Behrens III, *The Limits to Growth*.
15. Donella H. Meadows, Jørgen Randers, and Dennis L. Meadows, *Limits to Growth: the 30-Year Update*.
16. See, for example, Janine M. Benyus, *Biomimicry: Innovation Inspired by Nature* for a discussion of species that destroy their own habitats.
17. John D. Hamaker and Donald A. Weaver, *The Survival of Civilization*.
18. This series of colloquia called "Peacebuilding for the 21st Century" was initiated by Willis Harman in collabouration with Avon Mattison of Pathways to Peace, and convened twice a year from 1996 to 2000, mostly at the Fetzer Institute campus in Michigan.
19. I was first introduced to this idea by one of my brilliant colleagues in Tucson, Dr Laurence Victor; then later on by another friend, Norrie Huddle, in her book called *Butterfly*; and more recently by evolutionary biologist Elizabet Sahtouris.
20. Personal correspondence from Elisabet Sahtouris, March 22, 2009.
21. See the Website at http://itstimereno.org/goodwill.asp.
22. Quoted from the June 2008 newsletter of the CCN. Available online at http://itstimereno.org/news.asp?area=FullNews&ID=28&iefix=67405338.
23. Friedrich von Hayek, *The Road to Serfdom*.
24. Ibid., p.149.
25. Laurence Victor, personal correspondence, December 28 2008.
26. H. L. Mencken, "Women as Outlaws" in *A Mencken Chrestomathy*, p. 29.
27. Naomi Wolf, *The End of America: Letter of Warning to a Young Patriot*.
28. Chalmers Johnson, *Blowback: The Costs and Consequences of American Empire*. The other titles are *The Sorrows of Empire* and *Nemesis*.
29. Arthur Schlesinger, *The Age of Jackson*, p. 9.

30. Ibid., p. 12.
31. Andrew A. Lipscomb, ed., *The Writings of Thomas Jefferson* vol. 1.
32. Ibid., p. 269.
33. Ibid., pp. 278–79.
34. Ibid., pp. 278–79.
35. Ibid., p. 278.
36. John Steele Gordon, *Hamilton's Blessing: The Extraordinary Life and Times of Our National Debt*, p. 20.
37. Ibid., pp. 30–31.
38. Ibid., pp. 29–30.
39. Ibid., p. 32.
40. Jeffrey Sachs, *The End of Poverty*, p. 39.
41. Carroll Quigley, *Tragedy and Hope*, p. 324.
42. See http://en.wikipedia.org/wiki/Bank_of_england#History. Accessed December 3, 2008.
43. From Riegel's essay *Breaking the English Tradition*. Available at www.reinventingmoney.com/documents/BreakingEnglishTradition.pdf.
44. Quigley, *Tragedy and Hope*, p. 48.
45. See http://en.wikipedia.org/wiki/Bank_of_North_America. Accessed November 25, 2008.
46. Murray Newton Rothbard, *A History of Money and Banking in the United States: The Colonial Era to World War II*, pp. 62–63.
47. Schlesinger, *The Age of Jackson*, p. 123.
48. Robert V. Remini, *Andrew Jackson and the Bank War: A Study in the Growth of Presidential Power*, p. 131.
49. Thomas Hart Benton in the Senate on February 2, 1831. Thomas Hart Benton, Register of Debates, 21st Cong., 2nd sess., 50–75; Benton, Thirty Years View, I, 187-205. Cited in Schlesinger, *The Age of Jackson*, p. 81.
50. The full text of Jackson's message has been made available by the Avalon Project at Yale Law School, and can be found at www.yale.edu/lawweb/avalon/presiden/veto/ajveto01.htm.
51. Ibid.
52. A more complete description of the cartoon can be found at http://hdl.loc.gov/loc.pnp/cph.3a05364. Accessed November 24, 2008.
53. Schlesinger, *The Age of Jackson*, p. 115.
54. The full quotation is, "I sincerely believe ...that banking establishments are more dangerous than standing armies, and that the principle of spending money to be paid by posterity under the name of funding is but swindling futurity on a large scale" (from Thomas Jefferson to John Taylor, 1816). Also see http://etext.lib.virginia.edu/jefferson/quotations/jeff1325.htm.
55. This quote is taken from the *Money Masters* video. Wikiquote has a somewhat different version: "Whosoever controls the volume of money in any country is absolute master of all industry and commerce." http://en.wikiquote.org/wiki/James_Garfield. Accessed January 4, 2009.
56. Alan Greenspan (remarks, Conference of State Bank Supervisors, Nashville, TN, May 2, 1998). www.federalreserve.gov/BoardDocs/Speeches/1998/19980502.htm.
57. Ibid.
58. Ibid.
59. G. Edward Griffin, *The Creature from Jekyll Island: A Second Look at the Federal Reserve*.
60. See, for instance, the videos *The Money Masters* (www.themoneymasters.com) and *Money As Debt* (www.moneyasdebt.net).
61. Rothbard, *A History of Money and Banking in the United States*, p. 258.
62. Woodrow Wilson, *The New Freedom: A Call For the Emancipation of the Generous Energies of a People* (Project Gutenberg, 2005). www.gutenberg.org/etext/14811.
63. This exchange between Paul and Greenspan is in the Congressional Record and can be found at http://commdocs.house.gov/committees/bank/hba93425.000/hba93425_0f.htm, pp. 36–38. Accessed January 2, 2009.
64. Quigley, *Tragedy and Hope*, pp. 55–56.
65. Here I do not quote him verbatim but have extracted the general meaning from his book *Die Zentralnotenbank* [The History of Central Banks]

(Frankfurt a.M.: Knapp, 1962), pp. 18–19. This book was a standard university textbook for a long time. My thanks to Theo Megalli for translation assistance.

66. This development process is also described more precisely in Chapter B ("The Gradual Destruction of the Classical System from 1909 to 1932") of Rittershausen's, *Unemployment As A Problem Of Turnover Credits And The Supply Of Means Of Payment*, which is available at www.reinventingmoney.com/documents/RittershausenUnemployment.pdf. [First published "Zahlungsverkehr, Einkaufsscheine und Arbeitsbeschaffung" ("Payment Transactions, Purchasing Certificates and the Provision of Employment") in *Annalen der Gemeinwirtschaft* (*Annals of Cooperative Economy*), edited by Prof. Edgard Milhaud, 10th. year, vol. 1 (Jan/July 1934), pp. 153-207.]

67. Though it had been used many times previously, the phrase "new world order" was brought back into common usage by Bush, especially following his speech on September 11, 1990, in which he laid out the policies that would lead to the first Gulf War against Iraq. See http://en.wikipedia.org/wiki/New_world_order#The_Gulf_War_and_Bush.27s_formulation. Accessed Sept. 28, 2008.

68. Quigley, *Tragedy and Hope*, pp. 326–27.

69. Given the persistent long term inflation of political currencies, this statement might seem to contradict the argument that the investment banks are in control of the money system and the political process. This point may be an oversimplification on Quigley's part, but it must be realized in any case that control of money enables the controllers to enhance their power and wealth in both the inflationary and deflationary phases. It is by alternating easy credit with tight credit that their object is achieved. Easy credit entices the fish to bite; tight credit sets the hook.

If deflation is defined as a falling general price level resulting from restriction of credit to the *private* sector, it enables those who control the money creation process to acquire ownership and/or control of real assets at distress sale prices. Such a policy does not preclude the inflationary expansion of credit into the *public* sector by monetizing government debt, which takes real value (goods and services) out of the market. The two can happen sequentially or even simultaneously. The counterfeiter profits regardless of whether prices are falling or rising because he is first to spend his bogus money into the economy. It is, in fact, his bogus money that causes prices eventually to rise. Not all counterfeiting is illegal; the worst of it is official policy.

70. Quigley, *Tragedy and Hope*, p. 52.

71. Quigley, *Tragedy and Hope*, p. 945.

72. Skousen's foreword to *The Naked Capitalist* can been seen online at www.amazon.com/gp/reader/0899683231/ref=sib_dp_pop_cr?ie=UTF8&p=S006#reader-link. Accessed January 4, 2009.

73. "Canada, US Agree to Use Each Other's Troops in Civil Emergencies," *Ottawa Citizen*, February 22, 2008. www.canada.com/topics/news/story.html?id=403d90d6-7a61-41ac-8cef-902a1d14879d. Accessed January 2, 2009.

74. "UN rips police and refugee systems," *The Copenhagen Post*, May 22, 2007. http://jp.dk/uknews/article947497.ece. Accessed November 18, 2008.

75. E. C. Riegel, *Breaking the English Tradition*. This essay, with my comments, has been published at www.reinventingmoney.com/documents/BreakingEnglishTradition.pdf.

76. Quigley, *Tragedy and Hope*, p. 324.

77. Benn Steil, "The End of National Currency," *Foreign Affairs*, May/June 2007. www.foreignaffairs.org/20070501faessay86308/benn-steil/the-end-of-national-currency.html.

78. "The Future of North America," *Foreign Affairs*, July/August 2008. www.foreignaffairs. org/20080701faessay87406/robert-a-pastor/the-future-of-north-america. html.

79. Jack Weatherford, *Indian Givers*, p. 6.

80. Adam Smith, *Wealth of Nations*, p. 29.

81. I have provided a more complete exposition of the "money problem" in my previous books and other writings. See especially *Money: Understanding and Creating Alternatives to Legal Tender* (Part 1) and *Money and Debt: A Solution to the Global Crisis*, which can be seen at http://reinventingmoney. com, along with expository slide shows and other writings on the subject.

82. Kevin Phillips, *Bad Money*.

83. *The Worsening Debt Crisis, An Interview with Economist Michael Hudson by Mike Whitney*. Global Research, September 9, 2008. www.globalresearch.ca/index. php?context=va&aid=10129.

84. Letter of Calvin: *De Usuris Responsum*. Quoted in Calvin Elliott, *Usury: A Scriptural, Ethical and Economic View* (1902). Available at www.gutenberg. org/files/21623/21623-h/21623-h. htm#CHAPTER_XI.

85. See, for example, Richard Moore, "Responding to the Collapse (Ireland)". At https://lists.riseup.net/www/arc/ cyberjournal/2008-10/msg00001.html.

86. The real bills doctrine, often attributed to Adam Smith, holds that money issued by banks on the basis of bills for actual goods already sold and due for payment within about sixty days will not be inflationary.

87. Ralph Borsodi, *Inflation and the Coming Keynesian Catastrophe*.

88. E. C. Riegel, *New Approach to Freedom*.

89. Fisher, *The Money Illusion*, p. 177.

90. Fisher, *The Money Illusion*, p. 145.

91. Ulrich von Beckerath expresses it in quantitative terms: "Inflation results, when government issues more legal tender money than the market would accept at face value without legal tender... " Contained in a letter to Mr Humbert dated August 21, 1951.

Available at www.reinventingmoney. com/documents/1939.html. Accessed December 3, 2008.

92. Colour of law: n. the appearance of an act being performed based upon legal right or enforcement of statute, when in reality no such right exists. An outstanding example is found in the civil rights acts which penalize law enforcement officers for violating civil rights by making arrests "under colour of law" of peaceful protestors or to disrupt voter registration. It could apply to phony traffic arrests in order to raise revenue from fines or extort payoffs to forget the ticket. [From the Farlex Free Dictionary at http://legal-dictionary. thefreedictionary.com/Colour+(law).]

93. *Federal Reserve Has Monopoly over Money and Credit in United States*, *Congressional Record*, (April 28, 1997): H 1901. www.house.gov/paul/congrec/ congrec97/cr042897.htm.

94. Robert L. Hetzel, "German Monetary History in the First Half of the Twentieth Century," *Federal Reserve Bank of Richmond Economic Quarterly*, Winter 2002, p. 8. www.richmondfed. org/publications/research/economic_ quarterly/2002/winter/pdf/hetzel.pdf.

95. Ibid., p. 2.

96. Ibid., p. 6.

97. Chris Trueman, The History Learning site, www.historylearningsite.co.uk/ hyperinf.htm.

98. Hetzel, "German Monetary History," p. 9.

99. Ulrich von Beckerath, letter to Mr Runge dated July 5, 1949.

100. Ulrich von Beckerath, *Does the Provision of Employment Necessitate Money Expenditure*. Reprint taken from Peace Plans #10, compiled by John Zube and available at www. reinventingmoney.com/documents/ full-employment.html. Accessed December 3, 2008.

101. Hetzel, "German Monetary History," p. 12.

102. Heinrich Rittershausen, *The Central Bank*, p. 245.

103. Unpublished letter provided by Theo Megalli; translated by Theo Megalli and

Philip Beard.

104. Thayer Watkins, "The Worst Episode of Hyperinflation in History: Yugoslavia 1993–94." www.rogershermansociety. org/yugoslavia.htm.

105. Jonga Kandemiiri, "Amid Roaring Hyperinflation, Zimbabwe Sets New Cash Holding Limits," *Voice of America*, March 4, 2008. www.voanews.com/ english/archive/2008-03/2008-03-04- voa56.cfm?CFID=8210719&CFTOK EN=84725646.

106. Letter to Henry Meulen contained in the Beckerath papers at www. reinventingmoney.com/documents/ mag1.html. Accessed January 4, 2009.

107. Walter Zander, *Railway Money and Unemployment* (Geneva: Annals of Collective Economy, vol. IX, 1933). Available at www.reinventingmoney. com/zanderRailway.php. Accessed December 3, 2008.

108. John Zube, personal correspondence, June 25, 2008.

109. From www.pbs.org/jefferson/enlight/ religi.htm.

110. Most of the factual content in this section was taken from the Wikipedia entry on Separation of Church and State: http://en.wikipedia.org/wiki/ Separation_of_church_and_state. Accessed September 29, 2008.

111. According to Wikipedia, this quote appeared in Jefferson's 1811 letter to Baptist Churches.

112. Robert Somers, *The Scotch Banks and System of Issue*, p. 206.

113. See my book *Money: Understanding and Creating Alternatives to Legal Tender*, pp. 145–63.

114. *Money and Debt* is available free of charge as a downloadable PDF document at www.reinventingmoney.com.

115. Hartley Withers, *The Meaning of Money*, 7th ed.

116. Jack Weatherford, *The History of Money*, p. 118.

117. Edwin Vieira, *What Is a "Dollar"?: An Historical Analysis of the Fundamental Question in Monetary Policy*, Monograph No. 6. At www.fame.org/ HTM/Vieira_Edwin_What_is_a_ Dollar_EV-002.HTM.

118. Withers, *The Meaning of Money*, p. 18.

119. RKO Pictures, 1946.

120. Withers, *The Meaning of Money*, p. 21.

121. Ibid., p. 24.

122. Ibid., p. 26.

123. Quigley, *Tragedy and Hope*, p. 55.

124. Hugo Bilgram, and L. E. Levy, *The Cause of Business Depressions*.

125. Steil, *The End of National Currency*.

126. R. Buckminster Fuller, *Critical Path*, p. 237.

127. From Riegel's essay *Breaking the English Tradition*. Available at www. reinventingmoney.com/documents/ BreakingEnglishTradition.pdf.

128. Ibid.

129. Clayton M. Christensen, *The Innovator's Dilemma*, pp. xxvii–xix.

130. Walter Zander, "A Way Out of the Monetary Chaos," *Annals of Public and Cooperative Economics* vol. 12, no. 1 (1936), pp. 285–305. Available at www. reinventingmoney.com/documents/ wayout1.html.

131. Steil, *The End of National Currency*.

132. That presentation is available at www. reinventingmoney.com/documents/ Malaysia+sound.pps. Accessed December 24, 2008.

133. Zander, "A Way Out of the Monetary Chaos."

134. Christine Ammer and Dean Ammer, *Dictionary of Business and Economics*.

135. William Bridgwater and Seymour Kurtz, eds., *The Illustrated Columbia Encyclopedia* (1972).

136. John Zube, personal correspondence, February 14, 2006.

137. LETS is an acronym that stands variously for Local Exchange Trading System or Local Employment and Trading System.

138. In banking terms, this is referred to as the "reflux" rate, which is the rate at which a currency is redeemed by an issuer. The rule of thumb from experience says that there should be a minimum daily reflux of 1 percent of the amount of currency issued. That means the entire issue could be redeemed within a one hundred day period, or roughly three months.

139. However there are other aspects of microcredit, as developed thus far, that have negative consequences, so this should not be taken as a blanket endorsement.

140. Greco, *Money: Understanding and Creating Alternatives to Legal Tender*, and *New Money for Healthy Communities*.

141. Michael Linton and Thomas Greco, "The Local Employment and Trading System," *Whole Earth Review*, no. 55 (Summer 1987).

142. I described this kind of voucher system in my earlier book, *Money: Understanding and Creating Alternatives to Legal Tender*, pp. 191–96.

143. Dan Dorsey, personal correspondence, April 13, 2008.

144. The levels of the supply chain are retailers, wholesalers, manufacturers, basic commodity producers, employees, and consumers. These are depicted in the chart that appears in Chapter 15 (Figure 15.1).

145. Riegel, *Flight from Inflation*, p. 16.

146. Riegel, *Flight from Inflation*, p. 24.

147. A paper currency or voucher has the possibility of being hoarded, so these should have an expiration date to assure that they will be redeemed within a reasonable time frame. But most currency units will reside in accounts. Account credits cannot be hoarded if there is an agreement that surplus credits above a certain amount in an account will be automatically loaned out or otherwise invested.

148. Riegel, *Flight From Inflation*, p. 95.

149. Malcolm Gladwell, *The Tipping Point*, p. 19.

150. Gladwell, *The Tipping Point*, p. 7.

151. Gladwell, *The Tipping Point*, p. 70.

152. Laszlo Barabasi, *Linked: The New Science of Networks*.

153. Ibid., pp. 214–15.

154. Tobias Studer, *WIR and the Swiss National Economy*, p. 32.

155. Professor Studer, personal correspondence, May 6, 2005.

156. WIR Annual Reports from www.wir.ch.

157. *Small and Medium-sized Enterprises: Local Strength, Global Reach*, OECD Policy Brief (2000), p. 1. Available at www.oecd.org/dataoecd/3/30/1918307.pdf.

158. Jacobs, *Cities and the Wealth of Nations*.

159. Mark Buchanan, *Nexus: Small Worlds and the Groundbreaking Science of Networks*, p. 47.

160. Christensen, *The Innovator's Dilemma*, p. xv.

161. These cases were discussed in my previous book, *Money: Understanding and Creating Alternatives to Legal Tender*, pp. 64–69, and additional materials about them can be found at www.reinventingmoney.com.

162. Christensen, *The Innovator's Dilemma*, pp. 170–71.

163. The Living Directory is designed in such a way as to be especially effective in building a network of trusting relationships. It does this by requiring that each person be invited by someone who knows them personally, and by providing various levels of "referral" that determine one's level of access to the information in the database.

164. Greco, *Money and Debt*, Part 3, Appendices.

165. See, for example, Benyus, *Biomimicry: Innovation Inspired by Nature*.

166. The effectiveness of this approach has been amply demonstrated by the work of such innovators as Carolyn Lukensmeyer (America Speaks: www.americaspeaks.org), Jim Rough (The Center for Wise Democracy: www.wisedemocracy.org), Jean Francois Noubel (http://thetransitioner.org), and Richard K. Moore, *Escaping the Matrix: How We the People Can Change the World*. http://EscapingTheMatrix.org.

167. Much of this information is taken from the Bali Blog at www.baliblog.com/travel-tips/banjar-bali-village-level-government.html. Accessed January 4, 2009.

168. S. DeMeulenaere and B. Lietaer, "Sustaining Cultural Vitality in a Globalizing World: The Balinese Example," *International Journal of Social Economics* 30, no. 9 (2003), pp. 967–84.

169. Ibid.
170. Taken from the Mondragon document, *Corporate Management Model*, March 2007, p. 17.
171. *The History of an Experience*, p. 2. www.mcc.es/ing/quienessomos/historiaMCC_ing.pdf.
172. Ibid., p. 6.
173. Ibid., p. 4.
174. Ibid., various pages.
175. Terry Mollner, *Mondragon: The Loving Society That Is Our Inevitable Future*. www.trusteeship.org/Articles/Trusteeship_Mondragon_theLovingSociety.html. Accessed Dec. 31, 2008.
176. Ibid.
177. Owners of corporate shares often complain that they must pay income tax on the dividends they receive on their shares, even though the corporation has already paid a tax on its corporate profits. Whether this constitutes double taxation, and whether it is fair or not, is an arguable point. One could argue that the corporate income tax is a legitimate charge for the privilege of limited liability that corporations enjoy — which is something wholly distinct from the tax on personal income.
178. Open Capital Website, www.opencapital.net.
179. Chris Cook, *If Not Global Capitalism — Then What?* www.moq.org/forum/chriscook/ifnotglobal.html
180. See Cook's Website at www.opencapital.net.
181. *An Examination of the Banking Crises of the 1980s and Early 1990s*, Chapter 6. Available at www.fdic.gov/bank/historical/history/211_234.pdf, p. 230.
182. Ibid., p. 231.
183. A historical sketch of one long-established mutual savings bank, now called Mutual Bank, can be found at www.mymutualbank.com/about_history.htm. Accessed, January 4, 2009.
184. Gladwell, *The Tipping Point*, p. 182.
185. Gladwell, *The Tipping Point*, p. 192.
186. These proposals are inspired by, and draw heavily upon, The Four Law Drafts that were proposed by Dr Gustav Ramin, Heinrich Rittershausen, Dr Munzer, Ulrich von Beckerath, Hans Meis, Walter Unger, and Dr Walter Zander for implementation in Germany in 1932. The assistance of Theo Megalli and John Zube is also acknowledged.
187. Ulrich von Beckerath, *Does the Provision of Employment Necessitate Money Expenditure*. Available at, www.reinventingmoney.com/documents/full-employment.html.
188. From Henry George Jr., *The Life of Henry George*, pp. 557–58.
189. www.usafedcu.org/page.php?page=75.
190. www.prosper.com/welcome/how_it_works.aspx.
191. www.prosper.com/help/topics/start-faq.aspx.
192. www.prosper.com/help/topics/lender-quiet_period.aspx.
193. Nassim Nicholas Taleb, *The Black Swan: The Impact of the Highly Improbable*.
194. Mills, *The Power Élite*, p. 355.
195. Quigley, *Tragedy and Hope*, pp. 1200–1.
196. Woodrow Wilson, *The New Freedom*.
197. This draft agreement, while mainly original, has adapted the topical and hierarchical structure of an agreement of Ozone Barter Company, supplied by Daniel Evans.
198. A more complete account of the *Constant* currency experiment is provided in my book, *Money and Debt: A Solution to the Global Crisis*, Appendix C; and Ralph Borsodi, *Inflation and the Coming Keynesian Catastrophe: The Story of the Exeter Experiment with Constants*.

Index

Note: page numbers in italics refer to figures

Acton, Lord 24
Adams, John 100
affinity groups 21, 154, 230
Age of Jackson, The (Schlesinger) 26
alternative currencies. See complementary
 currencies
Amazon 211, 214
*American Capitalism: The Concept of
Countervailing Power* (Galbraith) 3
Argentina 176–80, 208, 239f
Arizmendiarrieta, Father José María 220–24
Arrasate 219
Articles of Confederation 27, 36
Auroville 225

Bad Money (Phillips) 62
Bali 217–19
banjar 218f
Bank Act of 1844 111
Bank for International Settlements 32
Bank of England 29, 31, 34–37, 45, 87, 111,
 137
Bank of North America 36
Bank of Scotland 227
Bank of the United States 36f
bank panics 107
"Bank War" 37
banknotes. See symbolic money
Barabasi, Laszlo 172f
Barnes, Peter 225
barter 35, 76, 102, 128f, 132, 177. See also
trade exchanges
BarterCard 182
basis of issue 72–75, 96f, 112f , 161f. See
 also issuing currency; market basket basis
"Battle of Seattle" 52
Beckerath, Ulrich von 78f, 81f, 84f, 127, 142,
 237
Benton, Thomas Hart 37f
Berkshares currency 160
Biddle, Nicholas 37, 39f
Bilderberg groups 49
Bilgram, Hugo 118
Bill of Rights 54, 91, 260
Blackwater 52
Blowback trilogy (Johnson) 26, 46
Borsodi, Ralph 67, 275
Brandeis, Louis 260

Britain 30, 96, 260
"bubbles" 44, 57, 108
Buchanan, Mark 205
Bush, George H. W. 47
Bush, George W. 52, 54

Caja Laboral Popular (CLP) 200, 221, 223
Calvin, John 64f
*Capitalism 3.0: A Guide to Reclaiming the
 Commons* (Barnes) 225
cashless trading 184, 187–89
Central Bank, The (Rittershausen) 81
central banking. See also Bank of England;
 Federal Reserve System
—, credit clearing and 143–47
—, élite class and 47–50, 136f
—, in Germany 75–82
—, inflation and 72–75
—, legal tender laws and 87, 96f, 124, 137,
 140
—, power and 33f
—, spread of 45f, 87
—, in United States 31f, 34–40, 45f, 73f
cheques 110–12
cherry-picking 185f
Chinese Tael system 135
Christensen, Clayton 127, 205–7, 209
civil emergencies 51
Civil War 42, 73, 125
Clinton, Bill 32
CLP (Caja Laboral Popular) 200, 221, 223
coins 33, 103f, 115, 135, 137. *See also* gold
 and silver
collateral 94f, 112f, 115, 153f, 249–51
Columbus 56
commercial barter exchanges. *See* trade
 exchanges
commodity money. *See also* gold and silver;
 gold standard
—, vs. credit money 109f, 169f. *See also* gold
 and silver; gold standard
—, evolution of 103–6, 109
—, as measure of value 96f, 103, 201, 213,
 234, 275–77
—, as monetary system basis 44, 125, 131f,
 134–38
community currencies. *See* complementary
currencies

complementary currencies. *See also*
    currencies
—, Berkshares 160
—, constant 275
—, credito 176–80
—, delinking with dollars 93–96
—, exchange system principles 164–71
—, failures of 161f
—, government roles 236–38
—, implementation strategies 171–73
—, inflation and 84–86
—, Jonestown flood railroad bonds 241f
—, Mark Banco 135f
—, Petroms 239, 240
—, regional 199f
—, Rentenmarks 78–80, 237f
—, savings and investments and 256–58
—, social justice and 208
—, trueque clubs 176–80
—, Tucson Traders 158–61
—, WIR Bank 173–76, 180, 208
compound interest 57–60
conflicts of interest 185, 265
Conscious Community Network 21
Constant (currency) 275
Constitution of the US 31, 36, 90f, 260
Constitutional Convention 28
Consumer Price index 89
Cook, Chris 226
cooperation vs. competition 215
corporations 225f
Council on Foreign Relations 49, 55, 125,
    136
counterfeiting 71f, 177, 180
Craigslist 211
Creature from Jekyll Island, The (Griffin) 43
credit cards 202–4, 207
credit clearing
—, balance limits and settlements 152f
—, credit balances and 94f
—, credit commons and 2
—, critical mass and 208
—, defined 68
—, examples 143–51
—, historical perspectives 141–43
—, LETSonora 158f
—, local exchange trading systems (LETS)
    6, 147, 152–55, 157f
—, locally controlled 137
—, membership agreement 264–76
—, membership base 186
—, organizational forms and structures
    224–31
—, process of 115–23
—, reciprocal exchange and 118, 122f, 141,
    161

—, regional economic development and
    196, 198–201
—, savings and investments in 256–58
—, surety of contract 153f
—, trade exchanges and 184, 187–90
—, Tucson Traders (TT) 158–61
—, in web-based trading platforms 213f
—, WIR Bank 153, 156, 173–76, 180, 207
credit commons 2, 95, 125, 154, 198, 216,
    232
credit money 105–14, 119f, 132, 138, 169f,
    235
credito currencies 176–80
currencies 5. *See also* complementary
currencies
—, as credit obligations 133, 164, 235
—, fiat 44, 134
—, global reserve 87f
—, government issued 236–38
—, historical perspectives 84–86
—, inflation and 67, 72–74, 77–83
—, issued by private banks 41, 45
—, issued by private companies 166–71,
    177, 199
—, legal tender laws and 87, 93, 122f, 139f,
    235f
—, measure of value and 45, 60, 95f, 131,
    134–39
—, national 54, 60, 93f, 137, 140, 213
—, symbolic 104–6, 110

debit cards 202f
debt bomb 15
debt financing vs. equity financing 249–56
debt financing vs. equity financing 61, 69,
    249–56
debt imperative 50, 58, 61f
debt monetization 62, 76, 87f, 96f, 116,
    119–21, 237
debt-money system 57f, 62f, 119, 203, 261
DEC (Digital Equipment Company) 209
deficit spending 45, 74f, 83, 87–89, 124–26,
    237
deflation 80f, 234f
demand deposits 106. *See also* deposits
DeMeulenaere, Stephen 217–19
depositories 37, 68, 73, 116f
deposits
—, as bank account balances 62, 133
—, bank loans and 34, 73
—, cheques and 110–12
—, as commodity money 105f
—, credit clearing and 115f, 120, 143–47
—, as credit instruments 107–10
—, demand 106
—, in mutual savings banks 229f

—, savings 245f
—, sight 106
—, volume of 83
Digital Equipment Company (DEC) 209
direct credit clearing. *See* credit clearing
Disraeli, Benjamin 47
disruptive technologies vs. sustaining
    technologies 205
dissent 51, 259f
dominant companies 205f
Dorsey, Dan 160f
Drucker, Peter 211, 213
Dumais, Marc 50
Dunbar, Robin 230
Eastman Kodak 210
eBay 211, 214
economic development 194–201
economy, steady state 13, 17, 69
Ecuador 55, 234
egalitarianism 23–26
élite class
—, in American society 3, 17, 23–26, 43,
    124f, 262
—, central banks and 47–50, 136f
—, historical perspectives 31, 35–37
—, mega-crisis and 65
—, national sovereignty and 54f, 57, 136f
—, war financing and 52–54
End of America, The (Wolf) 26
"End of National Currency, The" (Steil) 54
equity financing vs. debt financing 61, 69,
    249–56
Esssay on the Principle of Population
    (Malthus) 15
European Union 55, 96
exchange alternatives 127–29, 156f, 161,
    207. *See also* WIR Bank
exchange function vs. finance function
    65–69, 243
exchange process. *See* medium of exchange;
reciprocal exchange
exponential growth 13f, 57f, 62

Facebook 211
Federal Deposit Insurance Corporation 229
Federal Reserve System 42–44, 72–74, 87,
    96f. *See also* central banking
Feil, Chuck 180
fiat currencies 44, 134
finance function vs. exchange function
    65–69, 243
financial "bubbles" 44, 57, 108
First Amendment 91
Fisher, Irving 10, 70, 84
Flyer, Richard 21
fractional reserve system 41, 107

France 28, 30, 34
Franco, Francisco 220, 223
Free Banking (Meulen) 84
free banking era 40f
free trade 49, 55, 193
Friedman, Milton 70
Friendster 211
Fuller, Buckminster 126

Galbraith, John Kenneth 3
Gandhi, Mahatma 7, 224, 261
Garfield, James A. 40
George, Henry 11, 240–42
George, Henry, Jr. 240
George Peabody and Company 48
German hyperinflation 75–78
German Rentenbank Act 80
German Rentenmarks 78–80, 237f
Gladwell, Malcolm 172, 230f
global monetary system 9f, 45f, 49f, 54f, 58f,
    61–64, 87f
Global Trading Network (Red Global de
    Trueque)
globalization 7f, 17, 34f, 193–95
gold and silver 33, 41, 57, 103f, 108, 113,
    115, 117, 132, 213. *See also* coins; gold
    standard
Gold Dinar Conference 138
gold standard
—, as constraint on debasement of money
    83f
—, German hyperinflation and 78–82
—, measurement of value and 134–39, 275
—, Rentenmark and 237f
—, in US 96f, 107f, 112, 125
Gono, Gideon 83
Google 173
Gordon, John Steele 30
Gore Associates 230
government bonds 72–75, 236, 250
Grameen Bank 154
Great Britain 30, 96, 260
Great Depression 8, 50, 156, 174, 207, 213
Greco, Thomas H. Jr. 7f
greenbacks 73, 125
Greenspan, Alan 41f, 44
growth
—, exponential 13f, 57f, 62
—, imperative 50, 58–63, 69
—, limits to 15
—, linear 13f
growth imperative 50, 58–63, 69

Halliburton 52
Hamaker, John 15
Hamburger Girobank 135

Hamilton, Alexander 26, 28–31, 33, 36, 40
Harman, Willis 16
Hayek, F.A. 23f
Hetzel, Robert 75, 77, 80
Hilton Hotel Group 227
historical perspectives
—, early America 26–32
—, commodity money 103–6, 109
—, credit clearing 141–43
—, currencies 84–86
—, élite class 31, 35–37
—, reciprocal exchange 102–6
—, trade exchanges 181f
Hock, Dee 1, 10
homeland security 16
Hotmail 173
House Financial Services Committee 44
House of Representatives Subcommittee on
    Domestic Finance 4f
Hudson, Michael 64
Hungary 82f
Hurricane Katrina 51
hyperinflation 75–78

IBM 209f
improper basis of money issue 72–75, 96,
    162
IMS 182
In the Wake of Inflation Can the Church
    Remain Silent? 4
India 225
inflation
—, central banking and 72–75
—, complementary currencies and 84–86
—, currencies and 67, 72–74, 77–83
—, defined 70–72
—, German hyperinflation 75–78
—, gold and 132
—, government deficits and 73–75
—, as a hidden tax 35
—, in Hungary 82f
—, improper basis and 72–75
—, legal tender laws and 67, 81, 84, 170,
    233–35
—, political money and 49, 170
—, turnover credit and 170
—, in United States 89
—, in Yugoslavia 82f
—, in Zimbabwe 83
Innovators Dilemma, The (Christensen) 205
    interest
—, central bank charges 34
—, compound 57–60
—, on credit card debt 202f
—, debt claims and 87–89, 116, 120, 149,
    249–51

—, on deposits 117
—, interest-free transactions 188f, 198, 204,
    211
—, money dysfunction and 64
—, on mortgages 252–56
—, and mutual savings banks (MSB) 229f
—, real estate bubble and 108
—, social lending movement and 247f
—, usury and 50, 60, 68f, 157
International Monetary Fund 54, 196
International Reciprocal Trade Association
    (IRTA) 181, 187
investment credits 167–69
investments. See saving and investment
Iraq war 52
IRTA (International Reciprocal Trade
    Association) 181, 187
issuing currency. See also basis of issue
—, by governments 236–38
—, by private banks 41, 45, 137
—, by private companies 166–71, 177, 199
ITEX 182
It's a Wonderful Life (film) 107

Jackson, Andrew 26, 31, 37–40, 113
Jacobs, Jane 197
Japan 52
Jefferson, Thomas 26–31, 40, 90, 104
Johnson, Chalmers 26, 46
Johnson, Tom L. 241
Jonestown flood railroad bonds 241f

KBR 52
Koressel, David 158
Korten, David 225
Kucinich, Dennis 11
Kuhn, Loeb & Company 43
Kuhn, Thomas 205

Lamont, Thomas W. 48
legal tender laws
—, cheques and 112
—, deficit spending and 124
—, forced circulation and 46, 87, 93, 123,
    235f
—, inflation and 67, 81, 84, 170, 233–35
—, legislative proposals 232–38
—, stable value reckoning and 96f, 131, 235
—, two meanings of dollar and 93, 133, 137,
    139f, 213
Leipzig Dresden Railway 85
LETS (local exchange trading systems) 6,
147f, 152–55, 157f. See also trade exchanges
LETSonora 158f
Levy, L.E. 118
Lezamiz, Mikel 220

Lietaer, Bernard 217–20
limited liability companies 226–28
limits to growth 15
Limits to Growth, The (Meadows) 15
Lincoln, Abraham 125
linear growth 13f
Linked: The New Science of Networks
    (Barabasi) 172
Linkedin 211
Linton, Michael 158
Living Directory 211
local currencies. *See* complementary
    currencies
local exchange trading systems (LETS) 6,
    147f, 152–55, 157f. *See also* trade exchanges
Locke, John 90
long-term vs. short-term credit 66–68,
    167–69, 243
Louis XIV 34
Lub, Sergio 180
Luther, Hans 78

MacCallum, Spencer 6
Madison, James 31, 40, 90f
Magna Carta 54
Malaysia 137f
Malthus, Thomas 15
Mark Banco 135f
market basket basis 138, 201, 213, 235,
    275–77
marketplace 211
Marshall Plan 2
Mary II 34
MasterCard 202f, 207
Meadows, Donella H. 15
Meaning of Money, The (Withers) 97
measure of value
—, commodity money and 96f, 103, 201,
    213, 234, 275–77
—, currency as 45, 60, 95f, 131, 134–39
—, lack of 124
—, objective 123, 129, 196
—, precious metals as 132
—, in web-based trading 211, 213
    medium of exchange
—, complementary currency as 199
—, credit as 208
—, German mark as 77
—, money as 7, 103, 112, 130, 139f, 204
—, US dollar as 54f, 93, 234
mega-crisis 5, 12–22, 65, 194
Mencken, H.L. 25
metamorphosis analogy 17–20
Metropolitan Life Insurance Company
    (MetLife) 229
Meulen, Henry 84

Mills, C. Wright 3, 259
Mollner, Terry 223
monarchy vs. republic 26–32
Mondragon Cooperative Corporation 200f,
    219–23
monetary principles 166–71
monetization of debt 62, 76, 87f, 96f, 116,
    119–21, 237
*Money and Debt: A Solution to the Global
    Crisis* (Greco) 7, 213
*Money Facts – 169 Questions and Answers
    On Money* (US House of Representatives
    Subcommittee on Domestic Finance) 4
*Money: Understanding and Creating
    Alternatives to Legal Tender* (Greco) 8
monopoly power
—, of central banking 36, 38, 43
—, credit money and 132f, 235
—, deficit spending and 64
—, inflation and 234f
—, of political money 34, 40, 92, 111f, 125
Morgan, J.P. 12, 43, 48f
Morris, Robert 36
mortgages 106, 108, 230, 252–56
Moxham, Arthur J. 241
mutual credit clearing. *See* credit clearing
mutual savings banks 228–30
MySpace 211

National Bank Act of 1863 42
national currencies 54, 60, 93f, 137, 140, 213
national sovereignty 54f, 57, 136f
New Freedom, The (Wilson) 43
New Money for Healthy Communities
    (Greco) 8
New York Clearing House 142
Nietzsche, Friedrich 11
nongovernmental currencies. See comple-
    mentary currencies
North American Union 55
note brokers 41
*Notes on the Establishment of a Money Unit
    and of a Coinage for the United States*
    (Jefferson) 104

Obama, Barack 54
open capital 226
Organization for Economic Cooperation
    and Development (OECD) 195
Öser, German Railway Minister 85
Ottawa Citizen 50

Pacheco, Dennis 74, 194
Pastor, Robert 55
Patterson, William 34f
Paul, Ron 44, 73, 125, 157

PayPal 211
Petersen, Herr 78
Petroms 239, 240
Phillips, Kevin 62
PJEC (Rochester Peace and Justice Education Center) 4
political consolidation 55
political money system 1
—, central banks and 47–50
—, dysfunctions of 7f, 65f, 190, 203, 206f
—, inflation and 49, 170
—, monopoly of 34, 40, 92, 111f, 125
—, war financing and 67
Polytechnic School, Mondragon 221
pooling 167
Power Élite, The (Mills) 3
precious metals 56f, 103f, 108, 115, 132, 137f, 245
Primavera, Heloisa 177
Primer on Money, A (US House of Representatives Subcommittee on Domestic Finance) 5
private currencies. *See* complementary currencies
Prosper.com 247f

Queen Victoria 47
Quigley, Carroll 32, 35, 45, 48f, 53, 55, 117, 260

railway money 85
Railway Money and Unemployment (Zander) 85
real bills doctrine 66
real estate bubble 108
reciprocal exchange
—, cashless payments and 191f
—, credit clearing and 118, 122f, 141, 161
—, evolution of 102–6
—, failures of 161f
—, free exchange and 97, 102
—, locally controlled/globally useful 230
—, as money's purpose 71, 166
—, process of 94, 164f
—, surety of contract and 153f
Red Global de Trueque (Global Trading Network) 177
reflux rate 167
regional currencies 199f. *See also* complementary currencies
regional economic development 194–201
Reichsbank 76
Rentenmarks 78–80, 237f
Renuart, Gene 51
Revolutionary War 30, 36
Riegel, E.C. 6, 46, 53, 67, 126–28, 166, 170

RIT (Rochester Institute of Technology) 2f, 8
Rittershausen, Heinrich 45, 81, 86
Rochester Institute of Technology (RIT) 2f, 8
Rochester Peace and Justice Education Center (PJEC) 4
Rockefeller, John D. 43
Roosevelt, Franklin 31
Rothbard, Murray 36, 43
Rothschild, Meyer Amschel 33
Rothschilds, the 48
"Rule of 150" 230
Runge, Dr 78

Sachs, Jeffrey 32
Sahtouris, Elisabet 20
Sampayo, Carlos 178
saving and investment 66, 168f, 200, 216, 243–49, 256–58
Schlesinger, Arthur 26, 40
Scottish banks 110
scrip 8, 156
Second Bank of the United States 37, 40, 113
settlements 141–43, 147–53
shared equity mortgages 252–56
short-term vs. long-term credit 66–68, 167–69, 243
sight deposits 106. *See also* deposits
silver and gold 33, 41, 57, 103f, 108, 113, 115, 117, 132, 213
Skousen, W. Cleon 49
Smith, Adam 61
Smith, Jeff 225
social justice 132, 208, 215, 251
social lending 247–49
Social Money Conference 177
social networks 211
Somers, Robert 92
Spain 200, 219–24
stable value reckoning 96f, 131, 235
steady state economy 13, 17, 69
Steil, Benn 54, 125, 136
Stewart, Jimmy 107
store of value 103, 131, 243f
Studer, Tobias 174f
subprime mortgage crisis 108
surety of contract 153f
Survival of Civilization, The (Hamaker) 15
sustaining technologies vs. disruptive technologies 205
Switzerland 32, 153, 174. *See also* WIR Bank
symbolic money 104–6, 110
Syracuse University 4

Taleb, Nassim 259
Taney, Roger B. 39f

Tipping Point, The (Gladwell) 172, 230
Toffler, Alvin 137
totalitarianism 25f
trade exchanges. *See also* local exchange
trading systems (LETS)
—, historical perspectives 181f
—, limiting factors 183–87
—, membership base 186–90
—, networks of 191f
—, taxes and 190f
—, value proposition 181–83, 187, 204f
trading clubs 176–80
Tragedy and Hope (Quigley) 49
Treaty of Versailles 76
Trilateral Commission 49
trueque clubs 176–80
Tucson Traders 158–61
turnover credits 132, 167–69

US Constitution 31, 36, 90f, 260
US House of Representatives Subcommittee
   on Domestic Finance
US Postal Service 210
USA Fed 248
Ubud 217–19
Ulgor 221
unit of account. *See* measure of value
University of Rochester 3
usury
—, vs. credit money 132
—, debt imperative and 62
—, vs. interest 50, 60, 68f, 157
—, religious prohibitions 64f, 253f

value proposition 181–83, 187, 204f
Veith, Edward 5
Victor, Laurence 21, 24
Victoria, Queen 47
Virginia Statute of Religious Freedom 90
Visa cards 202f, 207
von Stein, Lorenz 237
vouchers 159, 168, 199

Walker, Mr 85
Wallach, David 182
war financing 30, 36, 52, 67
War of the League of Augsburg 34
war on drugs 260
war on terror 25, 260
Washington, George 26–30, 36f
Watkins, Thayer 83
Weatherford, Jack 56
Web-based trading platforms 208–14
Wells Fargo Bank 248
When Corporations Rule the World (Korten) 225
William III (William of Orange) 34
Wilson, Woodrow 43, 261
WIR Bank 153, 156, 173–76, 180, 207
Withers, Hartley 97, 102, 106, 111f, 115
Wolf, Naomi 25f
Working Assets Long Distance 225
Working People's Bank (CLP) 200, 221, 223
World Bank 196
World Trade Center 54
World Trade Organization 52, 196
World War II 52
World Wide Web 208f

Xerox 210

Yacub, Ernie 158
Yahoo! 173
Yugoslavia 82f

Zander, Walter 85, 134, 139
Zimbabwe 83
Zimbardo, Philip 3
Zopa Limited 247f
Zopa USA 248
Zube, John 86, 98